Hitch

Patterns Inspired by the Films of Alfred Hitchcock

edited by
Stephannie Tallent

Hitch: Patterns Inspired by the Films of Alfred Hitchcock

Library of Congress Control Number: 2013949204
ISBN 13: 978-1-937513-27-6
First Edition
Published by Cooperative Press
http://www.cooperativepress.com

Patterns, charts, schematics, and text © 2013,
Stephannie Tallent and respective designers
Photography © 2013, Nick Murway, except where otherwise noted
Models: Marie Draz, Susan Enger, Leslie McCombs, Derek Grubaugh,
Nina Machlin Dayton, Anne Lecrivain-Cozzoli

A huge thank you to our test knitters: Amy Brondyke, Carrie
Patterson, Daria Bocciarello, Gina Polidoro, Jamie Hess, Jennifer
Almy, RiverPoet, sanomahead, Sarah Al-Amri, Simone Draeger, and
Stephanie Mann.

And special thanks to Cynthia Deering of Deering Vintage (Cleveland,
Ohio) for providing one of a kind vintage dresses and accessories for
photos.

Every effort has been made to ensure that all the information in this
book is accurate at the time of publication; however, Cooperative
Press neither endorses nor guarantees the content of external links
referenced in this book.

If you have questions or comments about this book, or need information
about licensing, custom editions, special sales, or academic/corporate
purchases, please contact Cooperative Press: info@cooperativepress.com
or 13000 Athens Ave C288, Lakewood, OH 44107 USA.

FOR COOPERATIVE PRESS

Senior Editor: Shannon Okey
Art Director and Assistant Editor: Elizabeth Green Musselman
Technical Editors: Katherine Vaughan, Stephannie Tallent
Illustrator: MJ Kim

For my father, Paul, who instilled in me
a great love of movies when I was child.

Contents

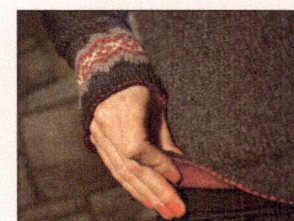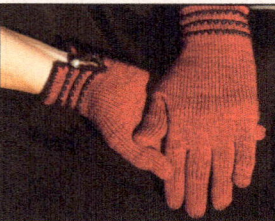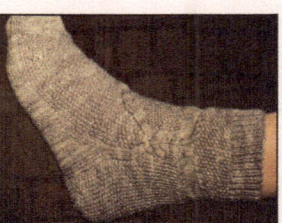

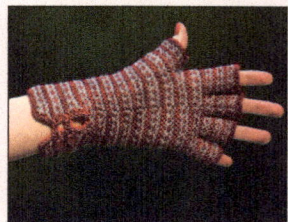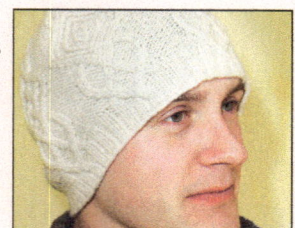
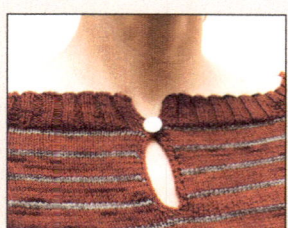

Robie
Sweater
[page 93]

Ambrose
Chapel
Capelet
[page 99]

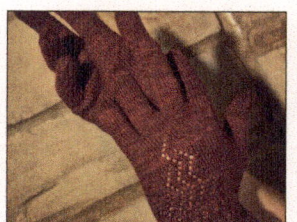

Madeleine
Gloves
[page 105]

San Juan
Bautista
Shawl
[page 111]

Souvenir
of a Killing
Beret
[page 115]

Cypress
Point
Sweater
[page 119]

Judy
Henley
[page 125]

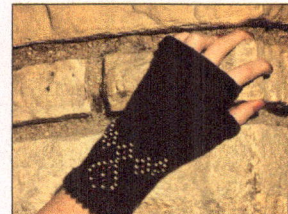

Stolen
Jewels
Mitts
[page 131]

Our Gal
Midge
Sweater
[page 135]

Thornhill
Cowl
[page 141]

Melanie
Shawl
[page 145]

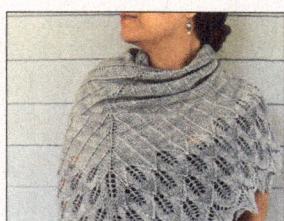

Bodega
Bay Stole
[page 151]

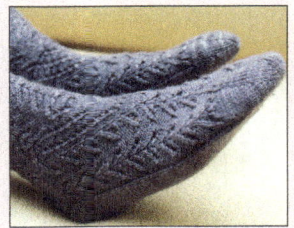

Tippi Toes
[page 154]

Annie
Pullover
[page 161]

Introduction

by Stephannie Tallent

I'd love to sound as if I was an expert in film studies, in particular the films of Alfred Hitchcock, but I'm afraid I'm just a fan of Alfred Hitchcock's movies. Not even a diehard, rabid fan; simply a fan.

Hitchcock's movies are just plain fun.

The fashion in the movies is to die for, especially when Edith Head (who dressed Ingrid Bergman in *Notorious*, Grace Kelly in *Rear Window* and *To Catch A Thief*, Doris Day in *The Man Who Knew Too Much*, Kim Novak in *Vertigo*, and Tippi Hedren in *The Birds* and *Marnie*) had her hand in the costume design.

Like Edith Head's fashions, Hitchcock's movies are essentially timeless. You can still enjoy them today without experiencing that jarring feeling that the films are dated. Hitchcock approached themes and ideas that are about people, not just the times in which the movies are set. This has been discussed in popular literature in reference to Hitchcock's use of "MacGuffins" (the object or person that sets the film's plot in motion). It's not the microfilm in the statue, nor even the uranium in the wine bottles that's so important. What matters is what happens to Thornhill (Cary Grant in *North By Northwest*) or Alicia (Ingrid Bergman in *Notorious*).

Of course, the proverbial elephant in the room is Hitchcock's alleged treatment of women, especially as portrayed in recent films such as *The Girl*, and in books such as Spoto's *Spellbound By Beauty*. How do you separate your admiration of Hitchcock's art from your distaste for his reported actions? I'll let you ponder that and decide for yourself.

Again, I'm coming at this as someone with an appreciation of films that rely on suspense as opposed to obvious depictions of blood, gore, and violence; films that rely on characterization and plot, instead of over-the-top action.

I remember watching some of his movies as a teenager. I remember being enthralled by how handsome and suave Cary Grant was, and how lovely and ethereal Grace Kelly was, for example, in *To Catch A Thief*. Even then, I loved the banter and sharp comments from various characters—the dialogue was clever.

We can still enjoy Hitchcock's movies and Edith Head's fashions today without experiencing that jarring feeling that they are dated.

Re-watching the films as an adult is a treat. I'm thrilled by the variety of movies that inspired our designers (although, no one came up with a pattern for *Psycho*, interestingly enough!). Some of these films are personal favorites, especially *Rear Window* and *Notorious*.

I hope you relish the explorations and reinterpretations of the fashions of the different time periods, and I hope that you sink your teeth into the bold designs inspired by the graphics of Saul Bass. The following is a variety of patterns to entice, tempt, and surprise you.

For more on MacGuffins, see Wikipedia's definition:

⬦ http://en.wikipedia.org/wiki/MacGuffin

... and this discussion of Hitchcock's use of the concept:

⬦ http://borgus.com/hitch/macguffins.htm

Constance Shawl

Anna Dalvi

SIZES

S (M, L); shown in size M

FINISHED (BLOCKED) MEASUREMENTS

Small: wingspan: 48" / 122cm; depth: 14.5" / 37cm
Medium: wingspan: 55" / 140cm; depth: 15.75" / 40cm
Large: wingspan: 62.25" / 158cm; depth: 17" / 43cm

MATERIALS

Zen Yarn Garden Serenity Silk Single (75% merino, 15% cashmere, 10% silk; 430 yds / 393m per 100g skein)

❧ [MC] Silver Moon; 1 (2, 2) skein(s)

❧ [CC] Flamenco; 1 skein (only 16 yds / 15m used)

32-inch US #6 / 4.0mm circular needle, or size needed to obtain gauge

2 removable stitch markers
Yarn needle

GAUGE

16 sts and 22 rows = 4" / 10cm in St st, blocked

REQUIRED SKILLS

Increases/decreases; cable cast on; short rows; working lace from chart; twisted stitches; picking up stitches; nupps

PATTERN NOTES

The edging is worked first.

Stitches for the main body of the shawl are picked up along the straight (left as you look at the RS) edge. The crescent shape of the main body is created by working short rows.

SPECIAL STITCHES

5×7: Knit 7 stitches together, then (yo, k, yo, k) into the same 7 stitches.

nupp-7: Knit, leaving the stitch on the needle, then (yo, k, yo, k, yo, k) into the same stitch (7 stitches total). On next row, purl all 7 stitches together as one.

PATTERN

Edging

CO 25 sts using a cable cast on (see Abbreviations & Techniques).
Start working Chart A. Work Rows 1–26, then work Rows 27–46 17 (19, 21) times.

Work Chart B.
BO 25 sts.

Body

With CC:
Row 1 (RS): Pick up and knit 194 (214, 234) sts along the edging.
Row 2 (WS): K3, p tbl 94 (104, 114), pm, p tbl 94 (104, 114), k3.
Row 3: K3, k tbl until 3 sts remain, k3.

This shawl is inspired by the 1945 movie Spellbound. *The snowflake motif represents the fateful skiing trip in the film, while the shawl's parallel lines remind us of the lines that frighten Dr. Anthony Edwardes. It's up to his colleague, Dr. Constance Petersen, to discover the true meaning of Edwardes' visions....*

With MC:
Row 4 (WS): K3, p tbl until 3 sts remain, k3.

Short rows:
Row 5 (RS): K3, k tbl to marker, rm, k tbl 3, turn work.
Row 6 (WS): Sl1, pm, p tbl 5 (5, 5), turn work.
Row 7: Sl1, pm, k tbl to marker, rm, k2tog, k tbl 3, turn work.
Row 8: Sl1, pm, p tbl to marker, rm, p2tog tbl, p tbl 3, turn work.
Rep Rows 7–8 until 4 unworked sts remain on each side.

Row 9: Sl1, pm, k tbl to marker, rm, k2tog, k3.
Row 10: K3, p tbl to marker, rm, p2togtbl, k3.
Row 11: K3, k tbl until 3 sts remain, k3.
Rows 12–14: Knit.

BO as follows: K2, *return sts to left needle, k2tog tbl, k1, repeat from * until no unworked sts remain.

FINISHING

Weave in loose ends. Block.

Chart A

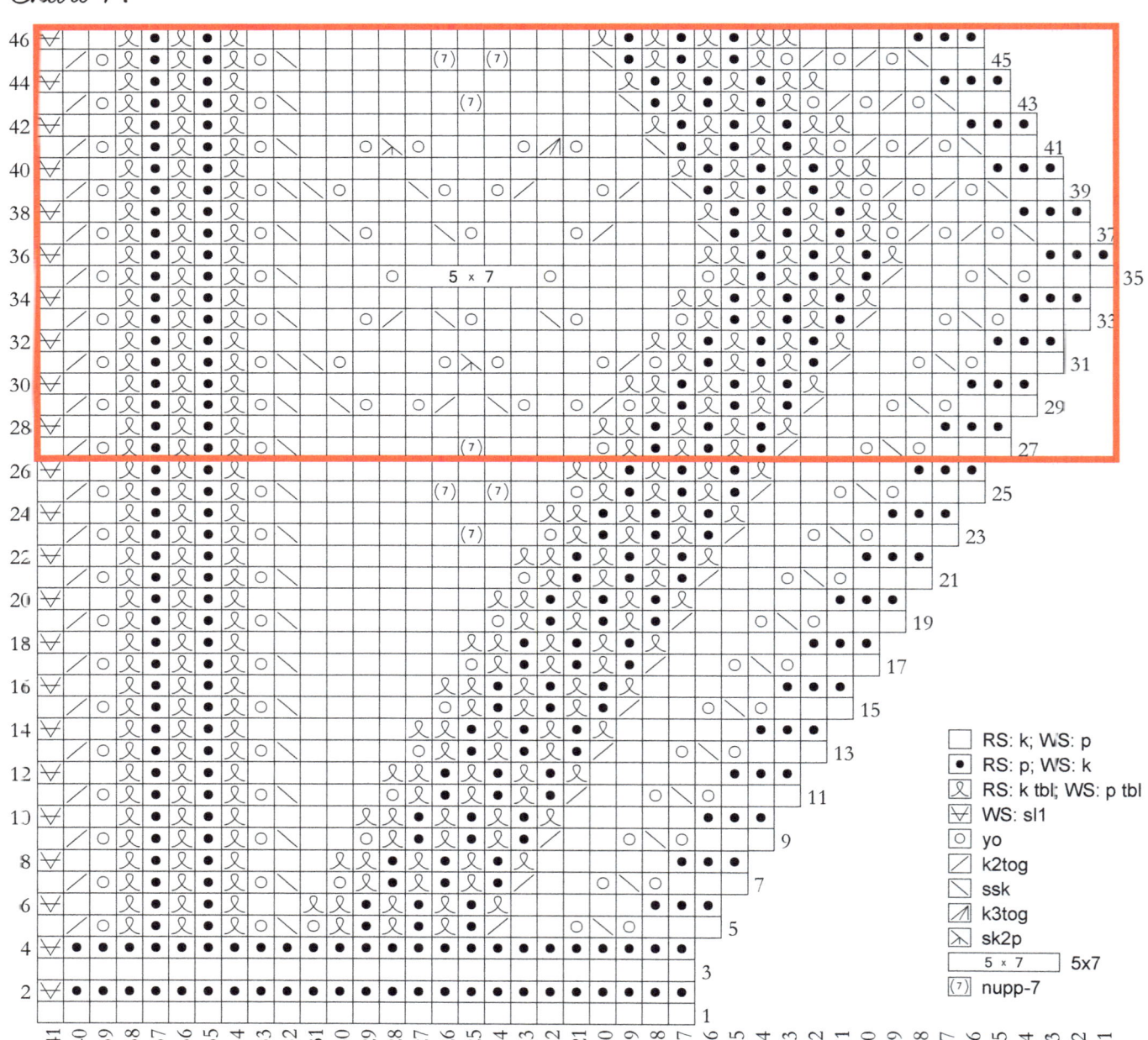

	RS: k; WS: p
•	RS: p; WS: k
႘	RS: k tbl; WS: p tbl
⅄	WS: sl1
○	yo
╱	k2tog
╲	ssk
⟋	k3tog
⅄	sk2p
5 × 7	5x7
(7)	nupp-7

Chart B

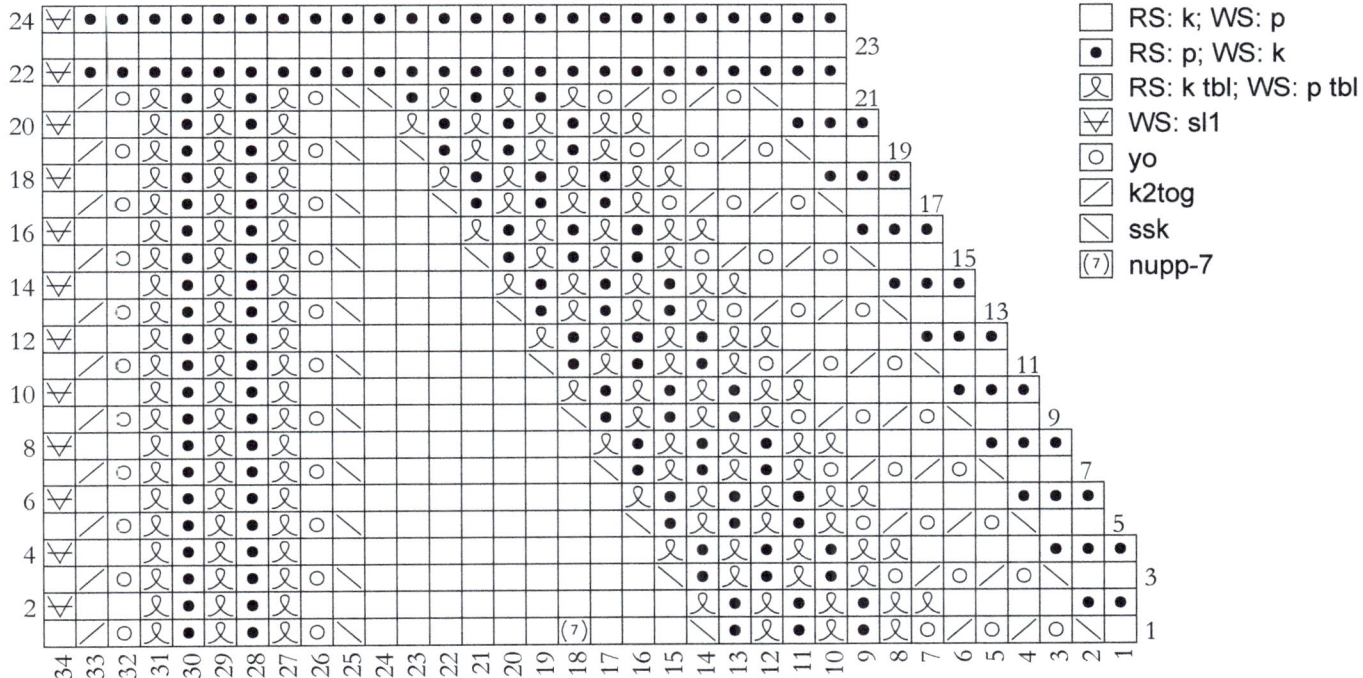

Legend:

- ☐ RS: k; WS: p
- ● RS: p; WS: k
- ℞ RS: k tbl; WS: p tbl
- ⋎ WS: sl1
- ○ yo
- ╱ k2tog
- ╲ ssk
- (7) nupp-7

Alicia Tam & Mitts

Dani Berg

Alicia Tam

SIZES

Sized to fit head circumferences: 17 (20, 23)" / 43 (51, 58.5)cm; shown in 20"/51cm size

FINISHED MEASUREMENTS

Circumference: 16 (18.75, 21.5)" / 40.5 (47.5, 54.5)cm
Length: 5 (5.5, 6)" / 12.5 (14, 15)cm

MATERIALS

Brooklyn Tweed Loft (100% wool; 275 yds / 251m per 50g skein)

- [Color A] Fossil #23; 1 skein
- [Color B] Long Johns #05; 1 skein
- [Color C] Cast Iron #20; 1 skein
- [Color D] Sweatshirt #28; 1 skein
- [Color E] Soot #24; 1 skein

16-inch US #3 / 3.25mm circular needle, or size needed to obtain gauge
16-inch US #1.5 / 2.5mm circular needle
1 set US #3 / 3.25mm double-point needles

Stitch marker
Yarn needle

GAUGE

26 sts and 36 rows = 4" / 10 cm in St st, on larger needle

REQUIRED SKILLS

Knitting in the round; increases/decreases; stranded colorwork techniques

PATTERN NOTES

To make the combined Tam and Mitt set (in any size), you will need 2 skeins of Color A and approximately 50 yards of each remaining color.

PATTERN

Brim

Using smaller needles, CO 104 (122, 140) sts with Color E. Join in the round, being careful not to twist. Pm for beginning of round.

Change to Color A and work in [k1, p1] ribbing for 1 (1.25, 1.5)" / 2.5 (3, 4) cm.

Change to larger needles and work [k2, m1] around to last 4 (2, 0) sts. Knit remaining 4 (2, 0) sts. 154 (182, 210) sts.

Body of Hat

Knit 3 (5, 7) rounds.

Work Alicia Chart 11 (13, 15) times around. All sts are knit in the colors indicated, and all rounds of the chart are read right to left.

With Color A, work in St st until piece measures 5 (5.5, 6)" / 12.5 (14, 15) cm from cast-on edge.

Bringing the classic 1940s into the 21st century is a cinch with this set inspired by Alfred Hitchcock's Notorious *(1946). Mirroring Hitchcock's style, touches of crimson make a cameo appearance in a stranded colorwork tam and mitt set. Shades of gray swirl together, reminiscent of the silhouettes and shadows famously used to create suspense and anticipation. Both hat and mitts are knit in the round with minimal finishing for an elegant design suitable for any leading lady.*

Alicia Chart

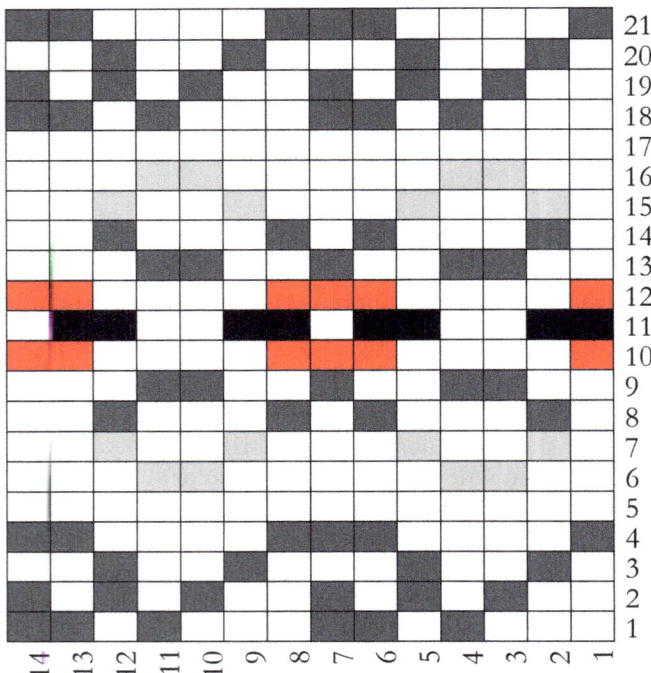

- ☐ Color A / Fossil
- ☐ Color B / Long Johns
- ☐ Color C / Cast Iron
- ☐ Color D / Sweatshirt
- ☐ Color E / Soot

Crown

Knit 1 round, evenly decreasing 4 (2, 0) sts. 150, (180, 210) sts.
Decrease Round 1: [K3, k2tog] around. 120 (144, 168) sts.

Work even for 1 (1.25, 1.5)" / 2.5 (3, 4) cm.
Decrease Round 2: [K2, k2tog] around. 90 (108, 126) sts.

Work even for 0.75 (1, 1.25)" / 2 (2.5, 3) cm.
Decrease Round 3: [K1, k2tog] around. 60 (72, 84) sts.

Work even for 0.5 (0.75, 1)" / 1.5 (2, 2.5) cm.
Decrease Round 4: [K2tog] around. 30 (36, 42) sts.

Work even for 0.25 (0.5, 0.75)" / 0.5 (1.5, 2) cm.
Decrease Round 5: [K2tog] around. 15 (18, 21) sts.

Decrease Round 6: [K2tog] to last 1 (0, 1) st, k1 (0, 1). 8 (9, 11) sts.

Finishing

Break yarn, leaving a 12" / 30cm tail. Thread tail through a yarn needle and draw through the remaining sts. Pull tightly and secure on the inside of the hat. Weave in ends. Block by soaking in wool wash and warm water. Spin or roll in a towel to remove excess water. Place a dinner plate upside down inside the tam to shape and allow to air dry completely.

Alicia Mitts

SIZES

Women's S/M (M/L); shown in size S/M

FINISHED MEASUREMENTS

Hand circumference: 6.5 (8.5)" / 16.5 (21.5) cm

MATERIALS

Brooklyn Tweed Loft (100% wool; 275 yds / 251m per 50g skein)

- ☽ [Color A] Fossil #23; 1 skein
- ☽ [Color B] Long Johns #05; 1 skein
- ☽ [Color C] Cast Iron #20; 1 skein
- ☽ [Color D] Sweatshirt #28; 1 skein
- ☽ [Color E] Soot #24; 1 skein

1 set US #3 / 3.25mm double-point needles or circular needles, or size needed to obtain gauge
US #5 / 3.75mm needle for bind off

3 stitch markers
Stitch holder or length of scrap yarn
Yarn needle

GAUGE

26 sts and 36 rows = 4" / 10 cm in St st, on smaller needle

REQUIRED SKILLS

Knitting in the round; increases/decreases; stranded colorwork techniques; provisional cast on

PATTERN

Work both mitts as described below.

Cuff

Using smaller needles and a provisional cast on, CO 42 (56) sts with Color A. Join in the round, being careful not to twist. Pm for beginning of round.

Knit 6 rounds.
Change to Color E. Knit 1 round.

Change to Color A. Purl 1 round. (Turning round for hemmed edge.)
Knit 6 more rounds.

Place the live sts from the provisional cast on onto a second needle.

Fold the work at the purl round so that the wrong side is on the inside, creating a hemmed edge. Knit 1 st from the front needle tog with 1 st from the back needle around.

Knit 1 round.
Work Alicia Chart 3 (4) times around.
Change to Color A. Knit 1 round.

Thumb Gusset

Round 1: M1, knit around. 43 (57) sts.
Round 2: Knit.
Round 3: K21 (28), pm, k1, pm, knit to end.
Round 4: Knit to marker, sm, m1L, knit to marker, m1R, sm, knit to end.
Round 5–8: Knit.

Repeat Rounds 4–8 until there are 13 (17) sts between the markers.

Next round: Knit to gusset marker, remove marker, place 13 (17) gusset sts onto waste yarn, remove second gusset marker, knit to end. 42 (56) sts.

Knit for 1 (1.5)" / 2.5 (4)cm.
Work [k1, p1] ribbing for 0.5 (0.75)" / 1.5 (2)cm.
Change to Color E and bind off loosely with larger needle.

Thumb

Place held sts on needles.

Knit 1 round, picking up and knitting an extra st at the base of the thumb, pm, and join to begin knitting in the round. Twist the picked up st by knitting it through the back loop to help prevent any holes. 14 (18) sts.

Work [k1, p1] ribbing for 0.5 (0.75)" / 1.5 (2)cm.

Change to Color E and BO loosely with larger needle.

Finishing

Break yarn, weave in ends. Block by socking in wool wash and warm water. Spin or roll in a towel to remove excess water. Lay flat, pat into shape, and allow to air dry completely.

Three-Second Kiss Sweater

Becky Herrick

SIZES

Women s XS (S, M, L, XL, 2X, 3X, 4X); shown in size M
Intended to be worn with no ease.

FINISHED MEASUREMENTS

Bust: 27.75 (33, 36.75, 41, 44, 48.5, 52.75, 57.5)" /
70.5 (84 93.5, 104, 112, 123, 134, 146)cm

MATERIALS

Sunday Knits Nirvana Sport (92% merino,
8% cashmere; 246 yds / 225m per 50g skein)

> [MC] Charcoal; 3 (4, 4, 4, 5, 5, 6, 6) skeins

Sunday Knits Eden Sport (100% merino; 99 yds /
90m per 20g skein)

> [CC1] Garnet; 2 (2, 2, 2, 2, 2, 3, 3) skeins
> [CC2] Red; 1 skein

Sunday Knits Angelic Sport (100% merino; 99 yds /
90m per 20g skein)

> [CC3] Smoke; 1 (1, 2, 2, 2, 2, 2, 2) skeins
> [CC4] Bone; 1 skein

Sunday Knits Nirvana Sport (92% merino,
8% cashmere; 99 yds / 90m per 20g skein)

> [CC5] Cream; 1 skein

32-inch US #3 / 3.25mm circular needle, or size
needed to obtain gauge in St st
32-inch US #2 / 2.75mm circular needle, or size
below that needed for gauge

32-inch US #4 / 3.5mm circular needle, or size
needed to obtain gauge in stranded patt
1 set US #3 / 3.25mm double-point needles
1 set US #2 / 2.75mm double-point needles

5 removable stitch markers
Stitch holders or waste yarn
Yarn needle

GAUGE

23 sts and 36 rounds = 4" / 10cm in St st, on middle-sized needle
23 sts and 36 rounds = 4" / 10cm in colorwork patt, on larger needle

REQUIRED SKILLS

Knitting in the round; knitting with double-pointed needles or magic loop or knitting in the round on two circulars; increases/decreases; short rows; stranded colorwork techniques; steeking; knit-on edging; knowledge of basic sweater construction; kitchener stitch (grafting); i-cord; seaming

PATTERN NOTES

This pullover is worked completely in the round with turned hems and a steeked neckline. The sleeves and body are worked from the bottom up and joined at the yoke. The steek band is added at the same time. After the colorwork chart a few short rows are added across the back. The neckline stitches are held live while the steek is worked. Attached i-cord edging trims the steek edges and binds off along the neckline for a single, polished edge.

I've always been fascinated by Bohus sweaters, the way the knit and purl stitches blend in the intricate colorwork yokes. I wanted to try a little knit-and-purl colorwork of my own. This sweater uses techniques similar to that of Bohus sweaters, but with just two strands of yarn in each round. The close shaping, short body length, and V-shaped neckline are all inspired by the fashions of the late 1940s. At the end of the Second World War resources were so limited that all fashionable clothing was trim and fitted—to use as little fabric or yarn as possible.

When working the stranded colorwork, white colors should be held dominant (closer to the fabric) over gray and reds should be dominant over white.

Stitches and Techniques

Attached i-cord edging: K2, ssk using the third st and the next st of the garment, sl 3 to the LH needle (1 st bound off). Repeat this process, binding off the given number of sts.

Pattern

Sleeves (identical)

With smaller needles and CC1, CO 42 (42, 48, 48, 54, 54, 60, 60). Pm and join to work in the round, being careful not to twist. Work in St st until piece measures 1.25 (1.25, 1.25, 1.5, 1.5, 1.5, 1.75, 1.75)" / 3, (3, 3, 4, 4, 4, 4.5, 4.5)cm. Break yarn.

Turning round: With middle-sized needles and MC, purl 1 round.

Knit 1 round. Continue in St st until piece measures 1.5 (1.5, 1.5, 1.75, 1.75, 1.75, 2, 2)" / 4 (4, 4, 4.5, 4.5, 4.5, 5, 5)cm from turning round.

With larger needles, join CC3 and work Row 1 of Cuff chart repeating to end of round.

Work Cuff Chart, breaking and joining colors as needed.

When Cuff Chart is complete, switch to middle-sized needles and work in St st until piece measures 5.75 (5.75, 5.75, 5.75, 6, 6, 6, 6)" / 14.5 (14.5, 14.5, 14.5, 15, 15, 15, 15)cm from turning round.

Inc Round: K1, m1, knit until 1 st remains, m1, k1. Work 7 (6, 6, 5, 4, 3, 3, 3) rounds even in St st. Repeat these 8 (7, 7, 6, 5, 4, 4, 4) rounds 8 (10, 10, 13, 14, 17, 19, 22) more times. 60 (64, 70, 76, 84, 90, 100, 106) sts.

Continue in St st until piece measures 19.25 (19.5, 19.75, 20, 20.25, 20.5, 20.75, 21)" / 49 (49.5, 50, 51, 51.5, 52, 52.5, 53.5)cm from turning round. Stop final round 7 (7, 8, 8, 9, 9, 10, 10) sts from marker. Place next 14 (14, 16, 16, 18, 18, 20, 20) sts on hold for underarm. Place remaining 46 (50, 54, 60, 66, 72, 80, 86) sts on hold for sleeve.

Body

Note: the end of round is at the center front of this sweater. This means the color changes for the yoke will line up with the steek line, which cuts back on having to weave in ends.

With smaller needles and CC1, CO 152 (182, 203, 228, 245, 271, 296, 322). Pm and join to work in the

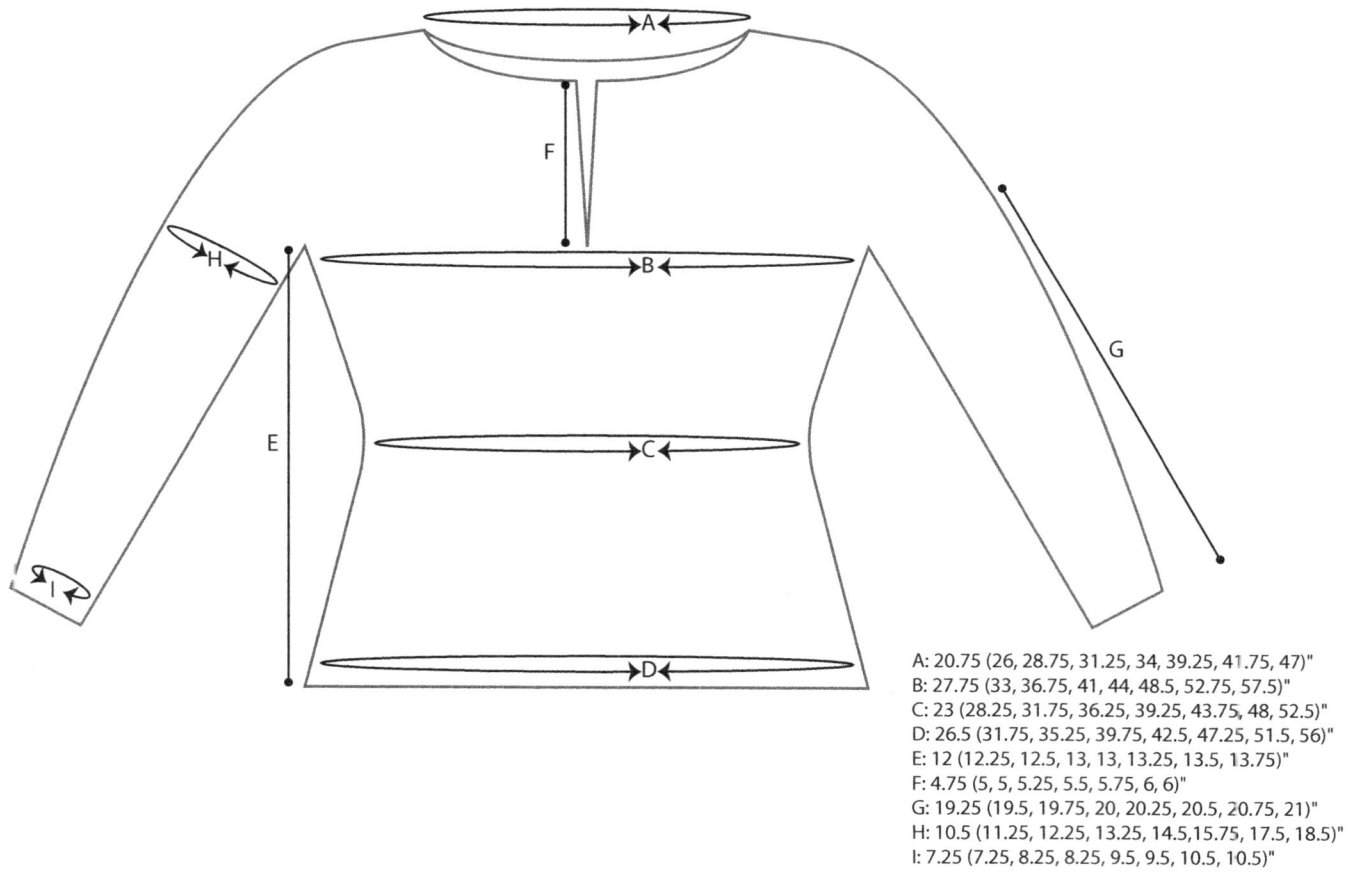

A: 20.75 (26, 28.75, 31.25, 34, 39.25, 41.75, 47)"
B: 27.75 (33, 36.75, 41, 44, 48.5, 52.75, 57.5)"
C: 23 (28.25, 31.75, 36.25, 39.25, 43.75, 48, 52.5)"
D: 26.5 (31.75, 35.25, 39.75, 42.5, 47.25, 51.5, 56)"
E: 12 (12.25, 12.5, 13, 13, 13.25, 13.5, 13.75)"
F: 4.75 (5, 5, 5.25, 5.5, 5.75, 6, 6)"
G: 19.25 (19.5, 19.75, 20, 20.25, 20.5, 20.75, 21)"
H: 10.5 (11.25, 12.25, 13.25, 14.5, 15.75, 17.5, 18.5)"
I: 7.25 (7.25, 8.25, 8.25, 9.5, 9.5, 10.5, 10.5)"

round, being careful not to twist. Work in St st until piece measures 1.25 (1.25, 1.25, 1.5, 1.5, 1.5, 1.75, 1.75)" / 3 (3, 3, 4, 4, 4, 4.5, 4.5)cm. Break yarn.

Turning round: With middle-sized needles and MC, purl 1 round.

Knit 1 round. Continue in St st until piece measures 1.75 (1.75, 2, 2.25, 2.25, 2.5, 2.5, 2.75)" / 4.5 (4.5, 5, 5.5, 5.5, 6.5, 6.5, 7)cm from turning round.

Waist shaping setup: K19 (23, 25, 29, 31, 34, 37, 40), pm, k44 (53, 59, 66, 71, 79, 86, 94), pm, k26 (30, 35, 38, 41, 45, 50, 54), pm, k44 (53, 59, 66, 71, 79, 86, 94), pm, knit to end of round.

Dec round: [Knit until 2 sts before m, k2tog, sm, knit to m, sm, ssk] twice, knit to end of round.
Work 4 rounds even in St st.
Repeat these 5 rounds 4 more times. 132 (162, 183, 208, 225, 251, 276, 302) sts.

Work even in St st until piece measures 6.75 (6.75, 7, 7.5, 7.5, 7.75, 7.75, 8)" / 17 (17, 18, 19, 19, 19.5, 19.5, 20.5)cm from turning round.

Inc round: [Knit to m, LLI, sm, knit to m, sm, RLI] twice, knit to end of round.
Work 3 rounds even in St st.
Repeat these 4 rounds 6 more times. 160 (190, 211, 236, 253, 279, 304, 330) sts total.

Work even in St st until piece measures 12 (12.25, 12.5, 13, 13, 13.25, 13.5, 13.75)" / 30.5 (31, 32, 33, 33, 33.5, 34.5, 35)cm from turning round.

Yoke

Joining round: K12 (6, 6, 12, 12, 6, 12, 6), pm for neckline, k21 (34, 39, 39, 42, 54, 54, 66), place next 14 (14, 16, 16, 18, 18, 20, 20) sts on holder for underarm, k46 (50, 54, 60, 66, 72, 80, 86) from sleeve, k66 (82, 89, 102, 109, 123, 132, 146), place next 14 (14, 16, 16, 18, 18, 20, 20) sts on holder for underarm, k46 (50, 54, 60, 66, 72, 80, 86) from sleeve, k21 (34, 39, 39, 42, 54, 54, 66), pm for neckline, k12 (6, 6, 12, 12, 6, 12, 6), CO 4 sts for steek, sm for end of round, CO 4 sts for steek. Knit to end of round. 232 (270, 295, 332, 357, 395, 432, 470) sts total. 32 (20, 20, 32, 32, 20, 32, 20) between neckline markers including steek sts and 200 (250, 275, 300, 325, 375, 400, 450) around yoke.

Work 0 (1, 1, 2, 3, 4, 5, 6) rounds even in St st.

Note: Sizes S, M, 2X, 4X will work the Narrow Neckline chart and sizes XS, L, XL, 3X will work the Wide Neckline chart. Narrow and Wide refer to the width of the chart; the decs are the same for all sizes. Be sure to add or remove colors at the end of round marker. Steek sts can be worked either in a checkerboard or a striped pattern.

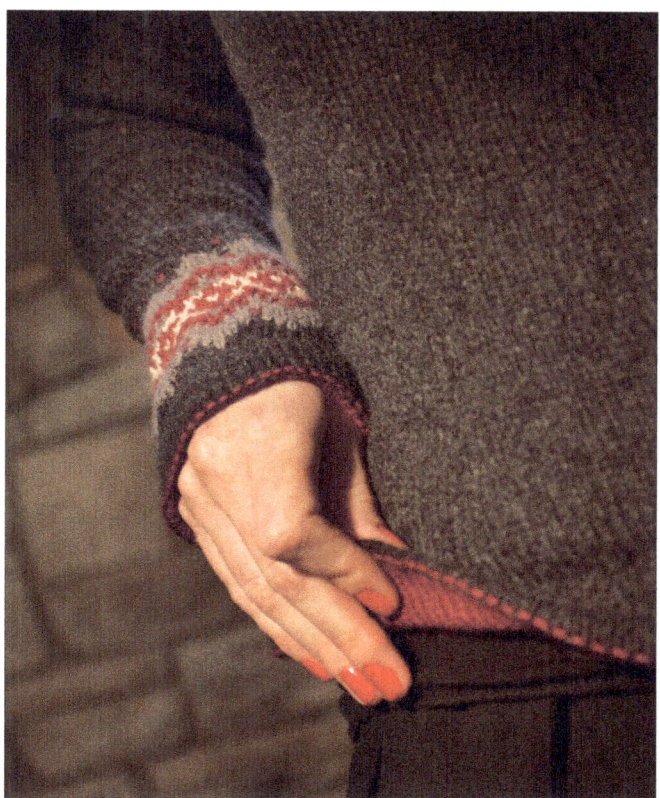

With larger needles, work 4 steek sts followed by Round 1 of Neckline chart, sm, work Round 1 of Yoke chart repeating to next marker, sm, work Round 1 of Neckline chart followed by 4 steek sts.

Work Neckline and Yoke charts, breaking and joining colors as needed through Round 37.

Note: If you are following the narrow neckline chart, on Round 34 you will need to remove the Neckline chart marker and work the last dec in the color of the next st of the Yoke chart. Once all neckline sts are used up cont to work the 8 steek sts and yoke sts in patt.

Row 38: Switch to middle-sized needle and work charts through Round 41. 140 (158, 173, 200, 215, 233, 260, 278) sts.

Shoulder short rows: K99 (113, 124, 144, 156, 169, 189, 203), w&t.
P66 (75, 83, 96, 104, 113, 126, 135), w&t.

Knit until 5 (5, 6, 6, 7, 7, 8, 8) sts from wrapped st, w&t.
Purl until 5 (5, 6, 6, 7, 7, 8, 8) sts from wrapped st, w&t.
Repeat these 2 rows once more.

Knit to end of round, picking up wraps and working them with the wrapped st.
Knit next round, picking up wraps and working them with the wrapped st.

Work 0 (0, 1, 1, 2, 2, 3, 3) more rounds even in St st. End last round 4 sts from marker.

BO 8 steek sts. Hold remaining 132 (150, 165, 192, 207, 225, 252, 270) sts.

Steek

Reinforce edges of steek with your preferred method. I used a crochet steek edging. Cut between sts 4 and 5 of steek. Trim all remaining yarn ends. Fold edges under and whipstitch in place.

Collar

With middle-sized needles, pick up 1 st for every row along edge of neckline. Hold needle with right front of sweater in left hand; with spare needle and MC, CO 3 sts, slip sts to LH needle and work i-cord edging along neckline. Work 1 round of unattached i-cord at corner, then work i-cord edging along neck, binding off held sts. Work 1 round of unattached i-cord at corner, then work i-cord edging along left front neckline.

Finishing

Weave in all ends. Graft held sts at underarms. Fold turned hems at cuffs and body to inside of sweater and whip-stitch. Tack the start and end of the i-cord trim together. Block to desired measurements and enjoy!

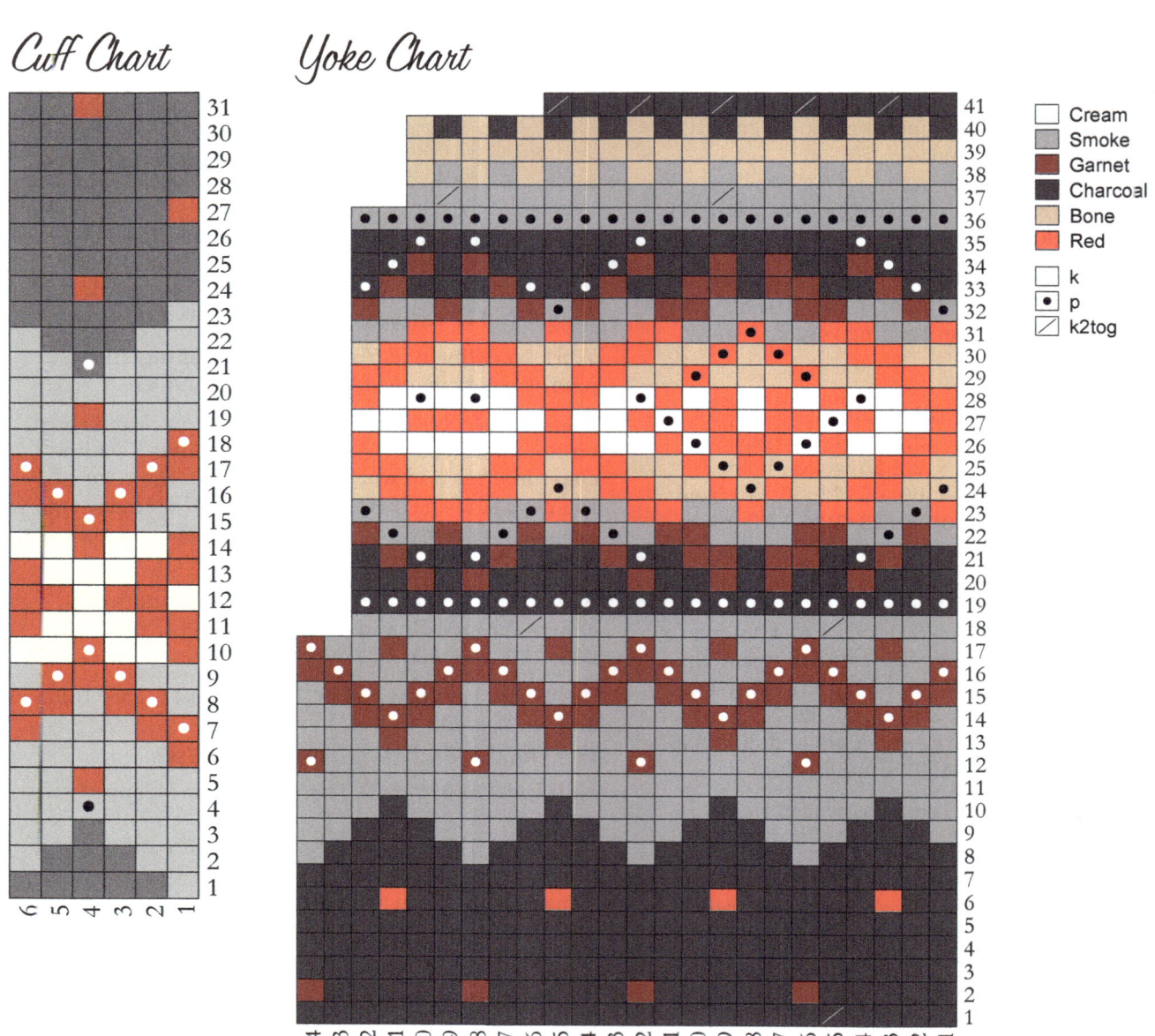

Narrow Neckline Chart

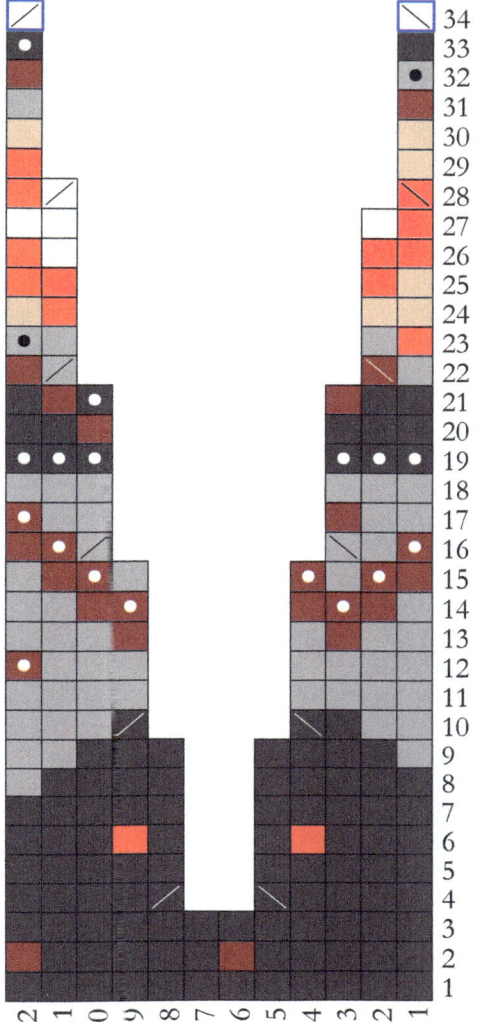

	Cream		k
	Smoke	●	p
	Garnet	⟋	k2tog
	Charcoal	⟍	ssk
	Bone		
	Red		

— Note: Use stitch before/after marker as appropriate to work these decreases

Wide Neckline Chart

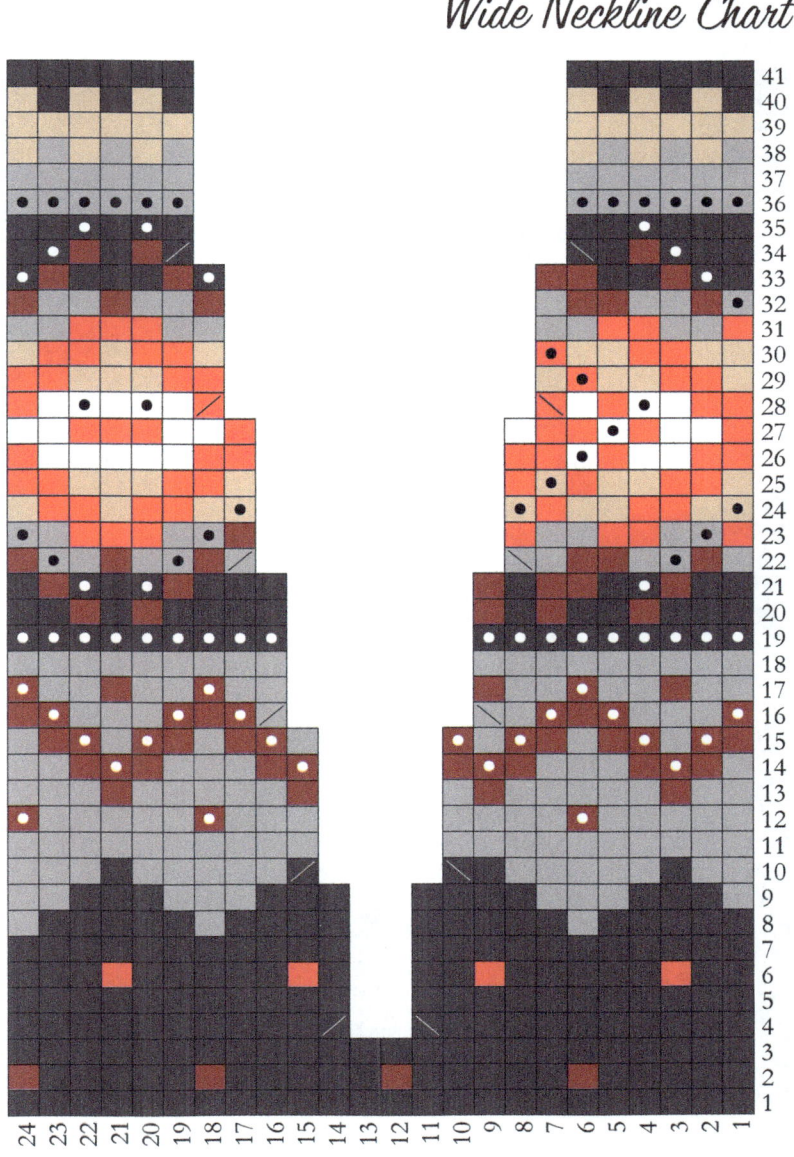

Rio Gloves

Stefanie Pollmeier

SIZES

Women's S (M, L); shown in size S (gray with red accents) and M (red with black accents)
Intended to be worn with no ease.

FINISHED MEASUREMENTS

Palm circumference: 7 (7.5, 8)" / 18 (19, 20.5)cm

MATERIALS

Long Cuff Version (grey with red accents)

Wollfarm Sockenwolle (75% new wool, 25% polyamid; 437 yds / 400m per 100g skein)

> [MC] Grey; 1 skein
> [CC] Red; 24 (26, 28) yds / 26 (28, 30)m

Short Cuff Version (red with black accents)

Drachenwolle Merino Extrafine Semisolid (100% merino; 350 yds / 320m per 100g skein)

> [MC] Bordeaux #4, 1 skein
> [CC] Anthrazit #25; 21 (23, 25) yds / 23 (25, 27)m

1 set US #2 / 2.5mm double-point needles
1 US #2 / 2.5mm circular or pair of straight needles
US #2.5 / 3mm crochet hook

2 removable stitch markers
8mm buttons: 4 for long cuff, 2 for short cuff version
Stitch holders or waste yarn
Yarn needle

GAUGE

28 sts and 40 rounds = 4" / 10cm in St st

REQUIRED SKILLS

Knitting in the round; knitting with double-pointed needles; increases/decreases; backward loop cast on; slipped stitches; picking up stitches; basic crochet stitches

PATTERN NOTES

Cuffs are knit flat before you join to knit in the round. The main part is knit in the round, with increases for the thumb gusset at the sides. The fingers are worked one after another from little finger to index finger, beginning at the side opposite the thumb gusset. While each finger is knit, the remaining hand stitches are placed on holders or scrap yarn. A few additional sts are cast on over the gap between the fingers, then knit in the round until the required length is reached. The thumb is knit last, but in the same manner as the other fingers, picking up sts over the gap between hand and gusset.

A note on fitting: Individual finger lengths can vary considerably from person to person. Try on the glove while knitting the fingers or measure the recipient's fingers whenever possible. In case this isn't practical, average measurements are provided in the instructions. If in doubt, err on the longer side and maybe cast on an additional stitch or two at the base of the fingers. Better a finger that is a little

These fitted, wrist-length gloves are my interpretation of the late-'40s / early-'50s New Look that Ingrid Bergman dons so spectacularly as Alicia Huberman in Notorious. *To re-create that uncluttered style, my gloves are mostly monochromatic and knit mainly in stockinette. Meanwhile, the split cuffs, rows of contrasting slip-stitch ridges, and simple crochet edgings add interest to the design. Knit them in stark, high-contrast colors for a dramatic effect, or choose softer grays and light reds for a more ladylike version.*

long and wide than too short and tight, which would make the glove unwearable. To adapt the pattern you can also combine the length measurements of one size with the width of another. (I have long fingers, but slim hands and need size S in width and M in length, for example).

When joining new yarn at the base of the fingers, make sure to leave a long tail (at least 8" / 20cm). You can use it later to cover gaps or misshapen stitches with duplicate stitch before you weave in ends.

STITCHES AND TECHNIQUES

Knot Ridge pattern

(worked flat over an odd number of sts)

Row 1 (RS): K1, [k1, yo, k1] into next st, *sl1 wyib, [k1, yo, k1] into next st; repeat from * to last st, k1.

Row 2 (WS): K1, k3tog tbl, *sl1 wyib, k3tog tbl; repeat from * to last st, k1.

Knit the pattern rows with slightly lesser tension than the St st sections of the gloves. This way the ridges really "pop" for a three-dimensional effect.

PATTERN—LEFT GLOVE

Cuff (Long Version)

CO 43 (47, 51) sts on straight or circular needles.
Row 1 (WS): Purl.
Continue in St st for 6 more rows.

Join CC and work first Knot Ridge.
Break CC and work St st in MC for 2 rows.

Inc row: K2, m1L, knit to last 2 sts, m1R, k2. 45 (49, 53) sts.
Continue in St st for 3 more rows.

Join CC and work second Knot Ridge.
Break CC and work St st in MC for 2 rows.

Inc row: K2, m1L, knit to last 2 sts, m1R, k2. 47 (51, 55) sts.
Purl 1 row, join CC and work third Knot Ridge.
Break CC and work St st in MC for 2 rows.

Inc row: K2, m1L, knit to last 2 sts, m1R, k2. 49 (53, 57) sts.

Purl 1 row.
Join CC and work last Knot Ridge.
Break CC and work St st in MC for 3 rows. Don't turn. Join for working in the round; pm to mark beginning of round.

Cuff should measure approx. 2.5" / 6.5cm.

Cuff (Short Version)

CO 45 (49, 53) sts on straight or circular needles.
Row 1 (WS): Purl.
Continue in St st for 4 more rows.

Join CC and work first Knot Ridge.
Break CC and work St st in MC for 2 rows.

Inc row: K2, m1L, knit to last 2 sts, m1R, k2. 47 (51, 55) sts.
Purl 1 row, join CC and work second Knot Ridge.
Break CC and work St st in MC for 2 rows.

Inc row: K2, m1L, knit to last 2 sts, m1R, k2. 49 (53, 57) sts.
Purl 1 row.
Join CC and work last Knot Ridge.
Break CC and work St st in MC for 3 rows. Don't turn. Join for working in the round; pm to mark beginning of round.

Cuff should measure approx. 2" / 5cm.

Thumb gusset

Knit 3 rounds.
K12 (13, 14) sts, pm, m1L, k1, m1R, pm, knit to end of round. 3 sts between markers.

Knit 3 rounds.
Knit to marker, sm, m1L, knit to marker, m1R, sm, knit to end of round.
Repeat last 4 rounds 2 (3, 3) more times. 9 (11, 11) sts between markers.

Knit 2 rounds.
Knit to marker, sm, m1L, knit to marker, m1R, sm, knit to end of round.
Repeat last 3 rounds 2 (2, 3) more times. 15 (17, 19) sts between markers.

Knit 2 more rounds. Knit to marker, sm, sl gusset sts onto stitch holder or scrap yarn. Using backwards-loop method, CO 5 (5, 7) sts over gap, sm, knit to end of round. 6 (6, 8) inside gusset markers; 48 (52, 56) on rest of hand.

Hand

Knit 2 rounds.
Knit to first marker, sm, k1 (1, 2), s2kp, k1, sm, knit to end of round. 3 (3, 5) sts between markers.

Knit 2 rounds.
Knit to first marker, sm, k– (–, 1), s2kp, k– (–, 1), sm, knit to end of round. 1 (1, 3) sts between markers.

Size L only: Knit 2 rounds.

All sizes: Knit to first marker, sm, s2kp, sm, knit to end of round. 49 (53, 57) sts.

Remove markers and cont in St st until piece measures 4.25 (4.25, 4.5)" / 10.5 (11, 11.5)cm from last Knot Ridge.

Little Finger

On the following round work to the last 7 (8, 10) sts, place next 38 (42, 44) sts on stitch holder or scrap yarn or leave them on spare dpns or circular needle. Using backwards-loop method, CO 3 sts over the gap, rejoin, and knit remaining sts, pm. 14 (14, 16) sts for little finger.

Arrange sts evenly over 3 dpns and work in the round.

Round 1: Knit.
Round 2: Sm, k5 (5, 7), ssk, k1, k2tog, knit to end of round. 12 (12, 14) sts.

Continue in St st until Little Finger measures 2 (2.25, 2.25)" / 5 (5.5, 6)cm or to desired length. (Measure from cast-on edge over the gap.)

Dec for top: [K2tog], repeat to end of round, end k3tog if there's an odd number of sts.

Break yarn, thread tail through remaining sts, pull tight to close the opening, and fasten off.

Upper Hand

Place held sts back on needles, join yarn at base of Little Finger, pick up and knit 4 sts along cast-on edge, knit around to 1 st before first picked up st, ssk, k1, pm, k1, k2tog. 40 (44, 46) sts.

Continue in St st to marker, work 1 more round.

Ring Finger

K7 (8, 8) sts, place 26 (28, 30) sts on holder or scrap yarn. Using backwards loop method, CO 3 (3, 4) sts over gap, k7 (8, 8), pm. 17 (19, 20) sts for Ring Finger.

Round 1: Knit.
Round 2: Sm, k6 (7, 7), ssk, k1 (1, 2), k2tog, knit to end of round. 15 (17, 18) sts.

Continue in St st until Ring Finger measures 2.25 (2.5, 2.75)" / 6 (6.5, 7)cm or to desired length.

Dec and finish as for Little Finger.

Middle Finger

Join yarn at base of Ring Finger, pick up and knit 4 sts along cast-on edge, k6 (7, 7), leave next 14 (14, 16) sts on holder. Using backwards loop method, CO 4 (3, 4) sts over gap, k5 (6, 6), ssk, k1, pm, k1, k2tog. 18 (19, 20) sts for Middle Finger.

Round 1: Knit to marker. New round begins here.
Round 2: Sm, k6 (7, 7), ssk, k2 (1, 2), k2tog, knit to end of round. 16 (17, 18) sts.

Continue in St st until Middle Finger measures 2.75 (3, 3.25)" / 7 (7.5, 8)cm or to desired length.

Dec and finish as for Little Finger.

Index Finger

Place remaining 14 (14, 16) sts back on needles. Join yarn at base of Middle Finger, pick up and knit 3 (4, 4) sts along cast-on edge, k13 (13, 15), ssk, k1, pm, k– (1, 1), k2tog. 15 (16, 18) sts for Index Finger.

Continue in St st until Index Finger measures 2.25 (2.5, 2.75)" / 6 (6.5, 7)cm or to desired length.

Dec and finish as for Little Finger.

Thumb

Place held gusset sts back on needles and join yarn.

Knit across gusset sts, pick up and knit 6 (6, 8) sts along cast-on edge above gap. 18 (20, 24) sts.

Round 1: Knit to last st before picked-up sts, ssk, k4 (4, 6), k2tog. 2 picked-up sts dec. 16 (18, 22) sts.
Round 2: Knit.

Sizes M & L only:
Round 3: Knit to last st before picked-up sts, ssk, k– (2, 4), k2tog. 2 picked-up sts dec. 16 (16, 20) sts.
Round 4: Knit.

All sizes:
Continue in St st until Thumb measures 1.75 (2, 2.25)" / 4.5 (5, 5.5)cm or to desired length.

Dec for top:
Round 1: [K2tog, k2], repeat to end of round.
Round 2: Knit.
Round 3: [K2tog], repeat to end of round, end k3tog if there's an odd number of sts. Finish as for other fingers.

Pattern—Right Glove

Cuff

Work as for Left Glove.

Thumb gusset

Knit 3 rounds.
K36 (39, 42) sts, pm, m1L, k1, m1R, pm, knit to end of round. 3 sts between markers.

Knit 3 rounds.
Knit to marker, sm, m1L, knit to marker, m1R, sm, knit to end of round.
Repeat last 4 rounds 2 (3, 3) more times.

Knit 2 rounds.
Knit to marker, sm, m1L, knit to marker, m1R, sm, knit to end of round.
Repeat last 3 rounds 2 (2, 3) more times. 15 (17, 19) sts between markers.

Knit 2 more rounds. Knit to marker, spm, k1, sl gusset sts onto stitch holder or scrap yarn. Using backwards-loop method CO 5 (5, 7) sts over gap, sm, knit to end of round.

Hand

Knit 2 rounds.
Knit to first marker, sm, k1 (1, 2), s2kp, k1, sm, knit to end of round.

Knit 2 rounds.
Knit to first marker, sm, k– (–, 1), s2kp, k1, sm, knit to end of round.

Size L only: Knit 2 rounds.

All sizes: Knit to first marker, sm, s2kp, k1, sm, knit to end of round. 49 (53, 57) sts.

Remove markers and cont in St st until piece measures 4.25 (4.25, 4.5)" / 10.5 (11, 11.5)cm from last Knot Ridge.

Little Finger

On the following round k7 (8, 10), pm, k11 (11, 13), place next 38 (42, 44) sts on stitch holder or scrap yarn or leave them on spare dpns or circular needle. Using backwards-loop method CO 3 st over the gap, rejoin and knit to marker. 14 (14, 16) sts for little finger.

Arrange sts evenly over 3 dpns and work in the round.

Round 1: Knit.
Round 2: K5 (5, 7), ssk, k1, k2tog, knit to end of round. 12 (12, 14) sts.

Continue in St st until Little Finger measures 2 (2.25, 2.25)" / 5 (5.5, 6)cm or to desired length. (Measure from cast-on edge over the gap.)

Dec for top: [K2tog] to end of round.

Break yarn, thread tail through remaining sts twice, pull tight, and fasten off.

Work Upper Hand, remaining fingers and thumb as for Left Glove.

Finishing

Weave in ends. Use cast-on tails at the base of fingers and thumbs to close any gaps and cover misshapen sts with duplicate st.

Crocheted edging

Left Glove (Long Version): With palm of the glove facing you and fingers pointing downwards, join CC at the left corner. Edging will be worked around the cast-on edge and the edges of the wrist slit. Work one sc into each cast-on st, 2 sc into the last cast-on st when you turn the corner to the wrist slit. Continue up the side of the slit to the first Knot Ridge. Ch 9 sts, work 1 sl st into each of the first 3 sts of the chain. That's the first button loop. Continue up the side to the third Knot Ridge. Ch 7 sts, work 1 sl st each into first st of chain and into sc at the bottom (second button loop). Continue around the edge, join to first st with a sl st. Break yarn and pull tail through. Weave in ends.

Left Glove (Short Version): With palm of the glove facing you and fingers pointing downwards, join CC at the left corner. Edging will be worked around the cast-on edge and the edges of the wrist slit. Work one sc into each cast-on st, 2 sc into the last cast-on st when you turn the corner to the wrist slit. Continue up the side to the first Knot Ridge. Ch 7 sts, work 1 sl st each into first st of chain and into sc at the bottom (button loop). Continue around the edge, join to first st with a sl st. Break yarn and pull tail through. Weave in ends.

Right Glove (Long Version): Start at the left corner, work along the cast-on edge as for Left Glove, cont up the slit WITHOUT working the button loops, turn the upper corner and work down to third Knot Ridge. Work 7 st chain as before, cont down to first Knot Ridge, work 9 st chain as before. Continue down and work sl st into first st to join. Finish as for Left Glove.

Right Glove (Short Version): Start at the left corner, work along the cast-on edge as for Left Glove, cont up the slit WITHOUT working the button loop, turn the upper corner and work down to first Knot Ridge. Work 7 st chain as before, cont down and work sl st into first st to join. Finish as for Left Glove.

Both gloves: Sew on buttons opposite button loops.

Lina Vest Coat

Nadya Stallings

SIZES

Women's S (M, L, XL, 2X, 3X); shown in size M
Intended to be worn with 3" / 7.5cm positive ease

FINISHED MEASUREMENTS

Bust: 37 (39, 43, 47, 51, 55)" / 94 (99, 109, 119.5,
129.5, 139.5)cm
Length 39.5 (40.5, 42, 43.5, 45, 46)" / 100.5 (103,
106.5, 110.5, 114.5, 117)cm

MATERIALS

Harrisville Designs Highland (100% wool; 200 yds /
183m per 100g skein);

> [MC] Charcoal; 7 (7, 8, 8, 9, 9) skeins

> [CC] White; 4 (4, 5, 5, 6, 6) skeins

48-inch US #5 / 3.75mm circular needle, or size
needed to obtain gauge

1 stitch marker (optional)
8 × 1" / 25mm buttons
Stitch holders or waste yarn
Yarn needle

GAUGE

22 sts and 22 rows = 4" / 10cm in charted pattern
stitch

REQUIRED SKILLS

Increases/decreases; reading simple charts; stranded
colorwork technique; picking up stitches; kitchener
stitch (grafting); seaming; sewing on buttons

PATTERN NOTES

Read the whole pattern before you begin working on
your garment; there are a few stages of the pattern
that are written separately but should be worked
simultaneously.

This work is made with selvedges: the first st is
slipped purlwise; last st is purled.

Seed stitch for even number of sts

Row 1: [K1, p1] to end of row.
Row 2: [P1, k1] to end of row.
Repeat Rows 1 & 2 for pattern.

Seed stitch for odd number of sts

Row 1: [K1, p1] to last st, k1.
Repeat Row 1 for pattern.

One-row buttonhole, worked in MC

Bring working yarn to front, sl 1, bring yarn to
back. [Sl one more st and pass the previous sl st
over it] 3 times. Sl first st from right needle back to
left needle, turn work. Bring working yarn to back,
passing it between needles. Make cable CO: [with
right needle pull the loop between first and second
sts of the left needle and place it on left needle
making it first st] 4 times.

I-cord BO

CO 3 extra sts and place them at the beg of the BO
row. [K2, skp, slip all 3 sts from right needle back
to the left needle], rep to last 3 sts, k3tog, fasten off
yarn.

In Suspicion *(1941), Lina (played by Joan Fontaine) wears a striped traveling coat that gave me an idea for
an unusual, stylish garment. All that remained was to add a few bold details. This sleeveless coat can be worn
over a shirt, blouse, or sleeved dress. Its textile-like fabric features striped and speckled stranded colorwork.
The double-breasted button closure is both functional and decorative.*

PATTERN

Back

With MC, CO 120 (132, 142, 154, 164, 176) sts.
Rows 1–3: Work in garter stitch.

Beginning on next row (RS), work 28 rows of Stranded Colorwork Chart, or until piece measures 5.5" / 14cm, ending with a WS row.

Dec Row (RS): Sl1, ssk, work to last 3 sts, k2tog, p1. Repeat Dec Row every 8th row, 11 more times. 96 (108, 118, 130, 140, 152) sts.

Work Dec Row every 6 (6, 8, 8, 8, 8)th row 3 (3, 1, 2, 2, 1) more times , and then every – (–, 6, 6, 6, 6)th row – (–, 2, 1, 1, 2) more times. 90 (102, 112, 124, 134, 146) sts.

Work 4 (6, 4, 4, 4, 8) more rows in Chart patt as established.

Inc Row: Sl1, m1, work to last st, m1, p1.

Repeat Inc Row every 6 (6, –, 8, 8, –)th row 2 (2, –, 1, 1, –) more times , and then every – (–, 6, 6, 6, 6)th row – (–, 2, 1, 1, 2) more times. 96 (108, 118, 130, 140, 152) sts.

Work 3 (5, 5, 3, 3, 3) more rows in Chart patt as established.

Underarm shaping

Put on waste yarn last 6 (6, 7, 7, 8, 8) sts of next 2 rows. 84 (96, 104, 116, 124, 136) sts.

Work Dec Row every 9th row once, and then every 8th row 3 (3, 4, 4, 5, 6) more times. 76 (88, 94, 106, 112, 122) sts.

Work 11 (15, 11, 15, 11, 9) more rows in Chart patt as established.

Neckline shaping

Row 1 (RS): Work in Chart patt for 22 (26, 28, 31, 34, 38) sts, put rem sts on holder.
Row 2 (WS): Work in Chart patt as established.
Row 3: Work in Chart patt as established to last 3 sts, ssk, p1.
Row 4: Work in Chart patt as established.

Put rem 21 (25, 27, 30, 33, 37) sts from working needle on holder (right shoulder), break yarn.

Divide sts from neckline holder in 2 parts: Leave 32 (36, 38, 44, 44, 46) central sts on holder for center neck, replace 22 (26, 28, 31, 34, 38) sts on needles for left shoulder.

Row 1 (RS): Work in Chart patt as established.
Row 2 (WS): Work in Chart patt as established.
Row 3: Sl1, k2tog, work in Chart patt as established to end of row.

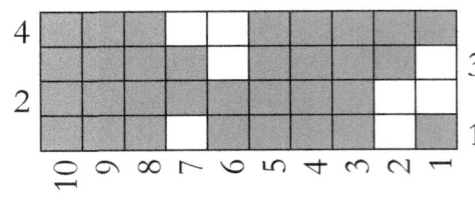

	CC		RS: k; WS: p
	MC		

Row 4: Work in Chart patt as established.

Put rem 21 (25, 27, 30, 33, 37) sts on holder (left shoulder), break yarn.

Left Front

With MC, CO 76 (82, 88, 96, 102, 110) sts.
Rows 1–3: Work in garter stitch.

Beginning on next row (RS), work 28 rows of Stranded Colorwork Chart, or until piece measures 5.5" / 14cm, ending by working a WS row.

Dec Row (RS): Sl1, ssk, work in Chart patt as established to end of row.

Repeat Dec Row every 8th row, 11 more times. 64 (70, 76, 84, 90, 98) sts.

Hip-to-waist decrease

Repeat Dec Row every 6 (6, 8, 8, 8, 8)th row 3 (3, 1, 2, 2, 1) more times , and then every 0 (0, 6, 6, 6, 6)th row 0 (0, 2, 1, 1, 2) more times . 61 (67, 73, 81, 87, 95) sts.

Work 4 (6, 4, 4, 4, 8) more rows in Chart patt as established.

Lapel

Note: Lapels are worked AT THE SAME TIME as Inc Rows. Lapel is worked in seed stitch using MC.

Row 1 (RS): Work in Chart patt until 3 sts from end, work in seed st with MC (Seed) to end.
Row 2 (WS): Sl1, Seed3, work in Chart patt to end.
Row 3: Work in Chart patt to 5 sts from end, Seed to end.
Row 4: Sl1, Seed4, work in Chart patt to end.

Row 5: Work in Chart patt to 1 before beginning of previous row's seed st section, work in seed st to end.
Row 6: Sl1, work in seed st section as previous row, work in Chart patt to end.

Rows 7–56: Repeat Rows 5–6. At end of Row 56, there will be 31 sts in seed st at the neck edge.

Row 57: Work in Chart patt to 32 sts from end, Seed to end.
Row 58: Sl1, Seed31 (31, 31, 31, 31, 32), work in Chart patt to end.
Row 59: Work in Chart patt to 33 sts from end, Seed to end.
Row 60: Sl1, Seed32 (32, 32, 32, 32, 33), work in Chart patt to end.
Row 61: Work in Chart patt to 34 sts from end, Seed to end
Row 62: Sl1, Seed33 (33, 33, 33, 33, 34), work in Chart patt to end.

Size XS only: Slip sts to waste yarn.

All other sizes:
Row 63: Work in Chart patt to – (35, 35, 35 35, 36) sts from end, Seed to end.
Row 64: Sl1, Seed– (34, 34, 34, 34, 35), work in Chart patt to end.
Row 65: Work in Chart patt to – (36, 36, 36, 36, 37) sts from end, Seed to end.
Row 66: Sl1, Seed– (35, 35, 35, 35, 36), work in Chart patt to end.
Row 67: Work in Chart patt to – (37, 37, 37, 37, 38) sts from end, Seed to end.
Row 68: Sl1, Seed– (37, 37, 37, 37, 38), work in Chart patt to end.

Size S only: Slip sts to waste yarn.

All other sizes:
Row 69: Work in Chart patt to – (–, 38, 38, 39, 39) sts from end, Seed to end.
Row 70: Sl1, Seed– (–, 37, 37, 38, 39), work in Chart patt to end.
Row 71: Work in Chart patt to – (–, 39, 39, 40, 40) sts from end, Seed to end.
Row 72: Sl1, Seed– (–, 38, 38, 39, 40), work in Chart patt to end.
Row 73: Work in Chart patt to – (–, 40, 40, 41, 42) sts from end, Seed to end.
Row 74: Sl1, Seed– (–, 39, 39, 40, 41), work in Chart patt to end.

Size M only: Slip sts to waste yarn.

All other sizes:
Row 75: Work in Chart patt to – (–, –, 41, 42, 43) sts from end, Seed to end.
Row 76: Sl1, Seed– (–, –, 41, 42, 42), work in Chart patt to end.
Row 77: Work in Chart patt to – (–, –, 42, 43, 44) sts from end, Seed to end.
Row 78: Sl1, Seed– (–, –, 42, 43, 44), work in Chart patt to end.

Size L only: Slip sts to waste yarn.

All other sizes:
Row 79: Work in Chart patt to – (–, –, –, 45, 45) sts from end, Seed to end.
Row 80: Sl1, Seed– (–, –, –, 44, 45), work in Chart patt to end.
Row 81: Work in Chart patt to – (–, –, –, 46, 46) sts from end, Seed to end.
Row 82: Sl1, Seed– (–, –, –, 45, 46), work in Chart patt to end.

Size XL only: Slip sts to waste yarn.

Size XXL only:
Row 83: Work in Chart patt to 48 sts from end, Seed to end.
Row 84: Sl1, Seed47, work in Chart patt to end.
Row 85: Work in Chart patt to 49 sts from end, Seed to end.
Row 86: Sl1, Seed48, work in Chart patt to end.
Slip sts to waste yarn.

Waist-to-armhole increase

Lapel and Inc Rows are begun on the same row.

Inc Row (RS): Sl1, m1, work in Chart patt as established to end of row (working Lapel as est). Repeat Inc Row every 6 (6, 8, 8, 8, 8)th row 2 (2, 0, 1, 1, 0) more times, and then every 0 (0, 6, 6, 6, 6)th row 0 (0, 2, 1, 1, 2) more times. 64 (70, 76, 84, 90, 98) sts.

Work 4 (6, 6, 4, 4, 4) more rows in Chart patt as est, ending with a RS row.

Underarm shaping

Work to last 6 (6, 7, 7, 8, 8) sts, put remaining sts on waste yarn. 58 (64, 69, 77, 82, 90) sts.

Work Dec Row every 9th row once, and then every 8th row 3 (3, 4, 4, 5, 6) more times. 54 (60, 64, 72, 76, 83) sts.

Cont working even until Lapel is complete.

Break yarn. Slip all sts to two holders: 21 (25, 27, 30, 33, 37) sts for left shoulder to one holder and 33 (38, 39, 44, 45, 48) sts for left lapel to the second holder.

Right Front

With MC, CO 76 (82, 88, 96, 102, 110) sts.
Rows 1–3: Work in garter stitch.

Beginning on next row (RS), work 28 rows of Stranded Colorwork Chart, or until piece measures 5.5" / 14cm, ending by working a WS row.

Dec Row (RS): Sl1, work in Chart patt as established to last 3 sts, k2tog, p1.

Repeat Dec Row every 8th row, 11 more times. 64 (70, 76, 84, 90, 98) sts rem

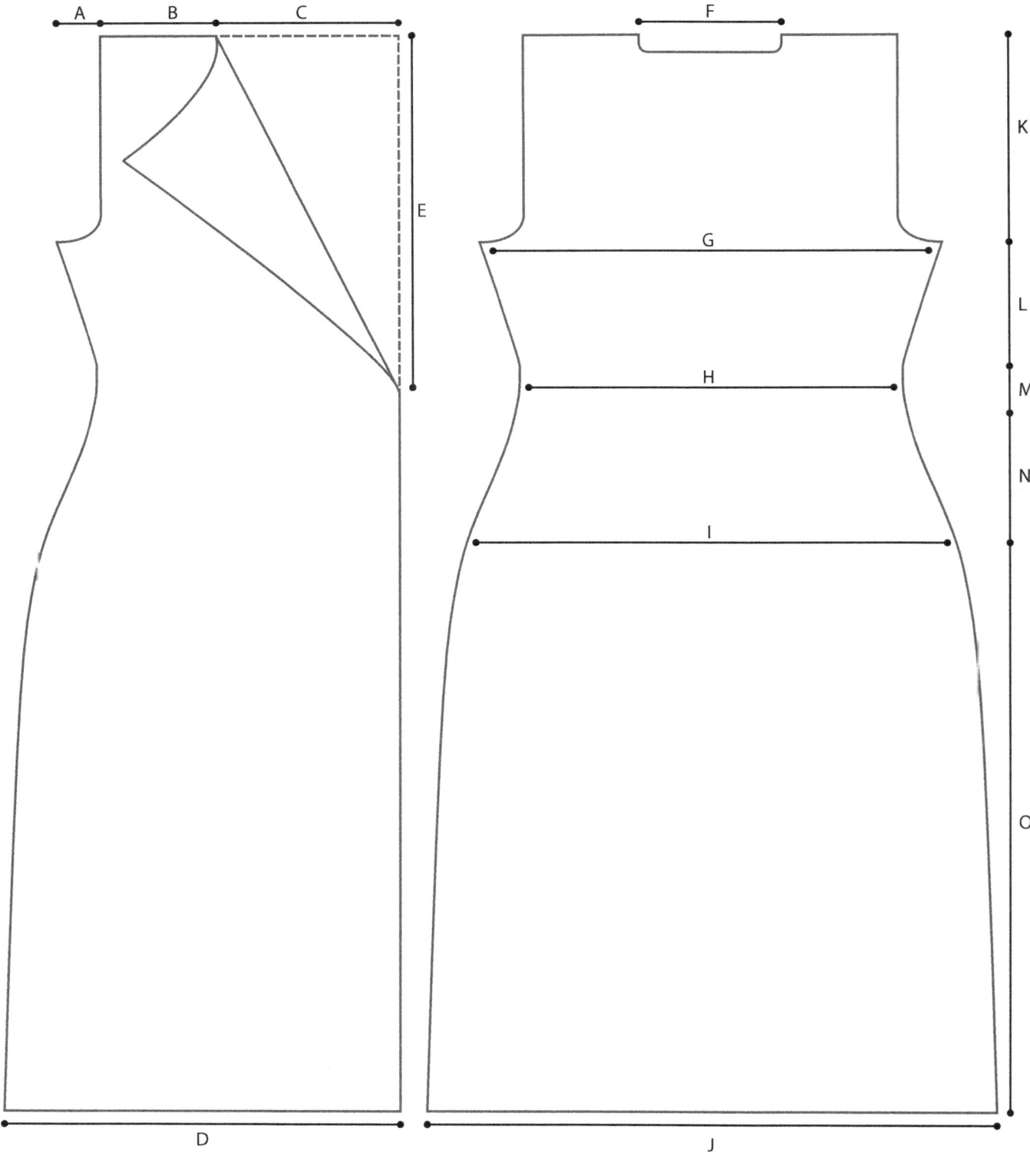

A: 1 (1, 1.25, 1.25, 1.5, 1.5, 1.5)"
B: 3.75 (4.5, 5, 5.5, 6, 6.75)"
C: 6 (7, 7, 8, 8.25, 8.75)"
D: 13.75 (15, 16, 17.5, 18.5, 20)"
E: 11.25 (12.5, 13.5, 14.25, 15, 15.5)"

K: 7.75 (8.75, 9.5, 10, 10.5, 12)"
L: 3.25 (3.25, 3.5, 4, 4, 4)"
M: 1 (1, 0.75, 0.75, 0.75, 0.75)"
N: 3.25 (3.25, 3.5, 4, 4, 4)"
O: 21" all sizes

F: 5.75 (6.5, 7, 8, 8, 8.5)"
G: 17.5 (19.5, 21.5, 23.5, 25.5, 27.5)"
H: 16.25 (18.5, 20.5, 22.5, 24.5, 26.5)"
I: 17.5 (19.5, 21.5, 23.5, 25.5, 27.5)"
J: 21.75 (24.25, 25.75, 28, 30, 32)"

Hip-to-waist decrease

Note: Buttonholes are worked AT THE SAME TIME as Dec Rows. See below.

Repeat Dec Row every 6 (6, 8, 8, 8, 8)th row 3 (3, 1, 2, 2, 1) more times, and then every 0 (0, 6, 6, 6, 6)th row 0 (0, 2, 1, 1, 2) more times. 61 (67, 73, 81, 87, 95) sts.

Work 4 (6, 4, 4, 4, 8) more rows in Chart patt as established.

Work buttonholes

First buttonhole row is worked at the same time as the first hip-to-waist dec row.

Buttonhole Row: K2, make buttonhole, work in Chart patt as established over next 20 (22, 24, 26, 28, 30) sts, make buttonhole, work in Chart patt as established to the end of the row.

Repeat Buttonhole Row every 14 (14, 12, 14, 14, 14)th row, two more times.

Lapel

Note: Lapels are worked AT THE SAME TIME as Inc Rows. Lapel is worked in seed stitch using MC.

Row 1 (RS): Sl1, work in Seed stitch with MC (Seed) for 2 sts, work in Chart patt to end.
Row 2 (WS): Work in Chart patt to 4 sts from end, Seed to end.
Row 3: Sl1, Seed4, work in Chart patt to end.
Row 4: Work in Chart patt to 5 sts from end, Seed to end.

Row 5: Sl1, Seed to 1 st past previous row's seed st section, work in Chart patt to end.
Row 6: Work in Chart patt to beginning of previous row's seed st, work in seed st to end.

Rows 7–56: Repeat Rows 5–6. At end of Row 56, there will be 31 sts in seed st at the neck edge.

Row 57: Sl1, Seed31, work in Chart patt to end.
Row 58: Work in Chart patt to 32 (32, 32, 32, 32, 33) sts from end, Seed to end.
Row 59: Sl1, Seed32, work in Chart patt to end.
Row 60: Work in Chart patt to 33 (33, 33, 33, 33, 34) sts from end, Seed to end.
Row 61: Sl1, Seed33, work in Chart patt to end.
Row 62: Work in Chart patt to 34 (34, 34, 34, 34, 35) sts from end, Seed to end.

Size XS only: Slip sts to waste yarn.

All other sizes:
Row 63: Sl1, Seed– (34, 34, 34, 34, 35), work in Chart patt to end.
Row 64: Work in Chart patt to – (35, 35, 35, 35, 36) sts from end, Seed to end.

Row 65: Sl1, Seed– (35, 35, 35, 35, 36), work in Chart patt to end.
Row 66: Work in Chart patt to – (36, 36, 36, 36, 37) sts from end, Seed to end.
Row 67: Sl1, Seed– (36, 36, 36, 36, 37), work in Chart patt to end.
Row 68: Work in Chart patt to – (38, 38, 38, 38, 38, 39) sts from end, Seed to end.

Size S only: Slip sts to waste yarn.

All other sizes:
Row 69: Sl1, Seed– (–, 37, 37, 37, 38), work in Chart patt to end.
Row 70: Work in Chart patt to – (–, 38, 38, 39, 40) sts from end, Seed to end.
Row 71: Sl1, Seed– (–, 37, 37, 38, 39), work in Chart patt to end.
Row 72: Work in Chart patt to – (–, 39, 39, 40, 41) sts from end, Seed to end.
Row 73: Sl1, Seed– (–, 38, 38, 39, 40), work in Chart patt to end.
Row 74: Work in Chart patt to – (–, 40, 40, 41, 42) sts from end, Seed to end.

Size M only: Slip sts to waste yarn.

All other sizes:
Row 75: Sl1, Seed– (–, –, 40, 41, 42), work in Chart patt to end.
Row 76: Work in Chart patt to – (–, –, 42, 43, 43) sts from end, Seed to end.
Row 77: Sl1, Seed– (–, –, 41, 42, 43), work in Chart patt to end.
Row 78: Work in Chart patt to – (–, –, 42, 43, 44) sts from end, Seed to end.

Size L only: Slip sts to waste yarn.

All other sizes:
Row 79: Sl1, Seed– (–, –, –, 44, 44), work in Chart patt to end.
Row 80: Work in Chart patt to – (–, –, –, 45, 46) sts from end, Seed to end.
Row 81: Sl1, Seed– (–, –, –, 45, 45), work in Chart patt to end.
Row 82: Work in Chart patt to – (–, –, –, 46, 47) sts from end, Seed to end.

Size XL only: Slip sts to waste yarn.

Size XXL only:
Row 83: Sl1, Seed– (–, –, –, –, 47), work in Chart patt to end.
Row 84: Work in Chart patt to 48 sts from end, Seed to end.
Row 85: Sl1, Seed47, work in Chart patt to end.
Row 86: Work in Chart patt to 49 sts from end, Seed to end.
Slip sts to waste yarn.

Waist-to-armhole increase

Lapel and Inc Rows are begun on the same row.

Inc Row (RS): Sl1, work in Chart patt (working Lapel as est) as established to last st, m1, p1.

Repeat Inc Row every 6 (6, 8, 8, 8, 8)th row 2 (2, 0, 1, 1, 0) more times, and then every 0 (0, 6, 6, 6, 6)th row 0 (0, 2, 1, 1, 2) more times. 64 (70, 76, 84, 90, 98) sts.

Work 3 (5, 5, 3, 3, 3) more rows in Chart patt as est, ending with a WS row.

Underarm shaping (RS):

Work in Chart patt to last 6 (6, 7, 7, 8, 8) sts, put remaining sts on waste yarn. 58 (64, 69, 77, 82, 90) sts.

Work Dec Row every 9th row once, and then every 8th row 3 (3, 4, 4, 5, 6) more times. 54 (60, 64, 72, 76, 83) sts.

Cont working even until Lapel is complete.

Break yarn. Slip all sts to two holders: 33 (38, 39, 44, 45, 48) sts of right lapel to first holder, and 21 (25, 27, 30, 33, 37) sts of right shoulder to second holder.

Back Strap

With MC, CO 9 sts and work in Seed st pattern for 6.5 (6.5, 6.5, 8, 8, 8)" / 16.5 (16.5, 16.5, 20.5, 20.5, 20.5)cm.

BO rem sts in patt.

Pick up and knit 86 [86, 86, 92, 92, 92] sts around the strap perimeter. With CC, work i-cord BO. Block. Sew two decorative buttons to RS of strap.

Finishing

Steam block back and front panels. Graft shoulders using Kitchener stitch.

With RS facing and using MC, pick up and knit 2 sts for every 3 rows up front opening, starting at right front corner. Knit across held sts for lapels and back neckline. Pick up and knit 2 sts for every 3 rows down front opening, finishing at left front hem corner. Break yarn. With CC, beginning at first picked up st, work i-cord BO.

With RS facing and using MC, knit across held sts, pick up and knit 2 sts for every 3 rows around left armhole. Slide needle back to the beg of RS row and with CC, use backward-loop cast on to CO 3 extra sts and make i-cord BO edging. Repeat for right armhole. Slightly steam block armholes. Sew side seams.

Steam block side seams and lightly block i-cord edging.
Sew back strap onto back panel at the waist line.
Sew buttons on left front panel.
Weave in ends.

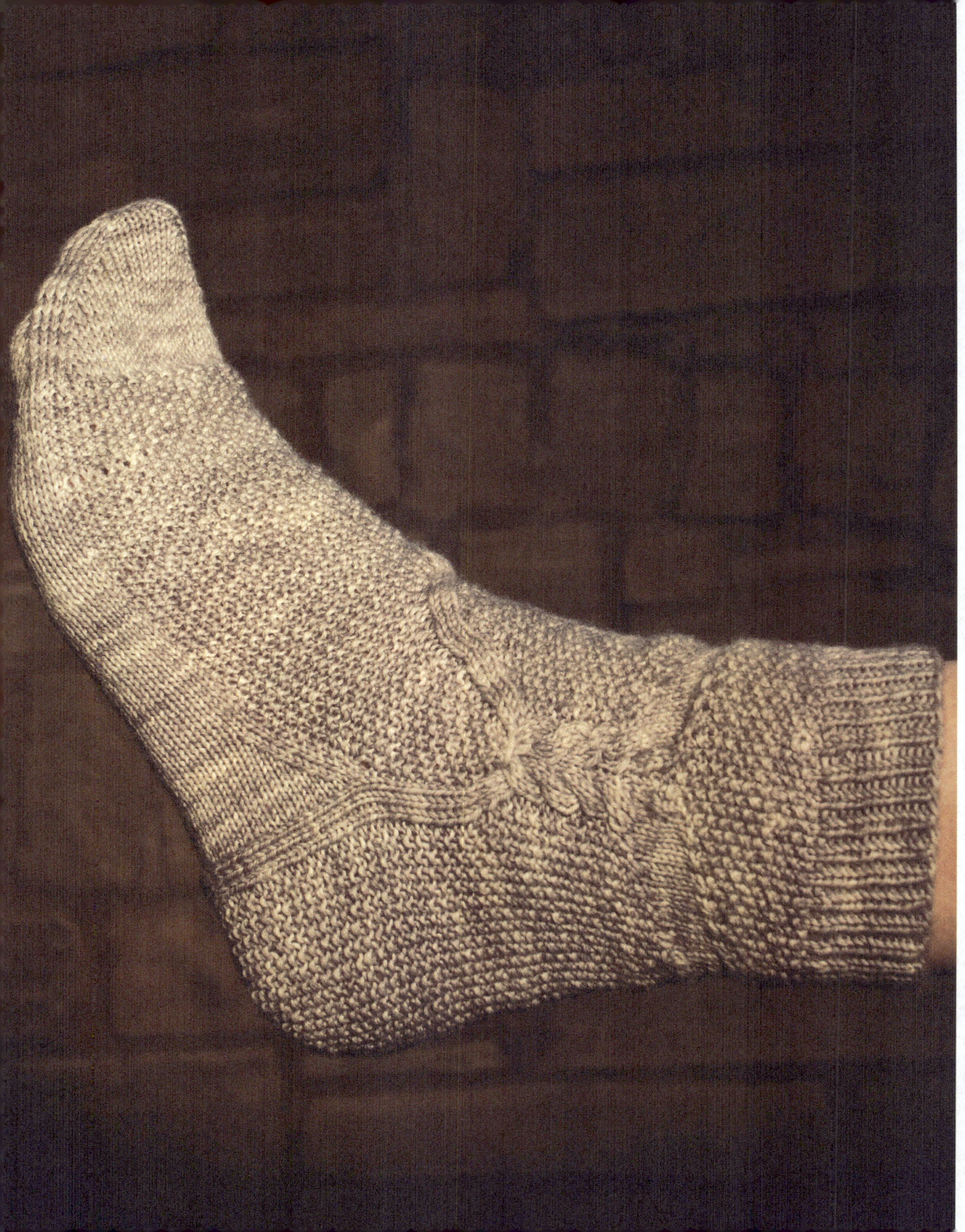

Kentley Socks

Heather Ordover

Sizes

Three sizes are included in the pattern:

- Size 1 corresponds to a Women's M (US sizes 6–8, European sizes 36–39) / Men's S (US size 6, European size 39).

- Size 2 corresponds to a Women's L (US sizes 9–10, European sizes 39–41) / Men's M (US sizes 7–8, European sizes 40–42).

- Size 3 corresponds to a Women's XL (US sizes 11–13, European sizes 41–44) / Men's L (US sizes 9–11, European sizes 42–45).

Shown in size 2 (Women's L / Men's M).

Finished Measurements

Foot circumference: 6.5 (7.5, 8.5)" / 16.5 (19, 21.5)cm
Finished leg length: 6" / 15.5cm
Finished foot length: adjustable to fit

Materials

Madeline Tosh Tosh Sock (100% superwash merino; 395 yds / 361m per 100g skein)], color: Charcoal; 1 (1, 2) skeins

Two 24-inch US #1 / 2.25mm circular needles
1 set US #1 / 2.25mm double-point needles

2 stitch markers
Yarn needle

Gauge

36 sts and 50 rounds = 4" / 10cm in St st in the round

Required Skills

Increases/decreases; knowledge of sock construction (helpful but not required); knitting in the round; reading charts; cables; twisted stitches

Pattern Notes

The pattern is written for two circular needles. Using this technique guarantees you won't accidentally knit two left socks and that you will be able to see the side patterning grow in tandem. However, this isn't required. The socks can easily be made on dpns or using magic loop.

This pattern is easy to resize. To be safe, measure the circumference of the ball of the foot (the part you stand on when you stand on tippy-toe). Multiply that number by your 1" / 2.5cm gauge (e.g., if 9 sts = 1" / 2.5cm and your foot is 9" / 23cm around, then multiply 9 × 9). Subtract 10% from that product (e.g., 81–8=73) then adjust to end at a number divisible by 4 (e.g., 72). The 10% stitch reduction guarantees a comfortably snug sock.

One of the most amazing Hitchcock movies is Rope (1948). *More like a stage play—and, in fact, based on one—*Rope *was filmed to look like it was one continuous "take," which put an enormous burden on director and actors. Luckily for us, Hitch was a genius, Jimmy Stewart stars, and the movie is a film-buff fave.*

These socks—among my faves—will wrap themselves around your calf and never let go. One strand of rope descends down the side of your ankle, the other wends its way across the top of your foot and down the side of your toe. The style can suit either women or men.

As indicated on the chart, a size 1 sock will begin at the blue border and end at the blue border (sts 9–64); size 2 will begin at the purple border and end at the purple border (sts 5–68); size 3 will include all sts 1–72. For sizes larger than this, repeat sts 1–4 and 69–72 as needed to achieve the circumference needed.

Welsh heels are not-your-normal-heel but are very comfy when done. The Welsh heel includes yarnovers and multiple decreases. This is not a "close-the-gap" heel, so a "seam stitch" has been added running down the center of the heel. This gives you both a mathematical and a visual reference point during the turn and adds extra cushiness and durability. If you are a tidy knitter, the yarnovers in the pattern may irk you. To address this, try the following: on WS rows, when you encounter the RS yo, you may wish to purl through the back loop—it tightens up the loose stitch.

PATTERN

CO 56 (64, 72) sts and distribute over two needles. Join to work in the round, being careful not to twist. Pm for beginning of round.

Leg

Rounds 1–4: [K1, p1] around.
Add additional rounds if you prefer more ribbing at the cuff.

Rounds 5–65: Follow appropriate Leg chart for size as indicated by blue and purple borders (see Pattern Notes above).

Heel Flap

This flap is worked in seed stitch with the rope motif continuing down the side of the flap in sts 30–34 on Right Leg chart and 39–43 on Left Leg chart. Those sts will become part of the heel turn.

Work Right Heel Flap over first 26 (30, 34) sts in seed stitch as follows:
Row 1 (RS): Sl1, [p1, k1] 10 (12, 14) times, p1, k3, p1 Turn.
Row 2 (WS): Sl1, p3, k1, [k1, p1] to end. Turn.
Repeat these 2 rows until there are 13 (15, 17) slipped sts on either side of the flap, ending with a WS row.

Work Left Heel Flap over last 26 (30, 34) sts in seed stitch as follows:
Set-up Round (Round 66 of Left Leg chart): Work Left Leg chart, then divide for heel after chart st 38 and begin heel flap. Remove beginning of round marker.

Row 1 (RS): Sl1, k3, p1, [p1, k1] 10 (12, 14) times, k1. Turn.
Row 2 (WS): Sl1, [k1, p1] to last 5 sts, k1, p3, k1. Turn.
Repeat these 2 rows until there are 13 (15, 17) slipped sts on either side of the flap, ending with a WS row.
End Rope motif.

Heel Turn

Row 1 (RS): Sl1, k2, p1, k1 (3, 5), yo, k2tog, k3, k2tog, k1, m1p‡, k1, ssk, k3, ssk, turn. (‡ indicates the seam st.)

Row 2 (WS): *Yo, purl to seam, knit seam st, p3, turn.
Row 3: Yo, k2tog, k3, k2tog, k1, purl seam st, k1, ssk, k3, ssk, turn.*
Repeat Rows 2 & 3 until 1 unworked st appears at each row-end.

Last WS row: *Sl1, purl to seam, knit seam st, p8, turn. (*Note:* no yo worked.)
Last RS row: Sl1, k2tog, k3, k2tog, k1, purl seam st, k1, ssk, k3, ssk. (*Note:* no yo worked.)

Gusset

Note: If using two circular needles, plan to keep all heel and gusset sts on one, and the instep sts on the other. If you have two needle lengths, place the instep sts on the shorter needle.

Pick up and knit 13 (15, 17) sts along the right heel side of the flap. Place marker between the last 2 sts. Work in patt across instep sts for Round 66 of Right Instep chart or Round 67 of Left Instep chart. Pick up and knit 13 (15, 17) sts along the left side of the heel flap, placing marker between the first and second sts. Knit to seam st. Place marker to indicate beginning of round before seam st.

If there are obvious gaps where the heel flap joins the heel or the instep, pick up sts from those areas too. The gusset decreases will take care of any extra sts.

From here to the toe, the sole will be worked in St st and the instep will be worked in patt as indicated on the appropriate Instep chart.

Round 1:
- Right gusset: Knit seam st, knit to 2 sts before marker, k2tog, sm, k1.
- Instep: Work appropriate Instep chart.
- Left gusset: K1, sm, ssk; knit to end of round.

Round 2: Knit across heel and right gusset, work appropriate Instep chart, knit across left gusset to end of round.

Repeat Rounds 1 & 2 until 56 (64, 72) sts remain. End by working Round 2.

Foot

Continue working last 2 rounds of chart on instep and St st on sole until the sock measures 2" / 5cm shorter than the desired finished length. Toe is worked in stockinette with the rope motif continuing to the end.

Left Toe

First st of Instep chart is now the beginning of the round and first st on the instep needle; move marker if desired. If not already in place, rearrange sts so instep and sole of foot needles have 28 (32, 36) sts each.

Round 1:
> Instep: P1, k3, p2tog, knit to the last 3 sts on the needle, k2tog, k1.
> Sole: K1, ssk, knit to the last 3 sts, k2tog, k1.

Round 2: Knit.
Repeat Rounds 1 & 2 until 8–10 sts remain on each needle. Cut yarn, leaving a 12" / 30cm tail.

Use Kitchener stitch to graft remaining sts tog.

Right Toe

First st of Instep chart is now the beginning of the round and first st on the instep needle; move marker if desired.

If not already in place, rearrange sts so instep and sole of foot have 28 (32, 36) sts.

Round 1:
> Instep: K1, ssk, knit to the last 6 sts on the needle, p2tog, k3, p1.
> Sole: K1, ssk, knit to the last 3 sts, k2tog, k1.

Round 2: Knit.
Repeat Rounds 1 & 2 until 8–10 sts remain on each needle. Cut yarn, leaving a 12" / 30cm tail.

Use Kitchener stitch to graft remaining sts tog.

Finishing

Weave in ends. Wear when you wish to tighten the yoke of unbridled envy in others.

Left Leg Chart

Legend:

- No stitch
- • k
- · P
- ✗ 1/1 RC
- ✗ 1/1 RCp
- ✗ 1/1 LC
- ✗ 1/1 LCp
- ✗ 3/1 RCp
- ✗ 2/2 RC
- ✗ 2/2 LC
- ✗ 3/1 LCp
- ⌐⌐ (k4) cluster
- small start/end
- medium start/end
- Heel flap begins

Left Instep Chart

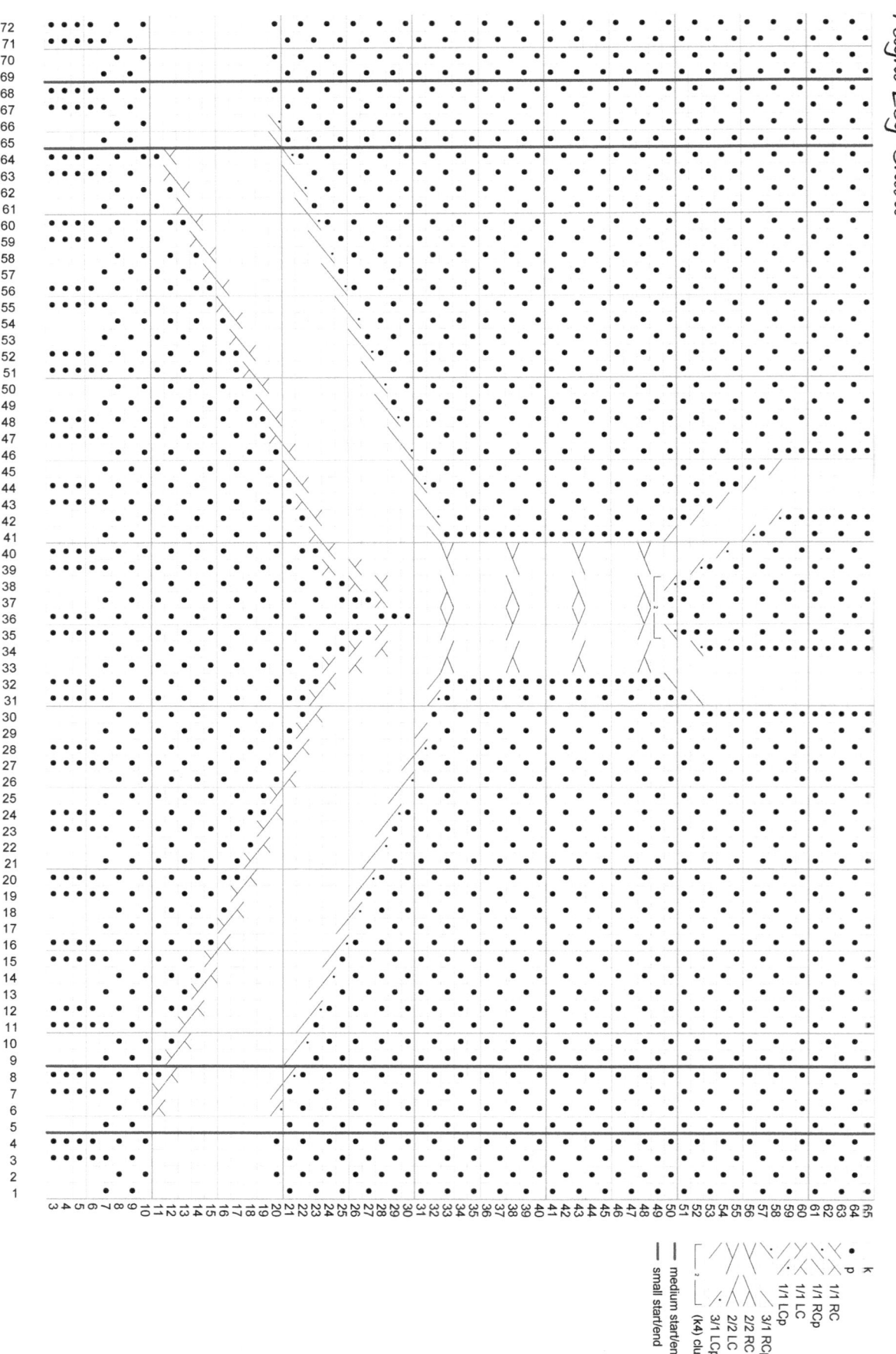

Right Instep Chart

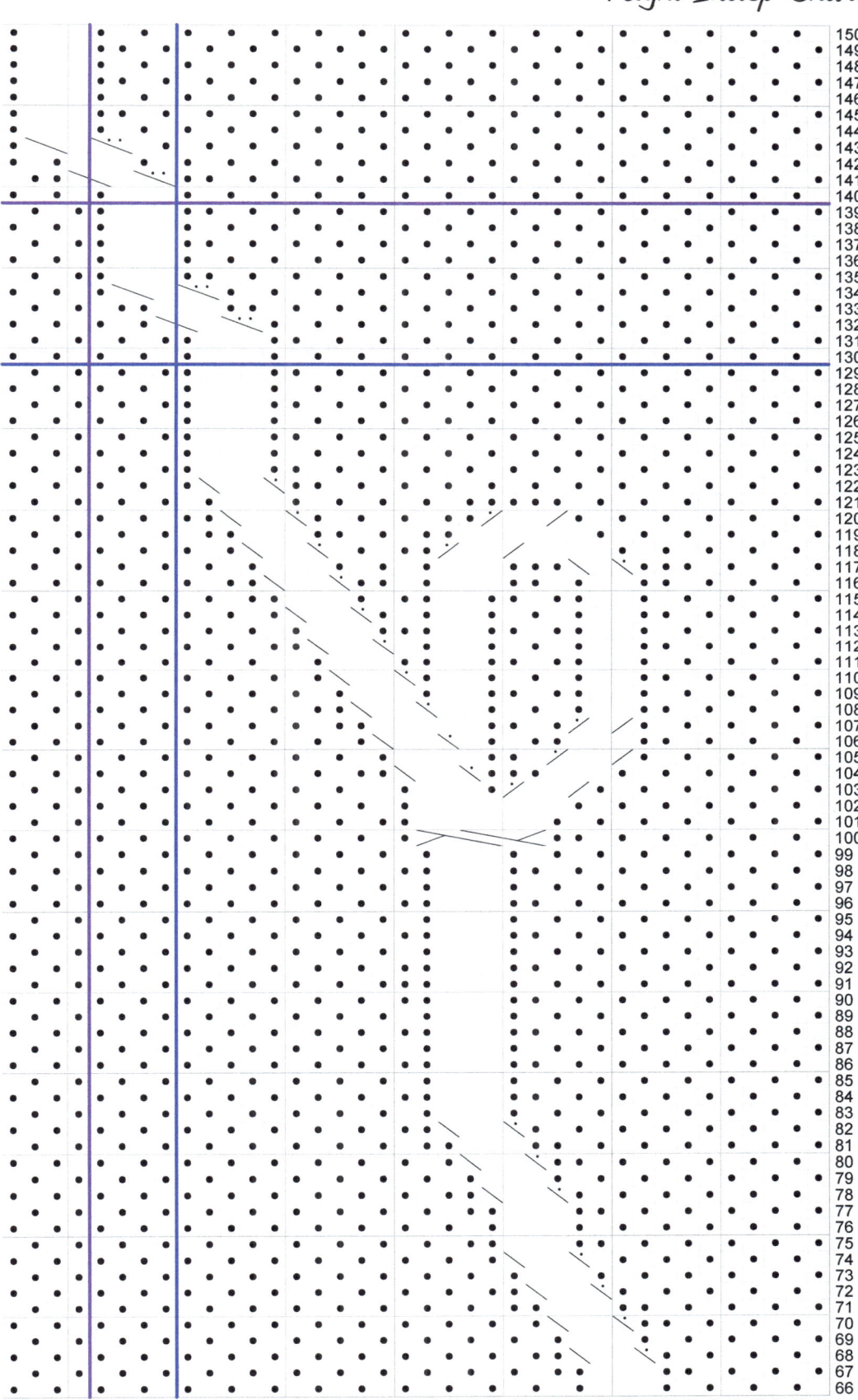

k
p
2/1 RPC
2/1 LPC
3/1 RCp
3/1 LCp
3/2 LCp
2/4 LC

— medium start/end
— small start/end

Wendice Socks

Rachel Coopey

SIZES

To fit foot circumferences: 7.5 (8.5, 9.5)" / 19 (21.5, 24)cm; shown in second size

FINISHED MEASUREMENTS

Finished leg length: 6" / 15cm
Finished foot length: adjustable to fit

MATERIALS

Hedgehog Fibres Twist Sock (80% Bluefaced Leicester, 20% nylon; 399 yds / 365m per 100g skein); color: Sin; 1 (1, 2) skeins

32-inch US #1 /2.25mm circular needle or 1 set US #1 /2.25mm double-point needles, or size needed to obtain gauge

Cable needle
1 stitch marker
Yarn needle

GAUGE

36 sts and 48 rounds = 4" / 10cm in St st

REQUIRED SKILLS

Knitting in the round; short rows; working intricate cables from chart; twisted stitches; knowledge of basic sock construction; picking up stitches; kitchener stitch (grafting)

PATTERN

Cuff

CO 68 (76, 84) sts. Join to work in the round, being careful not to twist. Pm for beginning of round.

Work Round 1 of Leg chart 6 times around.
Work Rounds 1–6 twice.

Leg

Work Rounds 1–24 of Leg chart twice.
Work Rounds 1–8 once more.

Heel Setup

[P2, k tbl] twice. Heel flap will be worked back and forth over 34 (38, 42) sts. Turn so WS is facing.

Heel Flap

Row 1 (WS): Sl1 wyif, k2, p tbl, k2, [p tbl, k1] 3 (4, 5) times, k1, p tbl, k2, p2 tbl, k2, p tbl, k2, [p tbl, k1] 3 (4, 5) times, k1, p tbl, k2, p1.

Row 2 (RS): Sl1 wyib, p2, k tbl, p2, [k tbl, p1] 3 (4, 5) times, p1, k tbl, p2, k2 tbl, p2, k tbl, p2, [k tbl, p1] 3 (4, 5) times, p1, k tbl, p2, k1.

Repeat these 2 rows 13 times. Work Row 1 once more.

Heel Turn

Row 1 (RS): Sl1 pwise wyib, k18 (20, 22), ssk, k1, turn.
Row 2 (WS): Sl1 pwise wyif, p5, p2tog, p1, turn.
Row 3 (RS): Sl1 pwise wyib, knit to 1 st before gap created on previous row, ssk, k1, turn.
Row 4 (WS): Sl1 pwise wyif, purl to 1 st before gap created on previous row, p2tog, p1, turn.

Inspired by a necktie worn by the character Tony Wendice in Dial M for Murder *(1954), these socks are elegant and charming. That's where the similarity between these two things ends—they definitely won't ask you to kill their wife with a smile and a glass of brandy!*

The ribbing incorporated into the leg pattern will hug the leg for an excellent fit.

Repeat Rows 3 & 4 until all sts have been worked.
20 (22, 24) heel sts.

Gusset

Set-up Round: Sl1, k19 (21, 23), pick up and knit 14
sts (1 st in each slipped st along edge of heel flap).
Continue across instep sts according to Leg Chart.
Pick up and knit 14 sts (1 st in each slipped st). Knit
to end of sole sts. Start of round is at start of instep
sts. 82 (88, 94) sts total: 34 (38, 42) on instep, 48 (50,
52) on sole.

Gusset Round 1: Work Foot Chart for your size
across instep sts; ssk, knit until 2 sts remain, k2tog.
Gusset Round 2: Work in patt.
Repeat these 2 rounds until 68 (76, 84) sts remain;
34 (38, 42) each on sole and instep.

Foot

Work in patt until sock measures 2" / 5cm less than
the desired finished length.

Toe

Round 1: Knit.
Round 2: K1, ssk, knit until 3 sts before end of instep,
k2tog, k2, ssk, knit until 3 sts remain, k2tog, k1.
Repeat these 2 rounds until 20 (24, 24) sts remain.
Cut yarn, leaving a 12" / 30.5cm tail. Graft sts tog.

Finishing

Weave in ends and block.

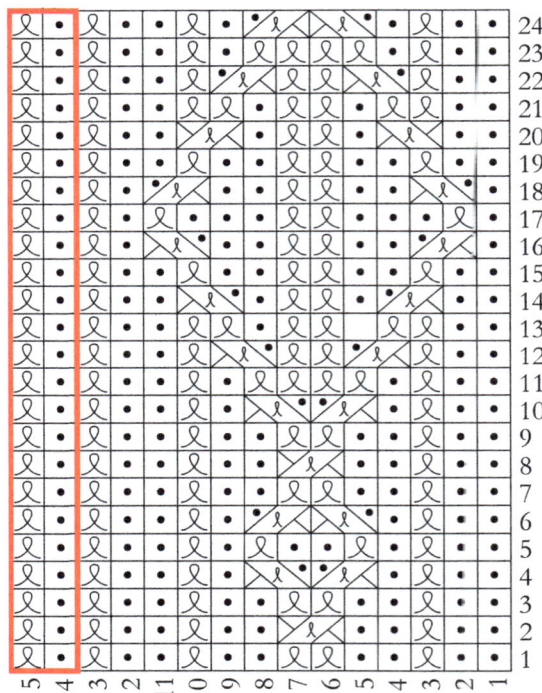

Leg Chart (all sizes)

□	k
•	p
ℓ	k tbl
⤫	1/1 LCt
⤫	1/1 RCt
⤫	1/1 LCtp
⤫	1/1 RCtp

*For cuff & leg, the
chart is worked 4 times
around, working sts
within the red border
2 (3, 4) times per repeat.*

Small Foot Chart

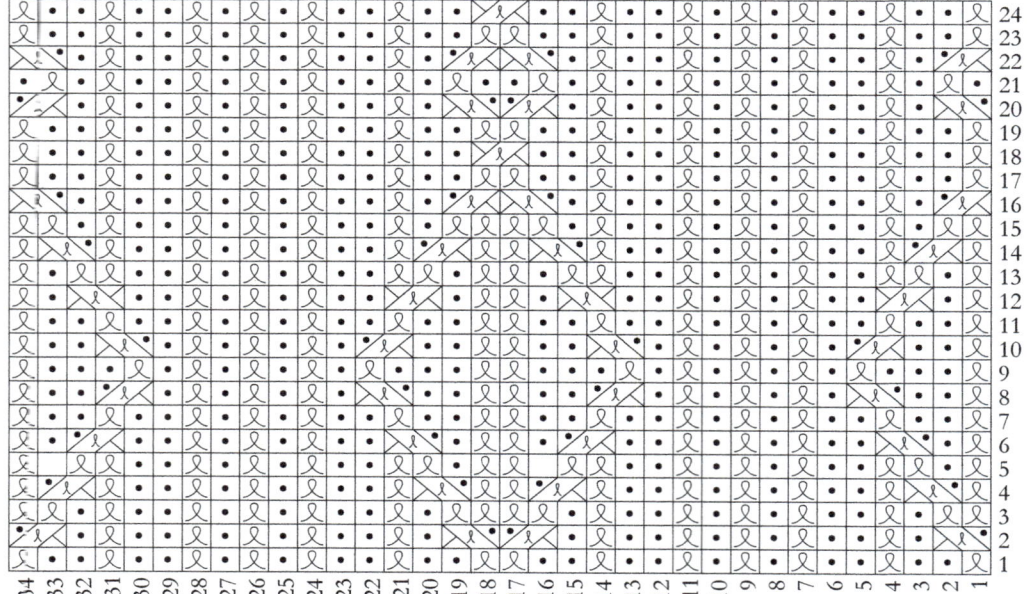

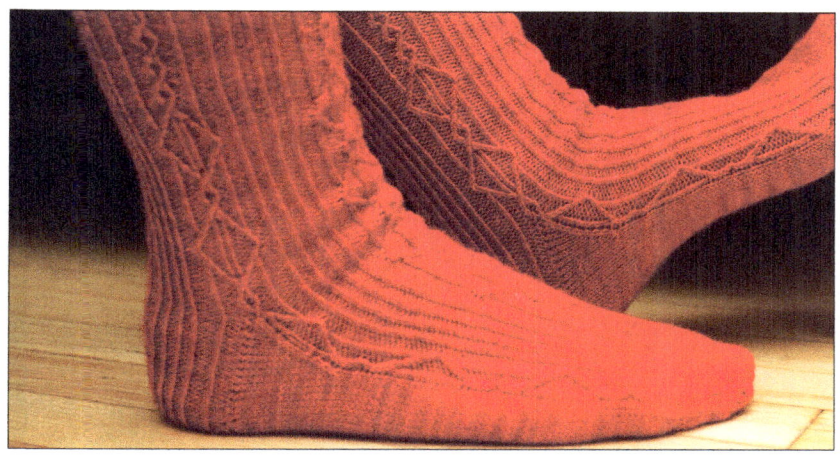

Medium Foot Chart

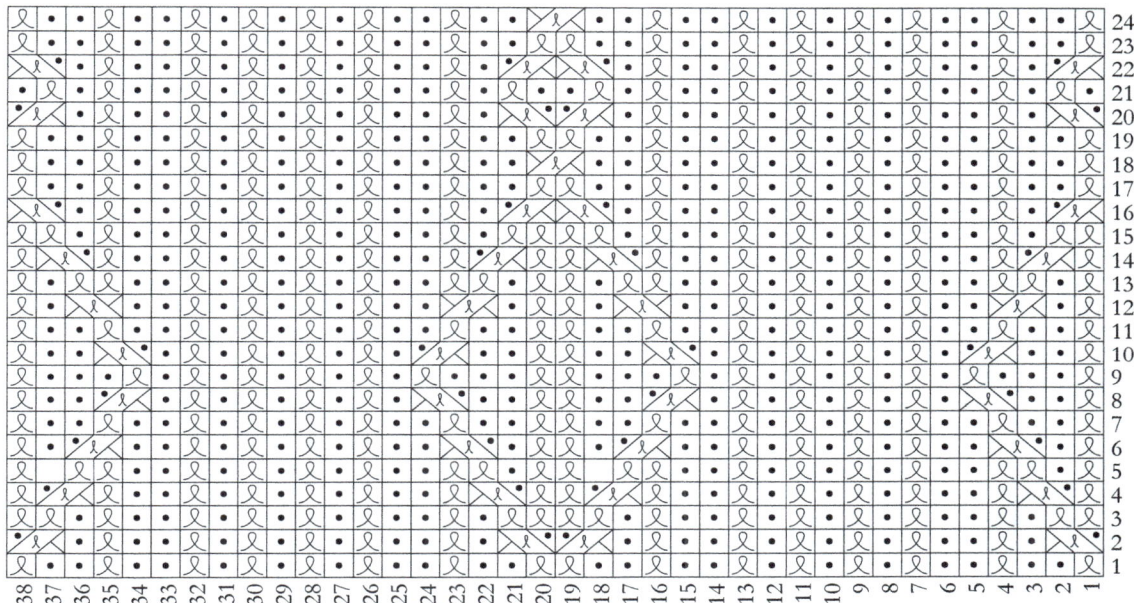

Large Foot Chart

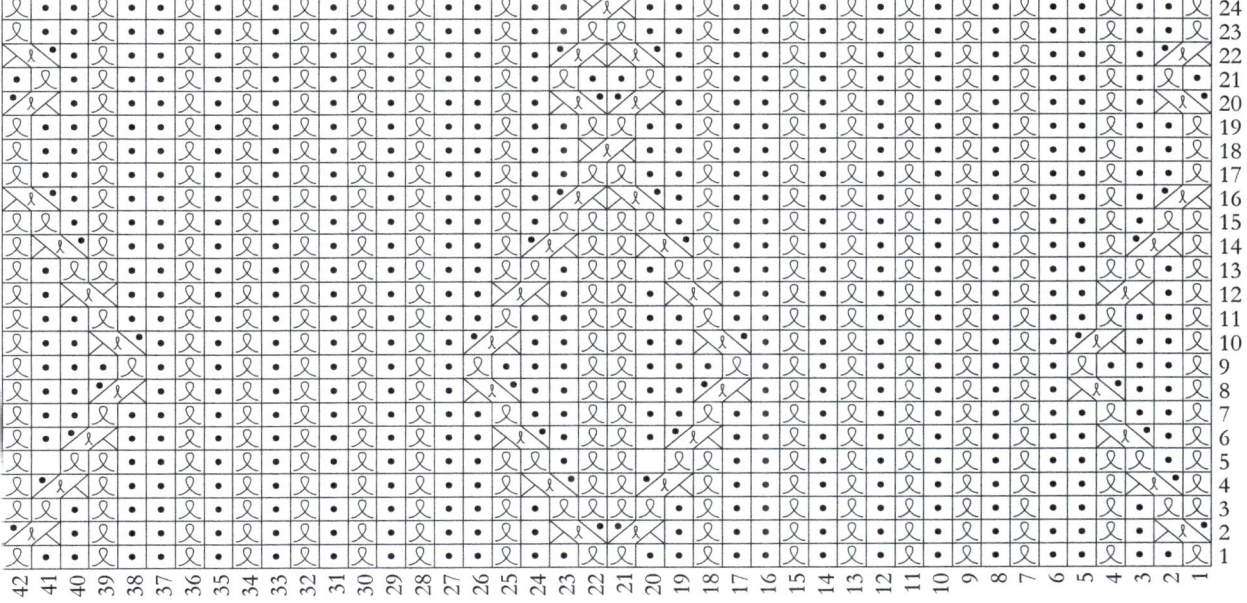

Eleven Hundred Dollars Sweater

Elanor King

SIZES

Women's 30 (33, 36, 39, 42, 45, 48, 51, 54)" / 76 (84, 91.5, 99, 106.5, 114.5, 122, 129.5, 137)cm; shown in size 36" / 91.5cm.

Intended to be worn with 3" / 7.5cm of positive ease in the main part of the top, and with no ease or negative ease at the waistband.

FINISHED MEASUREMENTS

Bust circumference: 33 (36, 39, 42, 45, 48, 51, 54, 57)" / 84 (91.5, 99, 106.5, 114.5, 122, 129.5, 137, 145)cm

MATERIALS

Fyberspates Scrumptious 4 Ply / Sport Superwash (45% silk, 55% superwash merino; 400 yds / 365m per 100g skein)

- ❥ [MC] Slate #307; 3 [3, 4, 4, 4, 4, 5, 5, 5] skeins
- ❥ [CC] Natural #310; 1 skein

32-inch US #4 / 3.5mm circular needle or size needed to obtain gauge
24-inch US #4 / 3.5mm circular needle or US #4 / 3.5mm dpns
US size C or D / 3mm crochet hook

9 removable stitch markers, at least 3 of them split-ring
2 × 3/8" / 12mm pearl buttons
4 yarn holders and 2 safety pins, or waste yarn for holding stitches
Yarn needle

GAUGE

27 sts and 36 rows = 4" / 10cm in St st
18 sts and 38.5 rows = 4" / 10cm in purse stitch
32 sts and 56 rounds = 4" / 10cm in zebra stitch
(One repeat of the zebra stitch is 3" / 17.5cm wide.)

REQUIRED SKILLS

Knitting flat and in the round; increases/decreases; long-tail cast on; provisional cast on; short rows; 3-needle bind off; working simple lace from chart or written instructions; slipped-stitch colorwork; knowledge of basic sweater construction; picking up stitches; basic crochet stitches; seaming i-cord, applied i-cord and applied i-cord bind off; sewing on buttons; kitchener stitch (grafting)

PATTERN NOTES

The sweater is worked from the bottom up. The waistband is worked in the round to the crossover, then the body is worked flat and splits into back and fronts at the armholes. The sleeves are worked flat, top-down.

STITCHES AND TECHNIQUES

Purse Stitch: [Yo, p2tog] to end of row.

Reverse Applied I-cord Bind Off: [P2, p2tog, sl 3 sts back to LH needle] to end.

The clothes worn by Lisa (Grace Kelly) in Rear Window *(1954) are fabulous celebrations of femininity: cross-over tops, wispy, floaty material, teeny-tiny nipped-in waists. I've tried to bring something of that glamour to this design. The geometric lines and princess seams flatter and curve with the waist and the sleeves are a flirty knit mesh with lots of shape. When Lisa shows off her Paris dress to Jeff she tells him it's "a steal at eleven hundred dollars." Well, I hope you get at least eleven hundred dollars' worth of compliments when you show off this top!*

PATTERN

Hem

With MC, CO 193 (212, 231, 251, 270, 289, 309, 328, 347) sts using long-tail cast on. Turn and purl 1 row. Join to work in the round, being careful not to twist. Pm for beginning of the round. This is also the center right underarm of the garment.
Purl 1 round in MC. Knit 3 rounds in CC. Knit 1 round in MC. Purl 2 rounds in MC.

Transition round:

> *Sizes 30, 33, 36, 39, 42, 45 & 54:* Increase 47 (52, 57, 61, 66, 71, –, –, 85) sts evenly by working [k3, kfb] to the last 7 or fewer sts, knit to end of round.

> *Sizes 48 & 51:* Increase – (–, –, –, –, –, 75, 80, –) sts evenly as above, but skip a kfb in the middle of the round. 240 (264, 288, 312, 336, 360, 384, 408, 432) sts.

Waistband

There are 4 "princess seams" on each waistband, worked using Chart B. Starting at center right underarm (beginning of round) and Row 1, work repeats from Charts A and B in the following ratios:

> Beginning of Right side: Start with st 13 (19, 1, 19, 1, 7, 13, 7, 13) of Chart A and work to st 24. Work 0 (1, 0, 1, 0, 1, 1, 1, 1) more repeats of Chart A. Pm, work 1 repeat of Chart B.

> Back: Work 2 (1, 2, 2, 3, 2, 3, 3, 4) repeats of Chart A. Pm, work 1 repeat of Chart B.

> Left side: Work 1 (2, 2, 2, 2, 3, 3, 3, 3) repeats of Chart A, placing a marker for the center left underarm in the middle of these Chart A sts. Pm, work 1 repeat of Chart B.

> Front: Work 2 (2, 2, 3, 3, 3, 3, 4, 4) repeats of Chart A. Pm, work 1 repeat of Chart B.

> Remainder of Right side: Work from st 1 to st 12 (18, 24, 18, 24, 6, 12, 6, 12) of Chart A, work 0 (0, 0, 0, 0, 1, 1, 1, 1) more repeats of Chart A.

Work 90 further zebra rounds in charted patterns as est. 192 (216, 240, 264, 288, 312, 336, 360, 384) sts.

Transition Round and Crossover Set-up

Cut CC; remainder of body is worked in St st using MC only.

Using MC, knit 1 round, decreasing 8 (12, 16, 20, 24, 24, 28, 36, 38) times evenly using k2tog. 184 (204, 224, 244, 264, 288, 308, 324, 346) sts. Make sure the center left underarm st is still halfway along the round. Move the princess seam markers so that they mark the central sts of the seams. Front and back should each have 92 (102, 112, 122, 132, 144, 154, 162, 173) sts.

Place a removable marker in the center front. Place markers 35 (36, 36, 36, 36, 36, 36, 37, 37) sts on either side of this central marker to mark the "points" of the crossover.

Break the yarn and join to the st at the left crossover point marker (as worn). Using a second circular needle, knit into each st to the next crossover point marker, but keep the st from the previous row live by slipping it pwise onto the end of the first circular needle. 70 (72, 72, 72, 72, 72, 72, 74, 74) sts added for the crossover. Knit to end. 254 (276, 296, 316, 336, 360, 380, 398, 420) sts total; 81 (87, 92, 97, 102, 108, 113, 118, 123) sts on each front, except size 54 will have an extra st on one front. Remove it with a p2togtbl on the next row.

Lower Body

The remainder of the body is worked flat.
All WS rows: Purl.
On all RS rows to shoulder rise, decrease for neckline as follows: K3, ssk, work to last 5 sts, k2tog, k3.

On Row 4 and repeated on 9 more 4th rows, work seam increases as follows: K3, ssk, work to princess seam marker, m1L, sm, work to next princess seam marker, sm, m1R, work to next princess seam marker, m1L, sm, work to last princess seam marker, sm, m1R, work to 5 sts before end, k2tog, k3. 40 rows worked since start of Body.

Continue working neckline decreases for 12 more rows. 242 (264, 284, 304, 324, 348, 368, 386, 407) sts.

Split for Back and Fronts

On the next RS row, k3, ssk, k58 (63, 68, 72, 77, 82, 87, 91, 96), BO 4 (6, 6, 8, 8, 10, 10, 12, 12), k108 (116, 126, 134, 144, 154, 164, 170, 181), BO 4 (6, 6, 8, 8, 10, 10, 12, 12), k58 (63, 68, 72, 77, 82, 87, 91, 96), k2tog, k3. Continue working on left front. Slip sts for right front and back onto yarn holders.

Left Front

Continue to decrease at neckline on RS rows as est throughout.

Row 1 (WS): Purl to last 3 sts, p2tog, p1.

Row 2 (RS): BO 1 (1, 1, 1, 1, 2, 2, 2, 2) sts at the armhole edge and work decrease at the neckline as est.

*

BO 1 st at armhole edge on each of the next 0 (0, 1, 1, 1, 1, 3, 3, 6) rows.

BO 1 st at armhole edge every other row 0 (1, 2, 4, 6, 6, 8, 9, 10) times.

BO 1 st at armhole edge every 4th row 1 (3, 4, 4, 5, 6, 5, 5, 4) times.

BO 1 st at armhole edge every 6th row 2 (2, 1, 2, 1, 1, 1, 1, 1) times.

BO 1 st at armhole edge every 8th row 2 (1, 1, 0, 0, 0, 0, 0, 0) times.

38 (40, 43, 44, 46, 47, 48, 50, 51) sts remaining. 7 (9, 11, 13 15, 17, 21, 21, 24) sts decreased at armhole edge and 17 (18, 18, 19, 20, 22, 23, 24, 25) sts decreased at neckline.

Continue decreasing at the neck edge only until 22 (23, 25, 25, 26, 28, 28, 29, 30) sts remain.

**

End by working a RS row.

Left Front Shoulder Rise

Throughout this section, continue working in patt: Purl on WS and knit on RS rows.
Row 1: Work 16 (18, 20, 20, 20, 23, 23, 24, 25), w&t.
Row 2: Work to end.
Row 3: Work 10 (13, 15, 15, 15, 18, 18, 19, 20), w&t.
Row 4: Work to end.
Row 5: Work 5 (8, 10, 10, 10, 13, 13, 14, 15), w&t.
Row 6: Work to end.
Size 30 only: Skip to Rise Finish.

Row 7: Work – (4, 5, 5, 5, 8, 8, 9, 10), w&t.
Row 8: Work to end.
Sizes 33, 36, 39 & 42 only: Skip to Rise Finish.

Row 9: Work – (–, –, –, –, 4, 4, 4, 5), w&t.
Row 10: Work to end.

Rise Finish

Work to end, picking up wraps as you go. Slip sts onto a yarn holder until finishing stage.

Right Front

Continue to decrease at neckline on RS rows as set throughout.

Replace held sts onto needle. Join yarn to WS of work at armhole edge.

Row 1 (WS): BO 1 (1, 1, 1, 1, 2, 2, 2, 2) sts at the start of this row, purl to end.
Row 2: Decrease at the neckline as est, knit to last 3 sts, k2tog, k1.

Work as for Left Front between * and **.
End by working a WS row.

Right Front Shoulder Rise

Work as for Left Front Shoulder Rise. Slip sts onto yarn holder until finishing stage.

Upper Back

Replace held sts onto needle. Join yarn to RS of work at right armhole edge.

Row 1 (RS): BO 1 (1, 1, 1, 1, 2, 2, 2, 2) sts at the start of this row, knit to last 3 sts, k2tog, k1.
Row 2: BO 1 (1, 1, 1, 1, 2, 2, 2, 2) sts at the start of this row, purl to last 3 sts, p2tog, p1.

BO 1 st at each armhole edge on each of the next 0 (0, 1, 1, 1, 1, 3, 3, 6) rows.

BO 1 st at each armhole edge every other row 0 (1, 2, 4, 6, 6, 8, 9, 10) times.

BO 1 st at each armhole edge every 4th row 1 (3, 4, 4, 5, 6, 5, 5, 4) times.

BO 1 st at each armhole edge every 6th row 2 (2, 1, 2, 1, 1, 1, 1, 1) times.

BO 1 st at each armhole edge every 8th row 2 (1, 1, 0, 0, 0, 0, 0, 0) times.

94 (98, 104, 108, 114, 120, 124, 128, 133) sts rem.

Work even for 34 (34, 37, 39, 41, 39, 42, 43, 44) rows. End by working a WS row.

Back Shoulder Rise and Back Neck

Row 1 (RS): K88 (93, 99, 103, 108, 115, 119, 123, 128), w&t.
Row 2: P82 (88, 94, 98, 102, 110, 114, 118, 123), w&t.

Size 30 only: Skip to Split for Back Neck.

Row 3: K– (83, 89, 93, 97, 105, 109, 113, 118), w&t.
Row 4: P– (78, 84, 88, 92, 100, 104, 108, 113), w&t.

Sizes 33, 36, 39 & 42 only: Skip to Split for Back Neck.

Row 5: K– (–, –, –, –, 95, 99, 103, 108), w&t.
Row 6: P– (–, –, –, –, 90, 94, 98, 103), w&t.

Split for Back Neck

K29 (26, 28, 28, 28, 26, 26, 27, 28), BO 30 (32, 34, 38, 42, 44, 48, 50, 53), k17 (15, 17, 17, 17, 15, 15, 16, 17), w&t.

35 (36, 38, 38, 39, 41, 41, 42, 43) sts rem for Right Shoulder and 29 (30, 32, 32, 33, 35, 35, 36, 37) sts rem for Left Shoulder.

Continue on back left shoulder. Place the sts for Right Back Shoulder onto a yarn holder.

Left Back Shoulder

*
Work to end.
BO 6 at neck edge, work 6 (5, 6, 6, 6, 5, 5, 5, 6) sts, w&t, work to end.

BO 1, work to end, picking up wraps as you go.
22 (23, 25, 25, 26, 28, 28, 29, 30) sts.

Place sts onto a yarn holder until finishing stage.

Right Back Shoulder

Join yarn to neck edge on WS of work.
BO 6 at neck edge, p17 (15, 17, 17, 17, 15, 15, 16, 17), w&t.

Continue as for Left Back Shoulder from *.

Sleeves, make 2 alike to cuff

Sleeve Cap

CO 6 (8, 8, 10, 10, 12, 12, 14, 14) sts using long-tail cast on.

Row 1: Knit to end.
Row 2: CO 3 sts using cable cast on (see Abbreviations & Techniques) and knit them, k1, work Purse Stitch to last st, k1.
Row 3: CO 1 st and knit it, k1, work Purse Stitch to last 2 sts, k2.

Row 4: CO 1 st and knit it, work Purse Stitch to last 2 sts, k2.
Row 5: CO 1 st and knit it, work Purse Stitch to last st, k1.
Row 6: CO 1 st and knit it, k1, work Purse Stitch to last st, k1.

Row 7: CO 1 st and knit it, k1, work Purse Stitch to last 2 sts, k2.

Repeat Rows 4 to 7, 2 (2, 1, 1, 2, 2, 2, 2, 3) more times. 22 (24, 20, 22, 26, 28, 28, 30, 34) sts.

Sizes 36, 39, 42, 48 & 51 only: Repeat Rows 4 & 5 once more, then continue from Row E below.

All other sizes: Continue from Row A below.

Row A: K2, work Purse Stitch to last 2 sts, k2.
Row B: K2, work Purse Stitch to last 2 sts, k2.
Row C: CO 1 st and knit it, work Purse Stitch to last 2 sts, k2.
Row D: CO 1 st and knit it, work Purse Stitch to last st, k1.
Row E: K1, work Purse Stitch to last st, k1.
Row F: K1, work Purse Stitch to last st, k1.
Row G: CO 1 st and knit it, k1, work Purse Stitch to last st, k1.
Row H: CO 1 st and knit it, k1, work Purse Stitch to last 2 sts, k2.

All sizes: Repeat Rows A–H, 3 (3, 5, 5, 4, 4, 5, 5, 5) more times. 38 (40, 44, 46, 46, 48, 52, 54, 58) sts.

Sizes 30, 33, 39, 42, 45, & 51 only: Repeat Rows A–D once more, then repeat Rows 6 & 7 again.

All sizes:
Repeat Rows 4–7 another 3 (3, 3, 2, 4, 3, 4, 3, 4) times. 54 (56, 56, 58, 66, 64, 68, 70, 74) sts.

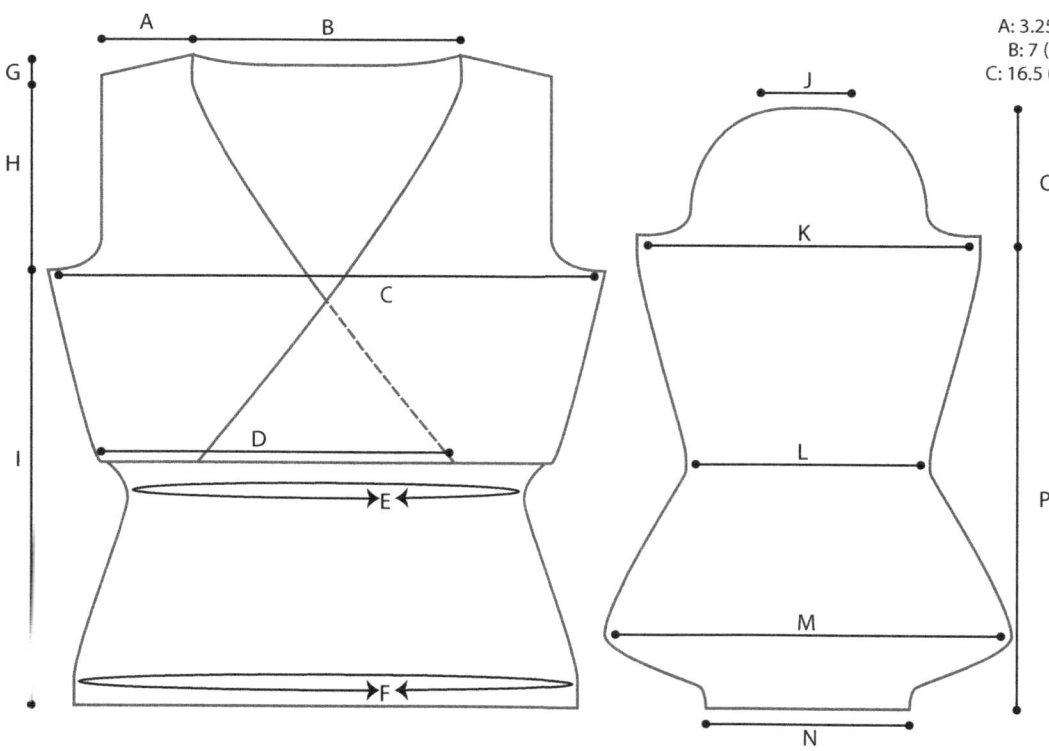

A: 3.25 (3.25, 3.5, 3.75, 3.75, 4, 4, 4.25, 4.5)"
B: 7 (7.75, 8, 8.25, 9, 9.25, 10, 10.25, 10.5)"
C: 16.5 (18, 19.5, 21, 22.5, 24, 25.5, 27, 28.5)"
D: 8.25 (9, 9.75, 10.5, 11.25, 12, 12.75, 13.5, 14.25)"
E: 11 (12.5, 14, 15.5, 17, 18.5, 20, 21.5, 23)"
F: 15 (16.5, 18, 19.5, 21, 22.5, 24, 25.5, 27)"
G: 0.75 (1, 1, 1, 1, 1.25, 1.25, 1.25, 1.25)"
H: 7.5 (8, 8.25, 8.75, 9, 9.5, 9.75, 10.25, 10.5)"
I: 5.75" all sizes

J: 2 (2.25, 2.5, 2.75, 3, 3.25, 3.5, 3.75, 4)"
K: 14 (14.5, 14.75, 15.25, 16.75, 17.5, 18.5, 19.75, 20.75)"
L: 12.25 (12.5, 13, 13.5, 14.75, 15.75, 16.75, 18, 19)"
M: 17.5 (18, 18.5, 19, 20.25, 21.25, 22, 23.5, 24.25)"
N: 9.25 (9.5, 9.75, 10.25, 11.25, 12, 12.75, 13.75, 14.5)"
O: 7 (7, 7.75, 8, 8.25, 8.25, 8.5, 8.75, 9.25)"
P: 13.75" all sizes

CO 4 (4, 5, 5, 4, 7, 7, 9, 9) and knit them, work Purse Stitch to last 2 sts, k2.
CO 4 (4, 5, 5, 4, 7, 7, 9, 9) and knit them, work Purse Stitch to last st, k1.
62 (64, 66, 68, 74, 78, 82, 88, 92) sts.

Sleeve Arm

Work even for 9 rows (k1, work Purse Stitch to last st, k1).

Row 10: K1, p2tog, work Purse Stitch to last st, k1.
Row 11: K1, work Purse Stitch to last 2 sts, k2.
Row 12: K2, work Purse Stitch to last st, k1.
Row 13: Repeat Row 11.
Row 14: Repeat Row 12.
Row 15: K1, p2tog, work Purse Stitch to last 2 sts, k2.
Rows 16–19: K2, work Purse Stitch to last 2 sts, k2.
Row 20: K1, yo, p3tog, work Purse Stitch to last 2 sts, k2.
Row 21 K2, work Purse Stitch to last st, k1.
Row 22 K1, work Purse Stitch to last 2 sts, k2.
Row 23 Repeat Row 21.
Row 24 Repeat Row 22.
Row 25 K1, yo, p3tog, work Purse Stitch to last st, k1.
Rows 26–29: K1, work Purse Stitch to last st, k1.

Repeat Rows 10–29 once more. 8 sts decreased.
54 (56, 58, 60, 66, 70, 74, 80, 84) sts.

Work even for 8 rows.

Increase Row: Work 9 sts in patt as est, yo, p1, yo, p1, work to 11 sts from end, yo, p1, yo, p1, work to end.
Work even for 8 rows.
Repeat last 9 rows 5 more times. 24 sts increased.
78 (80, 82, 84, 90, 94, 98, 104, 108) sts.

Work 12 (12, 12, 12, 14, 14, 16, 16, 16), pm, p2tog, omit the next yo, work 24 (26, 26, 26, 28, 30, 32, 34, 34), pm, p2tog, omit the next yo, work 22 (22, 24, 26, 26, 28, 26, 30, 34), pm, p2tog, omit the next yo, work to end.

Row 1: [Work to marker, p3tog] 3 times, work to end.
Row 2: [Work to 2 sts before marker, sm, p2tog, omit yo] 3 times, work to end.
Repeat these last 2 rows 2 more times, then 1st row once more. 24 sts decreased.

Left Sleeve Cuff

*

[K5, kfb] 9 (9, 9, 10, 11, 11, 12, 13, 14) times, knit to end. 63 (65, 67, 70, 77, 81, 86, 93, 98) sts.

With CC, purl 1 row, knit 1 row, purl 1 row.
With MC, knit 1 row.

**

Break yarn and re-join to other end of work.

Provisionally CO 3 sts and use applied i-cord bind off to end of row.

***

Make enough rows of unattached i-cord to form a loop for your choice of button. Continue to apply i-cord edging down side of cuff (at seam edge) for 2.5" / 6.5cm. Leave live i-cord sts on a safety pin or scrap yarn.

Right Sleeve Cuff

Break yarn and re-join to other end of work. Work as for Left Sleeve Cuff from * to **. Provisionally CO 3 sts and use reverse applied i-cord bind off to end of row. Continue from Left Sleeve Cuff ***.

Finishing

Sew up the 1-row split at the very beginning of the sweater using the tail from the cast on.

Seam each sleeve from the underarm to 2.5" / 6.5cm before the cuff edge. Pick up the live i-cord sts and continue to apply i-cord back up the other edge of cuff. Graft the two ends of the i-cord tog. Attach buttons.

Use 3-needle bind off to join the shoulders.

When seaming the sleeves onto the body, start at the underarm and ease the excess sleeve towards the shoulder to form a gentle gather there.

Using CC and a crochet hook, start at one of the crossover points and slip-stitch 1 st in from the edge once per row all around the neckline to the other crossover point. The natural tendency of the st st to roll will conceal this line when the sweater is worn. Start another slip-stitch line 3 sts in, and using the neckline decreases as your guide, work back around the neckline. At the back neck, maintain a distance of 3 to 4 rows from the first slip-stitch line. Continue down front to the next point.

With WS facing, whipstitch every outer edge st across the back neck to the "bump" of the second slipstitch line below it.

Chart A

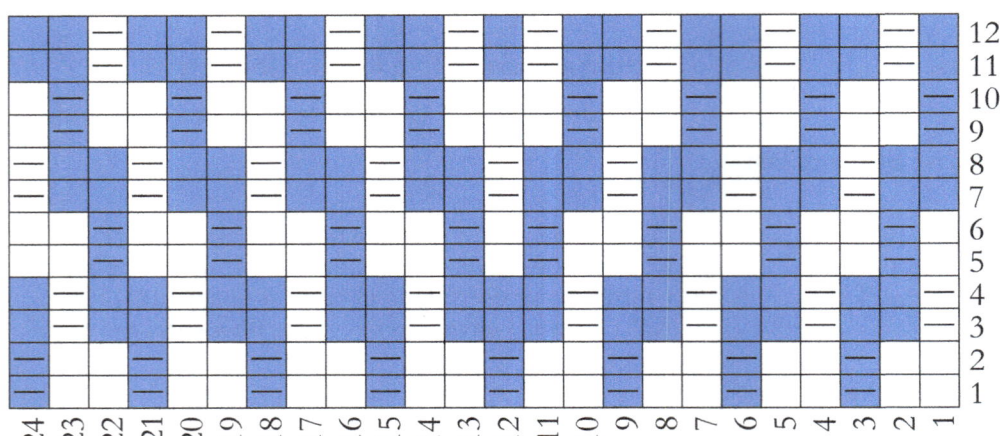

	CC		k
	MC	—	Sl st purlwise

Chart B

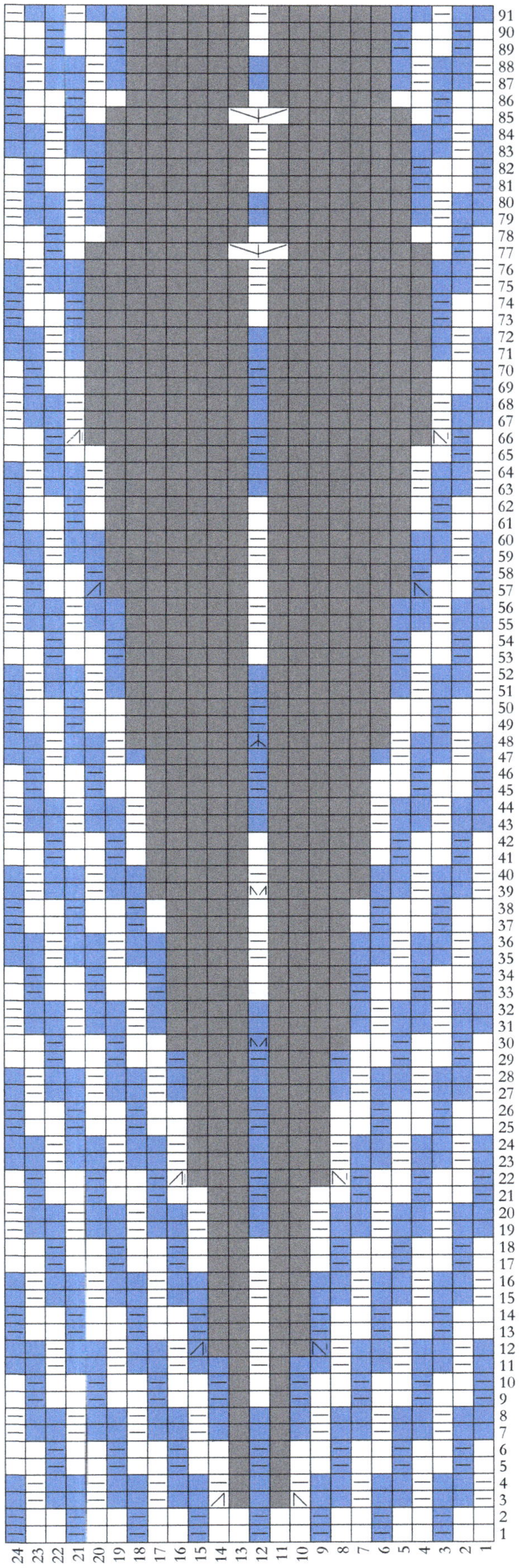

Purse Stitch Chart

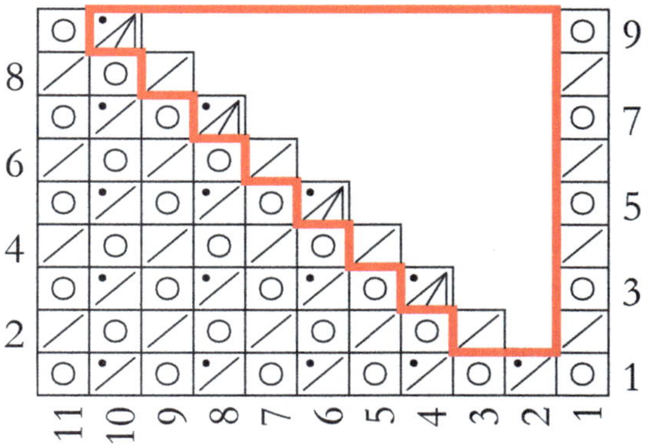

- yo
- WS: p2tog
- p2tog
- p3tog

Special Stitches for Charts

cdi: Knit through back loop, then front loop of the same stitch. Lift the vertical strand between the two stitches just created and knit into it.

ps: Pass second st on left needle over first stitch, slip to right needle.

psk: Pass 2nd st on left needle over 1st and knit.

spsp: Slip knitwise, pass 2nd st on left needle over 1st on left needle, slip to right needle, pass slipped st over.

spspk: Slip knitwise, pass 2nd st on left needle over 1st on left needle, slip to right needle, pass slipped st over, pass back to left needle and knit.

sspk: Slip, slip, pass slipped st over, pass back to the left needle and knit.

s2p: Slip, slip, pass slipped st over.

- CC
- MC

- No stitch
- k
- cdi
- Sl st purlwise
- s2p
- ps
- sspk
- psk
- spsp
- spspk

Stella Gloves

Katherine Vaughan

SIZES

Womens S (M, L); shown in size S
Intended to be worn with 0–2" / 0–5cm negative ease

FINISHED MEASUREMENTS

Hand circumference 7 (8, 9)" / 18 (20.5, 23)cm

MATERIALS

Hazel Knits Artisan Sock (90% superwash merino, 10% nylon; 400 yds / 366m per 120g skein)

- [Color A] Nickel, 0.5 (0.5, 0.5) skein
- [Color B] Vamp, 0.5 (0.5, 0.5) skein

1 set US #1 / 2.25mm double-point needles, or size needed to obtain gauge
US size B / 2.25mm crochet hook

3 stitch markers
4 × 7/16" / 13mm shanked buttons, in a coordinating color to Color B
3 stitch holders
Yarn needle

GAUGE

30 sts and 64 rounds = 4" / 10cm in pattern stitch in the round

REQUIRED SKILLS

Knitting in the round; knitting with double-pointed needles; increases; picking up stitches; basic crochet stitches (chain, single crochet); sewing on buttons; mosaic colorwork

PATTERN NOTES

Mosaic stitch requires you to use only one color of yarn on any given round. Be careful to carry the other yarn up the back of the work loosely, twisting every 1st round of the new color to prevent holes.

Always slip purlwise, with yarn held on the wrong side of the fabric.

STITCHES AND TECHNIQUES

Window Mosaic Flat
Worked over an odd number of sts. Odd rows are the RS.
Rows 1 & 2: With color A, knit.
Rows 3 & 4: With color B, k1, [sl1, k1] to end.
Rows 5 & 6: With color A, knit.
Rows 7 & 8: With color B, knit.

Window Mosaic in the Round
Worked over an even number of sts.
Round 1: With color A, knit.
Round 2: With color A, purl.
Round 3: With color B, [k1, sl1] to end.
Round 4: With color B, [p1, sl1] to end.
Round 5: With color A, knit.
Round 6: With color A, purl.
Round 7: With color B, knit.
Round 8: With color B, purl.

The smallest details jump out at me in movies. For instance, if I were to sit for hours on end watching my neighbors from my rear window, my hands would get cold. And if they did, I'd like to have a cozy pair of fingerless gloves—the better to tweak the focus on my binoculars, not to mention keep me warm.

These gloves use a garter-stitch-based mosaic stitch for interest and to evoke a highrise full of tantalizing neighbors. The buttoned cuff extends the retro feel from fingertips to wrist.

PATTERN—LEFT GLOVE

Cuff

With color A, CO 41 (49, 57) sts.
Work Window Mosaic Flat pattern 3 times.

With color A, work Row 1 of Window Mosaic Flat pattern. At end of row, CO 3 sts. Join for knitting in the round and place marker to indicate beginning of round. 44 (52, 60) sts.

Work Rounds 2–7 of Window Mosaic in the Round pattern.

Thumb Gusset

Next round: With color B, knit, placing thumb gusset markers as follows: K7 (9, 11), pm, k4, pm, knit to end of round.

Round 1: With color A, knit to marker, sm, m1, knit to marker, m1, sm, knit to end of round.

Rounds 2–8: Work Rounds 2–8 of Window Mosaic in the Round pattern.

Work these 8 rounds until there are 16 (18, 20) sts between the thumb markers, ending with Round 8.

Next round: With color A, knit to marker, rm, place next 16 (18, 20) sts on a holder, CO 4 sts across gap, remove second marker, knit to end of round.

Palm

Continue working in patt until you have worked Round 7 of Window Mosaic in the Round pattern 2 (3, 4) times after the thumb.

Pinky Finger

Next round: With color B, k26 (31, 36) and put these sts on a holder, k10 (12, 14), place remaining sts on a holder, CO 4 sts and join to other side of pinky, placing marker for beginning of round.

Continue in patt as established until you have worked Round 7 of Window Mosaic in the Round pattern 2 (3, 4) times for this finger.

BO using color B, purlwise.

Replace sts from the palm and back of hand onto needles. Join color B at the palm next to the pinky. Knit to end of round.

Next round: With color B, purl to pinky. Pick up and knit 4 sts from base of pinky. Join to palm sts and purl to end of round. 38 (44, 50) sts.

Ring Finger

Next round: With color A, k21 (25, 29) and put these sts on a holder, k14 (16, 18), place remaining sts on a holder, CO 4 sts and join to other side of ring finger, placing marker for beginning of round.

Continue in patt as established until you have worked Round 7 of Window Mosaic in the Round pattern 3 (4, 5) times for this finger.

BO using color B, purlwise.

Middle Finger

Replace 7 (8, 9) sts before and 7 (8, 9) sts after Ring Finger on needles. Join yarn at the palm next to the ring finger.

Working in patt as established, knit across palm sts, CO 4 sts, join to back of hand sts, knit across back of hand sts, pick up and knit 4 sts in all sizes from base of ring finger. Retain the position of the original beginning of round marker for this finger.

Continue in patt as established until you have worked Round 7 of Window Mosaic in the Round pattern 3 (4, 5) times for this finger.

BO using color B, purlwise.

Pointer Finger

Replace remaining sts on needles. Join yarn at the palm next to the middle finger.

Working in patt as established, knit across all sts, pick up and knit 4 sts from base of middle finger, join and place marker for beginning of round.

Continue in patt as established until you have worked Round 7 of Window Mosaic in the Round pattern 3 (4, 5) times for this finger.

BO using color B, purlwise.

Thumb

Replace sts from holder onto needles.

With color A, k1, pm for beginning of round, knit across remaining thumb sts, pick up and knit 6 sts from gap, p1.

Decrease round: With color A, k14 (16, 18), p2tog, p4, p2tog. 20 (22, 24) sts.

Continue in patt as established until you have worked Round 7 of Window Mosaic in the Round pattern 2 (3, 4) times for the thumb.

BO using color B, purlwise.

Cuff Trim

With crochet hook and color B, with RS facing and starting at the lower left corner of the cuff opening, work sc around edge.

Make button loops even with the color B stripes on the thumb size of the opening by working sc into the first st of the stripe, ch16, sc into the last sc of the edging, sc to next stripe or to end.

RIGHT GLOVE

Cuff

With color A, CO 41 (49, 57) sts.
Work Window Mosaic Flat pattern three times.

With color A, work Row 1 of Window Mosaic Flat pattern. At end of row, CO 3 sts. Join for knitting in the round and place marker to indicate beginning of round. 44 (52, 60) sts.

Work Rounds 2–7 of Window Mosaic in the Round pattern.

Thumb Gusset

Next round: With color B, knit, placing thumb gusset markers as follows: K30 (36, 42), pm, k4, pm, k10 (12, 14).

Round 1: With color A, knit to marker, sm, m1, knit to marker, m1, sm, knit to end of round.

Rounds 2–8: Work Rounds 2–8 of Window Mosaic in the Round pattern.

Work these 8 rounds until there are 16 (18, 20) sts between the thumb markers, ending with Round 8.

Next round: With color A, knit to marker, rm, place next 16 (18, 20) sts on a holder, CO 4 sts across gap, remove second marker, knit to end of round.

Palm

Continue working in patt until you have worked Round 7 of Window Mosaic in the Round pattern 2 (3, 4) times after the thumb.

Pinky Finger

Next round: With color B, 5 (6, 7) and put these sts on a holder, k10 (12, 14), place remaining sts on a holder, CO 4 sts and join to other side of pinky, placing marker for beginning of round.

Continue in patt as established until you have worked Round 7 of Window Mosaic in the Round pattern 2 (3, 4) times for this finger.

BO using color B, purlwise.

Replace sts from the palm and back of hand onto needles. With color B, pick up and knit 4 sts from base of pinky, join to next st on back of hand, knit to end of round. 38 (44, 50) sts.

Next round: With color B, purl.

Ring Finger

Next round: With color A, k10 (12, 14), place remaining sts on a holder, CO 4 sts and join to other side of ring finger. Retain the position of the original beginning of round marker for this finger.

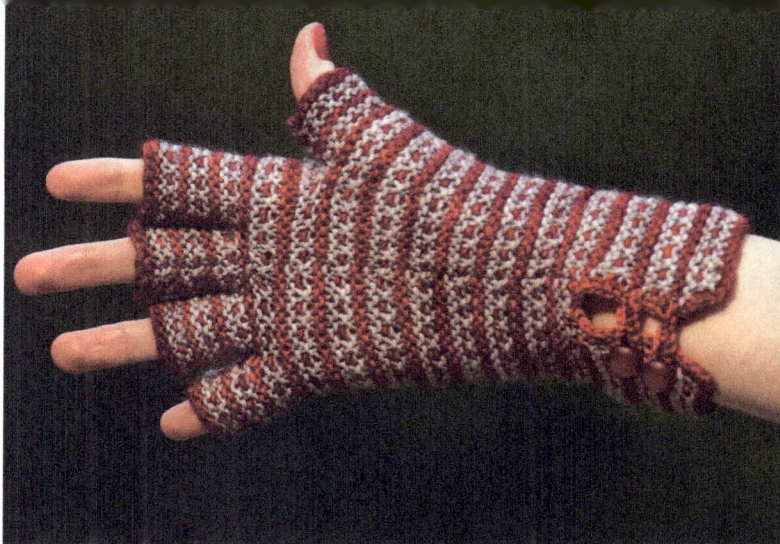

Continue in patt as established until you have worked Round 7 of Window Mosaic in the Round pattern 3 (4, 5) times for this finger.

BO using color B, purlwise.

Middle Finger

Replace 7 (8, 9) sts before and 7 (8, 9) sts after Ring Finger on needles. With A, pick up and knit 4 sts from base of ring finger, working in patt across back of hand sts, CO 4 sts, join to palm sts, work across palm sts, join and place marker for beginning of round.

Continue in patt as established until you have worked Round 7 of Window Mosaic in the Round pattern 3 (4, 5) times for this finger.

BO using color B, purlwise.

Pointer Finger

Replace remaining sts on needles. With color A, pick up and knit 4 sts from base of middle finger, work across remaining sts, join and place marker for beginning of round.

Continue in patt as established until you have worked Round 7 of Window Mosaic in the Round pattern 3 (4, 5) times for this finger.

BO using color B, purlwise.

Thumb and Cuff Trim

Work as for Left Glove.

Finishing (Both Gloves)

Block to even sts and to fit.

Attach buttons on pinky side of cuff opening. Mark position of buttons while glove is worn. Buttons should be even with the first column of "windows" formed by color B.

Weave in ends.

Greenwich Village Cardigan

Linda Wilgus

SIZES

Women's XS (S, M, L, XL, 2X, 3X); shown in size S. Intended to be worn with 1" / 2.5cm of positive ease.

FINISHED MEASUREMENTS

Bust: 31 (35, 39, 43, 47, 51, 55)" / 79 (89, 99, 109, 119.5, 129.5, 139.5)cm
Length: 17.5 (18.75, 18.75, 20.25, 21.5, 21.5, 23)" / 44.5 (47.5, 47.5, 51.5, 54.5, 54.5, 58.5)cm

MATERIALS

Blue Moon Fiber Arts Marine Silk Sport (51% silk, 29% merino, 20% sea cell rayon; 324 yds / 296m per 100g skein); color: "True Blood" Red; 3 (3, 4, 4, 5, 5, 6) skeins

32-inch or longer US #4 / 3.5mm circular needle, or size needed to obtain gauge
1 set US #4 / 3.5mm double-point needles

8 removable stitch markers
9 × ½" / 13mm buttons
2 stitch holders or waste yarn
Yarn needle

GAUGE

22 sts and 28 rows = 4" / 10cm in pattern stitch

REQUIRED SKILLS

Knitting in the round; knitting with double-pointed needles or magic loop; increases/decreases; working simple lace from chart or written instructions; picking up stitches; sewing on buttons

PATTERN NOTES

The cardigan is worked from the top down, working back and forth on a circular needle. The sleeves are worked in the round on double-pointed needles or using the magic loop technique. After the body and sleeves are finished, stitches are picked up on each front edge to work the button band.

STITCHES AND TECHNIQUES

Holland Lace Pattern worked FLAT:
Row 1 (RS): P2, k2, k2tog, yo, k1, yo, ssk, k2, p2.
Row 2 and all other WS rows: K2, p9, k2.
Row 3: P2, k1, k2tog, yo, k3, yo, ssk, k1, p2.
Rows 5 & 7: P2, k2tog, yo, k5, yo, ssk, p2.
Row 9: P2, k3, yo, sl2-k1-p2sso, yo, k3, p2.
Row 10: Repeat Row 2.

Holland Lace Pattern worked IN THE ROUND:
Round 1: P2, k2, k2tog, yo, k1, yo, ssk, k2, p2.
Round 2 and all other even-numbered rounds: P2, k9, p2.
Round 3: P2, k1, k2tog, yo, k3, yo, ssk, k1, p2.
Rounds 5 & 7: P2, k2tog, yo, k5, yo, ssk, p2.
Round 9: P2, k3, yo, sl2-k1-p2sso, yo, k3, p2.
Round 10: As Round 2.

No one who has seen Rear Window *can forget the awe-inspiring black-and-white dress that Grace Kelly's character Lisa Fremont wears. It was hot the day she wore it, but what if the weather had been different and she had needed a cardigan to keep warm? Greenwich Village is a fitted cardigan featuring a delicate lace panel down the front and on the sleeves. The cardigan is worked from the top down and is entirely seamless. Knit in a luxury sport-weight yarn with beautiful drape, Greenwich Village is just the cardigan to complement your Grace-inspired look.*

PATTERN

Yoke

CO 87 (92, 97, 107, 112, 112, 117) sts.
Rows 1 & 3 (RS): P2, [k3, p2] to end.
Rows 2 & 4 (WS): K2, [p3, k2] to end.

Sizes XS & L only:
Row 5: K1, k2tog, knit to end. 1 st dec.

Sizes S & XL only:
Row 5: K2, k2tog, knit to last 2 sts, ssk, k1. 2 sts dec.

Sizes M & 3X only:
Row 5: K1, m1, knit to end. 1 st inc.

Size 2X only:
Row 5: K1, m1, knit to last st, m1, k1. 2 sts inc.

All sizes:
86 (90, 98, 106, 110, 114, 118) sts.
Row 6: Purl.
Row 7: [K2tog, yo] to last 2 sts, k2.

Raglan Set-up Row (WS): P2, pm, p13, pm, p3 (4, 5, 6, 7, 8, 9), pm, p7 (7, 8, 9, 9, 9, 9), pm, p36 (38, 40, 42, 44, 46, 48), pm, p7 (7, 8, 9, 9, 9, 9), pm, p3 (4, 5, 6, 7, 8, 9), pm, p13, pm, p2.

Begin raglan inc:

Row 1: Knit to marker, sm, work Row 1 of Holland Lace Pattern, sm, [knit to 1 st before marker, kfb, sm, kfb] 4 times, knit to marker, sm, work Row 1 of Holland Lace Pattern, sm, k2. 94 (98, 106, 114, 118, 122, 126) sts; 19 (20, 21, 22, 23, 24, 25) each front, 38 (40, 42, 44, 46, 48, 50) back, 9 (9, 10, 11, 11, 11, 11) each sleeve.

Row 2: P2, sm, k2, p9, k2, purl to 7th marker, slipping markers as you go, k2, p9, k2, sm, p2.

Repeat Rows 1 & 2, working the next row of Holland Lace Pattern, 23 (27, 32, 36, 41, 41, 41) times more. 278 (314, 360, 398, 442, 446, 450) sts; 42 (47, 53, 58, 64, 65, 66) each front, 84 (94, 106, 116, 128, 130, 132) back, 55 (63, 74, 83, 93, 93, 93) each sleeve.

Separate sleeves from body:

Row 1 (RS): Knit to marker, sm, work the next row of Holland Lace Pattern, sm, [knit to marker, sm, place the next 55 (63, 74, 83, 93, 93, 93) sts on a stitch holder or waste yarn to be worked later, remove marker, CO 3 (3, 3, 3, 3, 11, 23) sts, pm] twice, knit to marker, sm, work the next row of Holland Lace Pattern, sm, k2. 174 (194, 218, 238, 262, 282, 306) sts.

Row 2 (WS): P2, sm, k2, p9, k2, purl to 5th marker, slipping markers as you go, k2, p9, k2, sm, p2.

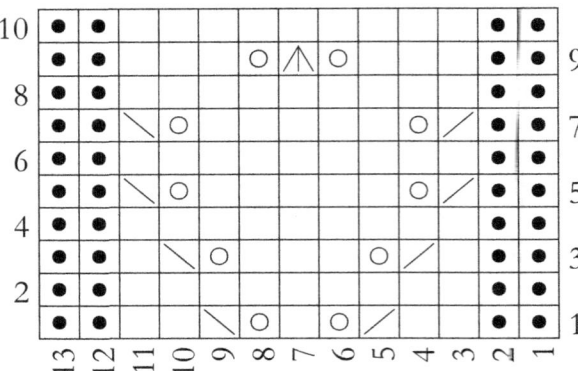

Holland Lace Chart

RS: k; WS: p	
▢	RS: k; WS: p
●	RS: p; WS: k
○	yo
╱	k2tog
╲	ssk
⋀	s2kp

Sizes XS & S only:
Row 3: K2, sm, work next row of Holland Lace Pattern, sm, [knit to marker, sm, s2kp, sm] twice, knit to marker, sm, work next row of Holland Lace Pattern, sm, k2. 4 sts dec.

Size M only:
Row 3: K2, sm, work next row of Holland Lace Pattern, [knit to marker, sm, k1, k2tog, sm] twice, knit to marker, sm, work next row of Holland Lace Pattern, sm, k2. 2 sts dec.

Sizes L, 1X, 2X & 3X only:
Row 3: Knit.

All sizes:
170 (190, 216, 238, 262, 282, 306) sts.

Lower Body

While continuing to work the Holland Lace Pattern on each front edge, work until the cardigan measures 12.5 (13.5, 13.5, 14.5, 15.5, 15.5, 16.5)" / 31.5 (34.5, 34.5, 37, 39.5, 39.5, 42)cm from the top, ending with a WS row.

While continuing to work the Holland Lace Pattern on each front edge, work dec row as follows:
Next row: [Work 15 (17, 19, 21, 24, 26, 28), k2tog] 10 times, work to end. 160 (180, 206, 228, 252, 272, 296) sts.

While continuing to work the Holland Lace Pattern on each front edge, work until the cardigan measures 13.5 (14.5, 14.5, 16, 17, 17, 18)" / 34.5 (37, 37, 40.5, 43, 43, 45.5)cm from the top, ending with a WS row.

While continuing to work the Holland Lace Pattern on each front edge, work dec row as follows:
Next row: [Work 18 (19, 23, 25, 28, 30, 33), k2tog] 8 times, work to end. 152 (172, 198, 220, 244, 264, 288) sts.

While continuing to work the Holland Lace Pattern on each front edge, work until the cardigan measures 14.5 (15.75, 15.75, 17.25, 18.5, 18.5, 20)" / 37 (40, 40, 44, 47, 47, 51)cm from the top, ending with a WS row that contains Row 10 of Holland Lace pattern on each front edge.

Eyelet and ribbed hem section:

Row 1 (RS): [K2tog, yo] to last 2 sts, k2.
Row 2 (WS): Purl.

Sizes XS & S only:
Row 3: K1, m1, knit to end. 1 st inc.

Sizes M & 3X only:
Row 3 Knit.

Size L only:
Row 3 K2tog, knit to last 2 sts, k2tog. 2 sts dec.

Sizes XL & 2X only:
Row 3 K2tog, knit to end. 1 st dec.

All sizes:
153 (173, 198, 218, 243, 263, 288) sts.
Row 4: Purl.
Row 5: [K3, p2] to last 3 sts, k3.
Row 6: [P3, k2] to last 3 sts, p3.
Repeat Rows 5 & 6 until the ribbed hem measures 2.5" / 6.5cm.
BO all sts in patt.

Sleeves

Pick up 2 (2, 2, 2, 2, 6, 12) sts from the left side of the underarm, add held sts of sleeve to needle, pick up 1 (1, 1, 1, 1, 5, 11) sts from the right side of the underarm. Pm and join to work in the round. 58 (66, 77, 86, 96, 104, 116) sts on needle.

Size 3X only:
Round 1: Knit.
Rounds 2 & 3: Ssk, knit to last 2 sts, k2tog. 2 sts dec.

All sizes:
58 (66, 77, 86, 96, 104, 114) sts on needles.
Work in St st until sleeve measures 3" / 7.5cm from underarm.

Next round (dec round): [K9 (11, 13, 15, 17, 18, 20), k2tog] 5 times, work to end. 53 (61, 72, 81, 91, 99, 109) sts.

Work in St st until sleeve measures 6.25 (6.5, 6.75, 7, 7.25, 7.75, 8.25)" / 16 (16.5, 17, 18, 18.5, 19.5, 21) cm from underarm.

Next round (dec round): [K11 (13, 22, 18, 20, 22, 25), k2tog] to last 1 (1, 0, 1, 3, 3, 1) sts, knit to end. 49 (57, 69, 77, 87, 95, 105) sts.

Next round: K18 (22, 28, 32, 37, 41, 46) pm, k13, pm, k18 (22, 28, 32, 37, 41, 46).

Begin Holland Lace section:

Round 1: K18 (22, 28, 32, 37, 41, 46), sm, work Row 1 of Holland Lace Pattern, sm, k18 (22, 28, 32, 37, 41, 46).
Round 2: Knit to marker, sm, p2, k9, p2, sm, knit to end.
Repeat Rounds 1 & 2, working the next round of the Holland Lace Pattern between the markers, 3 more times.

Round 9: K2tog, knit to marker, sm, work Row 9 of Holland Lace Pattern, sm, knit to last 2 sts, ssk. 47 (55, 67, 75, 85, 93, 103) sts.
Round 10: Repeat Round 2.

Repeat Rounds 1–10 once more, then rep Rounds 1–8 once more. 45 (53, 65, 73, 83, 91, 101) sts.

Next round: K2tog, knit to 2 sts before marker, ssk, sm, work Row 9 of Holland Lace Pattern, sm, k18, ssk. 42 (50, 62, 70, 80, 88, 98) sts.

Next round: Knit to marker, remove marker, p2, k9, p2, remove marker, knit to end.

Eyelet and ribbed edge section:

Round 1: K2tog, [k2tog, yo] to end. 41 (49, 61, 69, 79, 87, 97) sts.
Rounds 2 & 3: Knit.

Sizes XS & M only:
Round 4: K2tog, knit to end. 1 st dec.

Sizes S, L & XL only:
Round 4: K1, m1, knit to end. 1 st inc.

Sizes 2X & 3X only:
Round 4: K2tog, knit to last 2 sts, ssk. 2 sts dec.

All sizes:
40 (50, 60, 70, 80, 85, 95) sts.
Rounds 5–8: [K3, p2] to end.
BO all sts in patt.

Button Band

With the RS facing and starting at hem edge, pick up 80 (85, 85, 95, 100, 100, 105) sts on left front edge.

Beginning with a RS row, work in [k3, p2] rib for 4 rows.
BO all sts in patt.

Buttonhole Band

With the RS facing and starting at neck edge, pick up 80 (80, 90, 90, 100, 100, 110) sts on right front edge.

Row 1 (RS): [K3, p2] to end.
Row 2 (WS): While continuing to work [k3, p2] rib, [work 6 (6, 7, 7, 8, 8, 9) sts, k2tog, yo] 9 times, work to end.
Row 3: [K3, p2] to end.

Row 4: [K2, p3] to end.
BO all sts in patt.

Finishing

Weave in all yarn ends. Using a yarn needle, sew the buttons onto the left front of the cardigan to line up with the yarnovers on the right front edge. The yarnovers are the button holes, which you can reinforce if you like by threading yarn around the opening. Block the cardigan for best result.

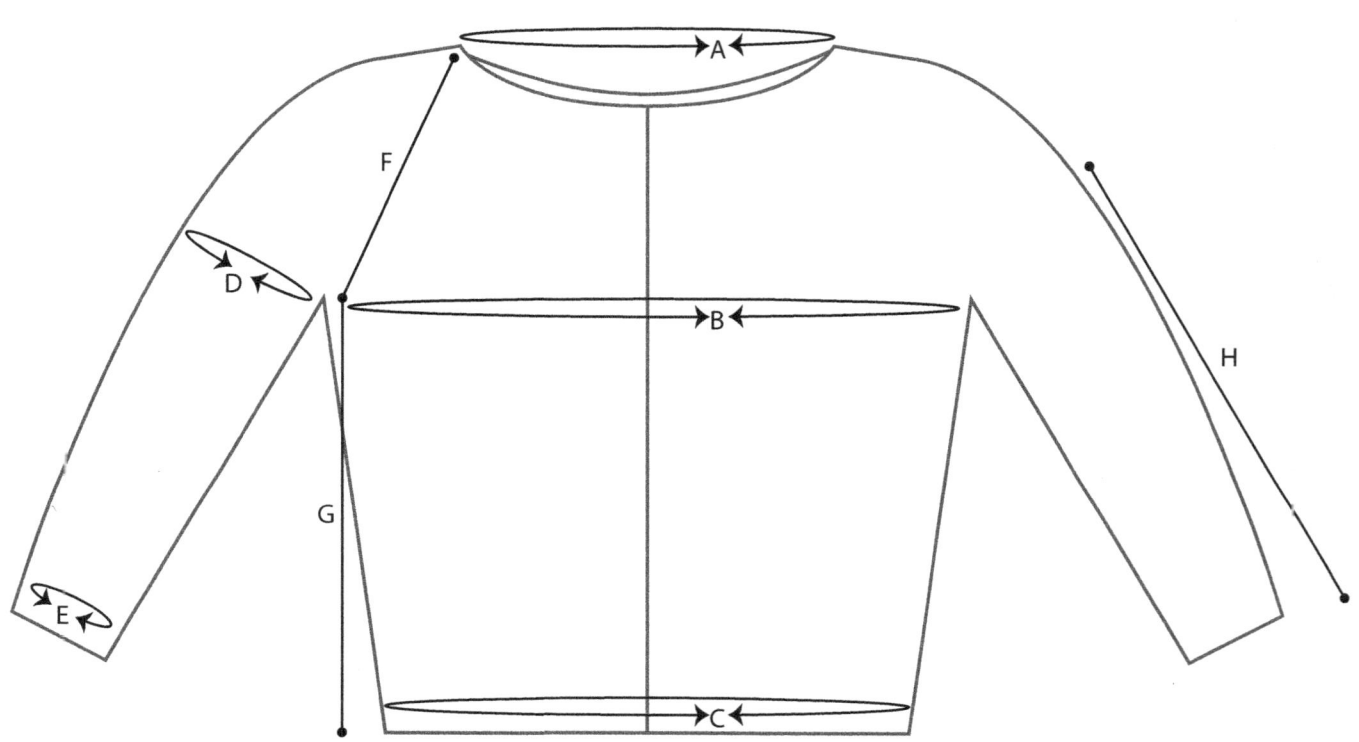

A: 15.5 (16.25, 17.5, 18.5, 19.5, 19.25, 20, 20.75)"
B: 31 (35, 39, 43, 47, 51, 55)"
C: 27 (31, 36, 40, 44, 48, 52)"
D: 10.5 (12, 14, 15.5, 17.5, 19.25, 21.5)"
E: 7.25 (9, 11, 12.75, 14.5, 15.5, 17.25)"
F: 6.75 (8, 9.5, 10.5, 12, 12, 12)"
G: 10.75 (10.75, 9.25, 9.75, 9.5, 9.5, 11)"
H: 12 (12.25, 12.5, 12.75, 13, 13.5, 14)"

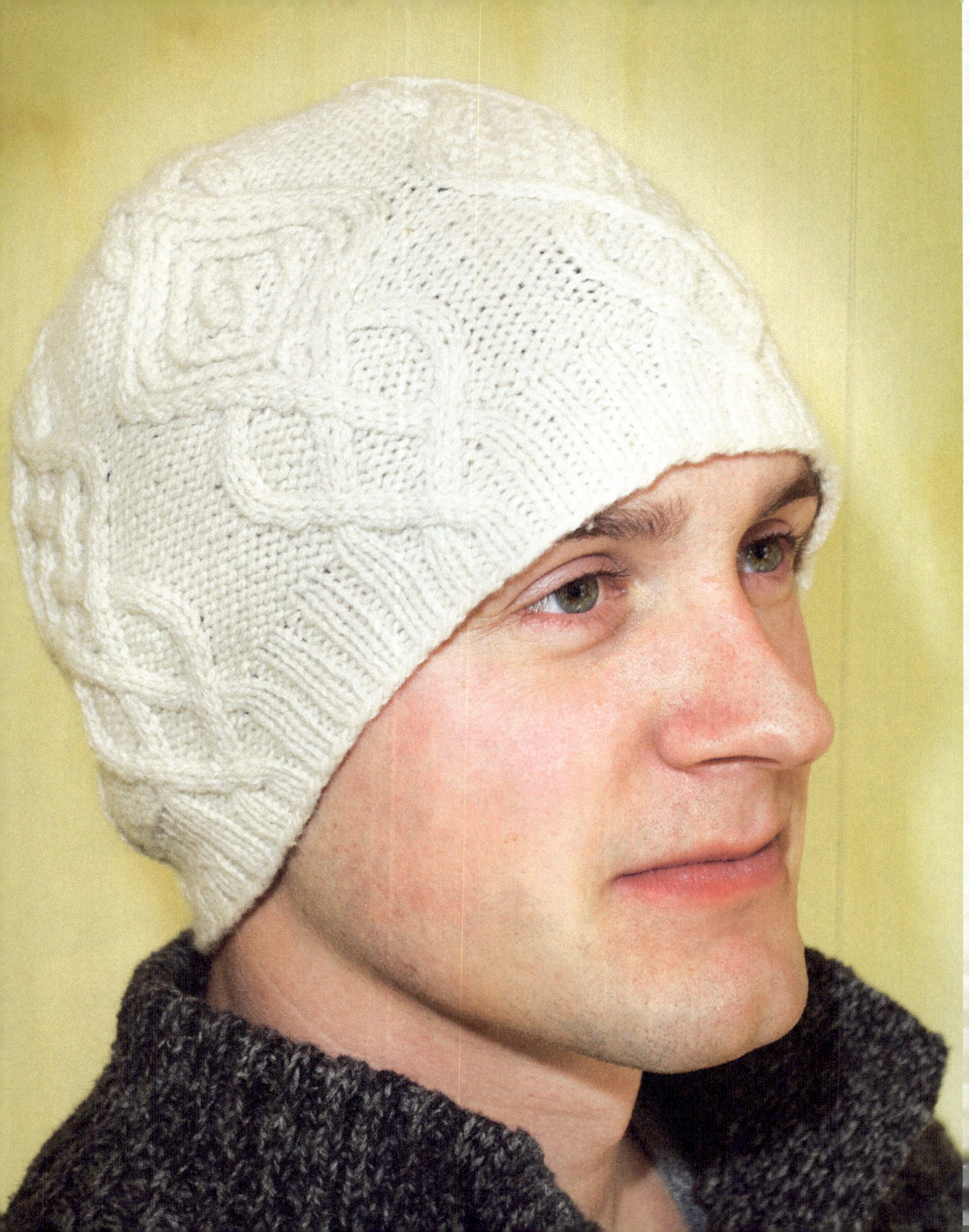

Exakta Hat

Stephannie Tallent

SIZES

Unisex S (M, L); shown in size M
Sized to fit head circumferences: 20 (23, 26)" /
51 (58.5, 66)cm

FINISHED MEASUREMENTS

Circumference: 18.5 (21.75, 24.75)" / 47 (55, 63)cm
Length: 7.5" / 19cm

MATERIALS

Bjiou Basin Ranch Bijou Bliss (50% Cormo wool,
50% yak; 150 yds / 137m per 56g skein); color:
Cream; 2 skeins

US #5 / 3.75mm needles, or size needed to obtain
gauge
US #4 / 3.5mm, or one size smaller than main needle
❧ For both needle sizes: your choice of magic loop,
    2 circulars or dpns for circular knitting

At least 1 stitch marker, more if desired to separate
pattern repeats
Yarn needle

GAUGE

Approx 31 sts and 36 rounds in 4" / 10cm in base
wedge pattern with larger needles. Note that gauge
will vary slightly depending on center motif chosen.

REQUIRED SKILLS

Knitting in the round; working cables and other
patterns from charts

PATTERN NOTES

For this hat, you get to choose what you knit in the
center of each "window." For the simplest option,
pick your favorite stitch pattern and use it in each
window. Of course, you can use a different pattern
for each window as well!

PATTERN

With smaller needles, CO 108 (126, 144) sts. Join to
work in the round, being careful not to twist. Pm for
beginning of round.

Work Rounds 1–12 of Chart A 6 (7, 8) times around.

Change to larger needles for remainder of hat.

When you get to the end of Chart A, choose which
center motif you'd like to work in each segment.
Work chosen center motif chart(s).

Work Chart B 6 (7, 8) times around. Complete chart.
Cut yarn, leaving a tail long enough to pull through
live sts & cinch hole at top of hat.

FINISHING

Weave in all ends. Block.

What do you do when you're housebound and used to looking at the world through a lens?

Do you see the same thing, or different things?

Fill the "window" of the center motif with your choice of stitch patterns.

Chart A

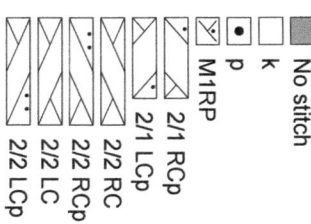

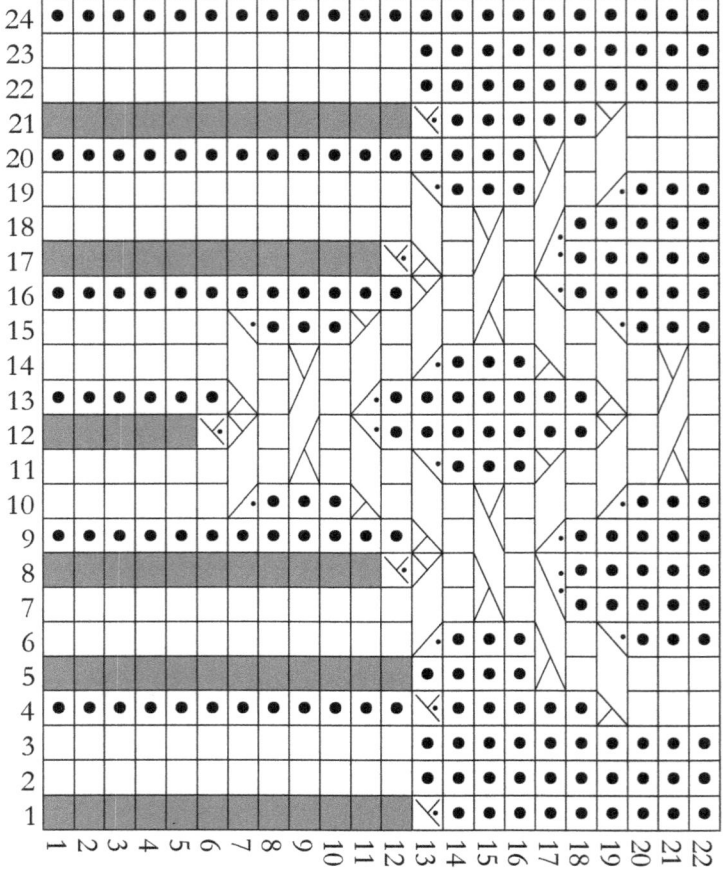

Chart B

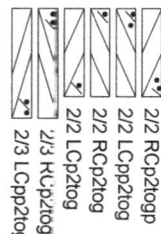

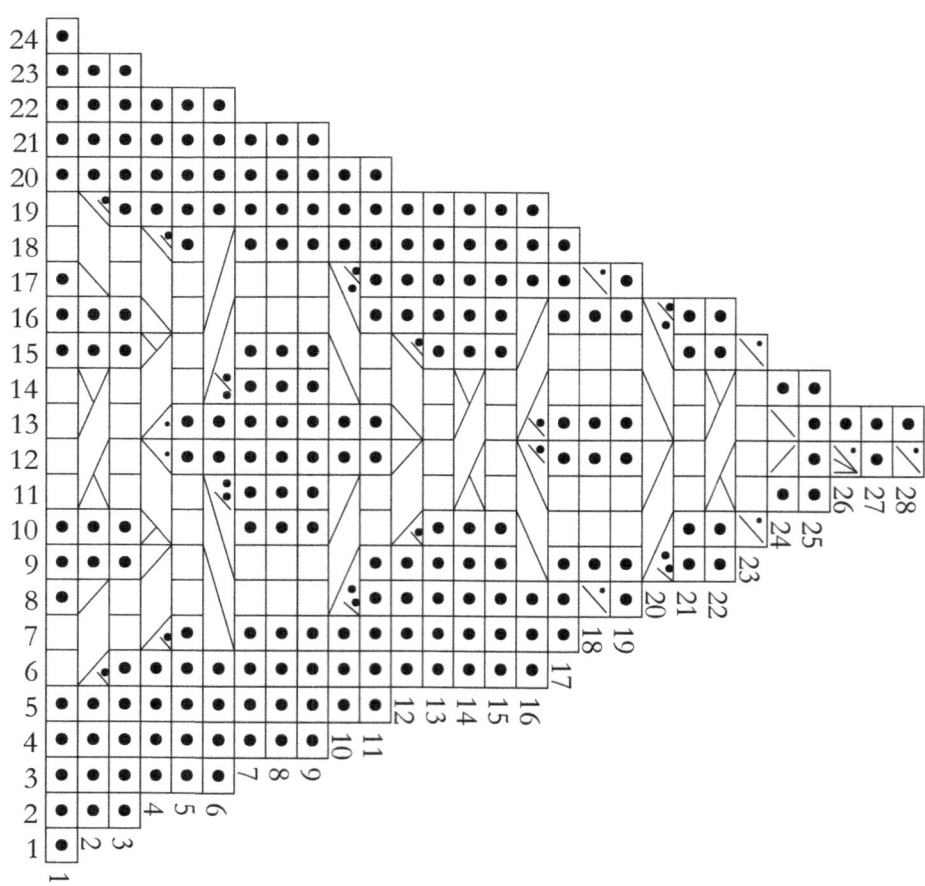

Center Motif Charts

Choose from any of the charts on the following four pages for your hat's center motif.

Cable

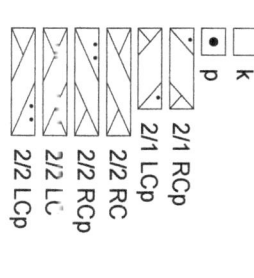

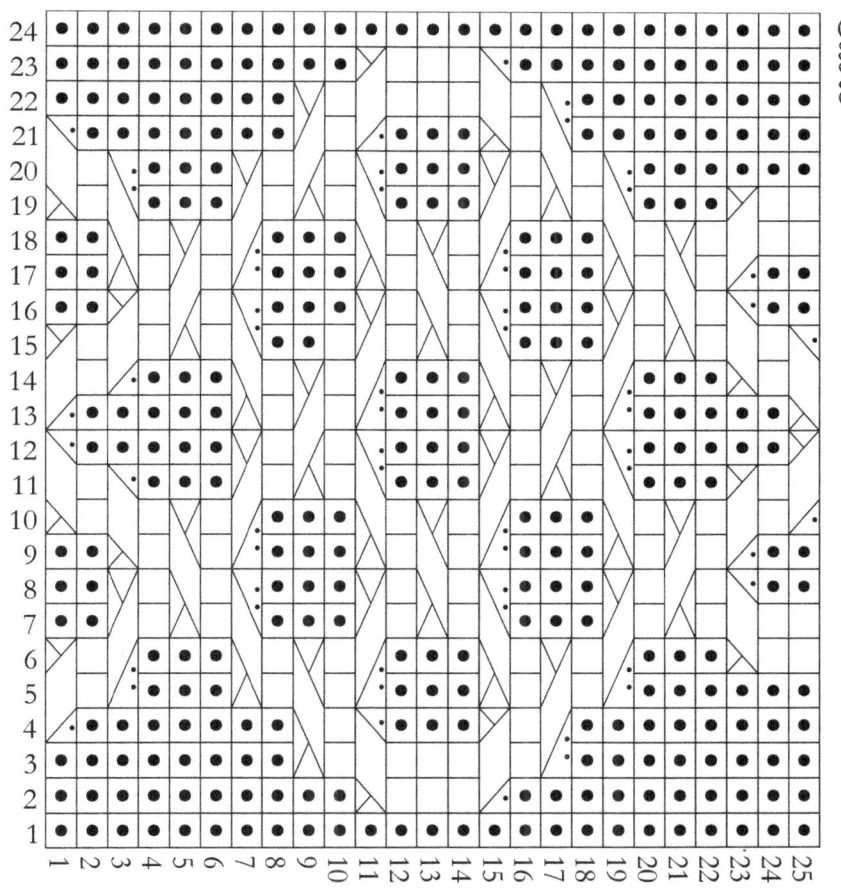

k
p

2/1 RCp
2/1 LCp
2/2 RC
2/2 RCp
2/2 LC
2/2 LCp

Honeycomb

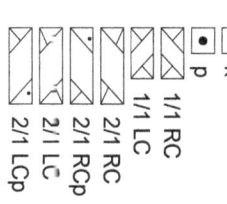

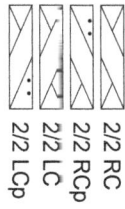

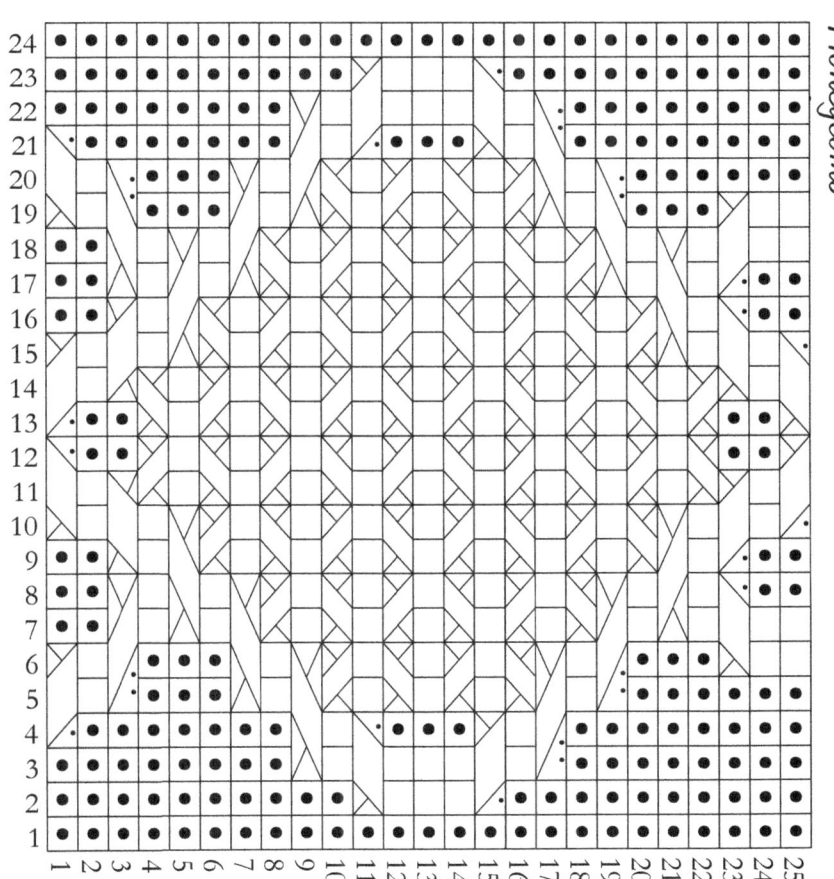

k
p

1/1 RC
1/1 LC
2/1 RC
2/1 RCp
2/1 LC
2/1 LCp

2/2 RC
2/2 RCp
2/2 LC
2/2 LCp

Onion

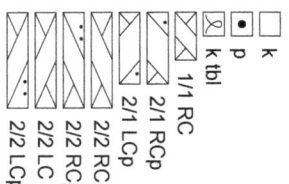

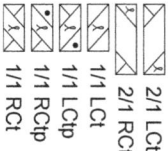

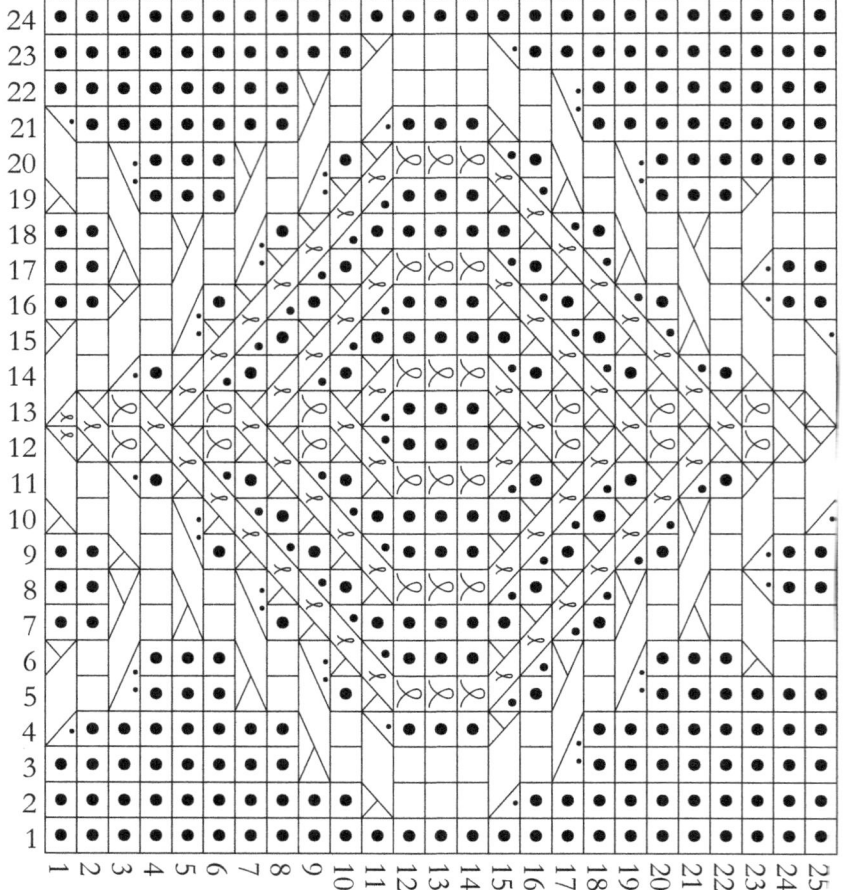

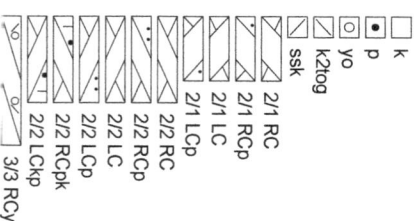

Aran Lace

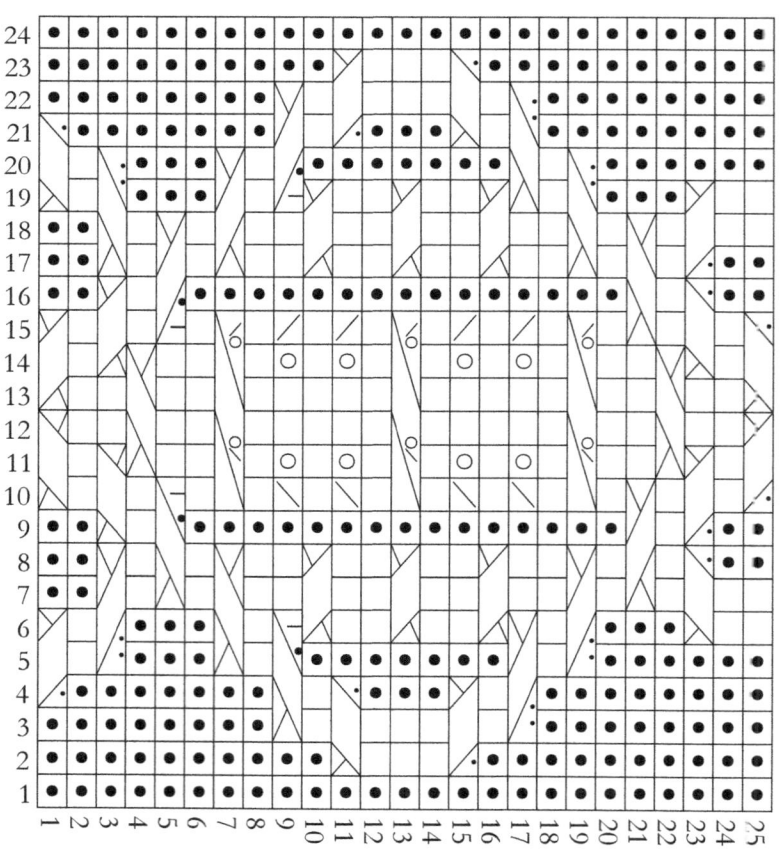

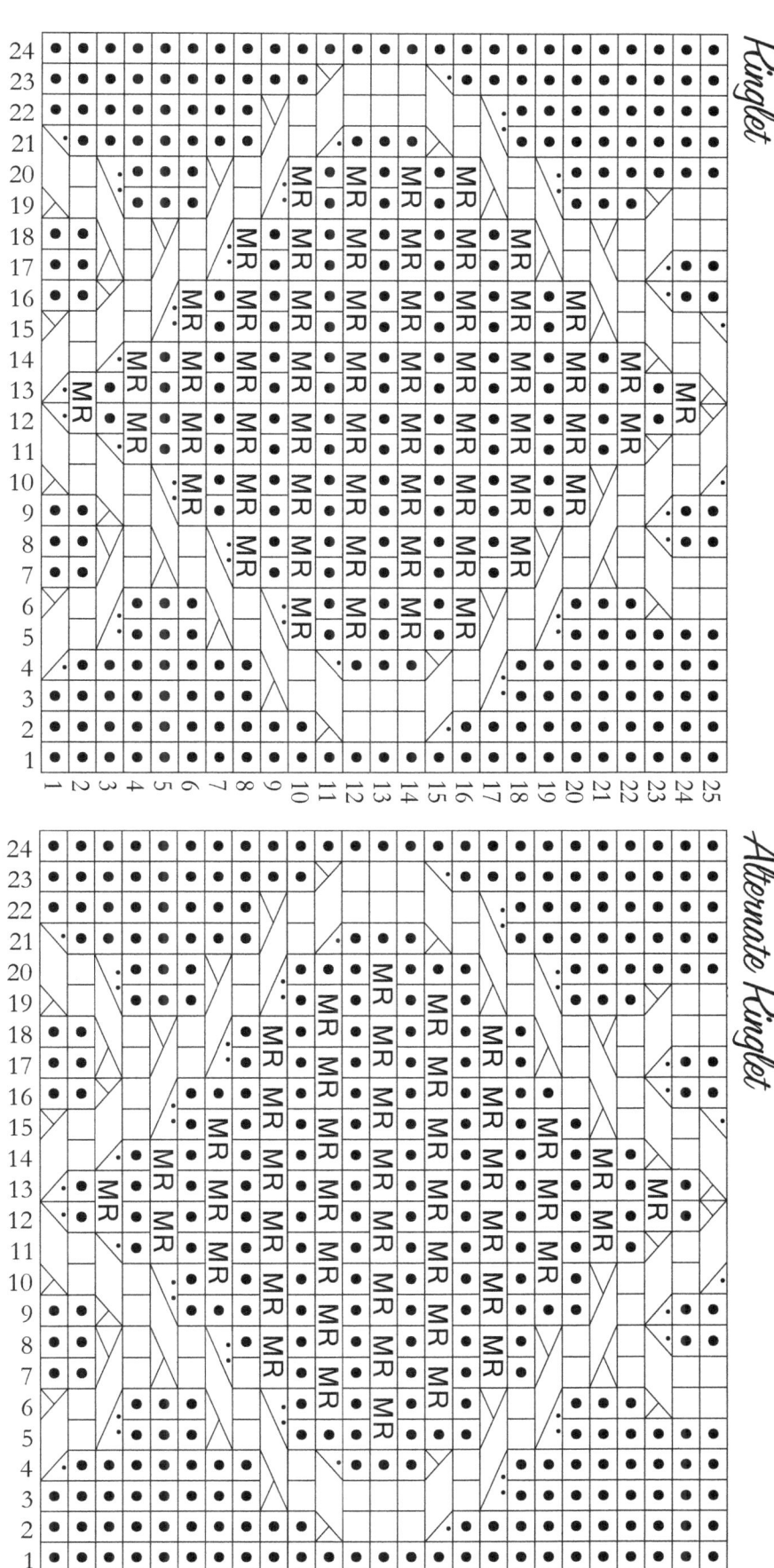

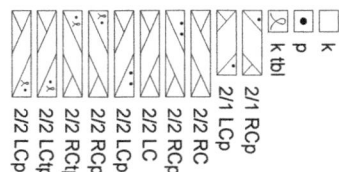

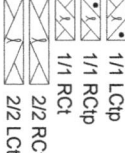

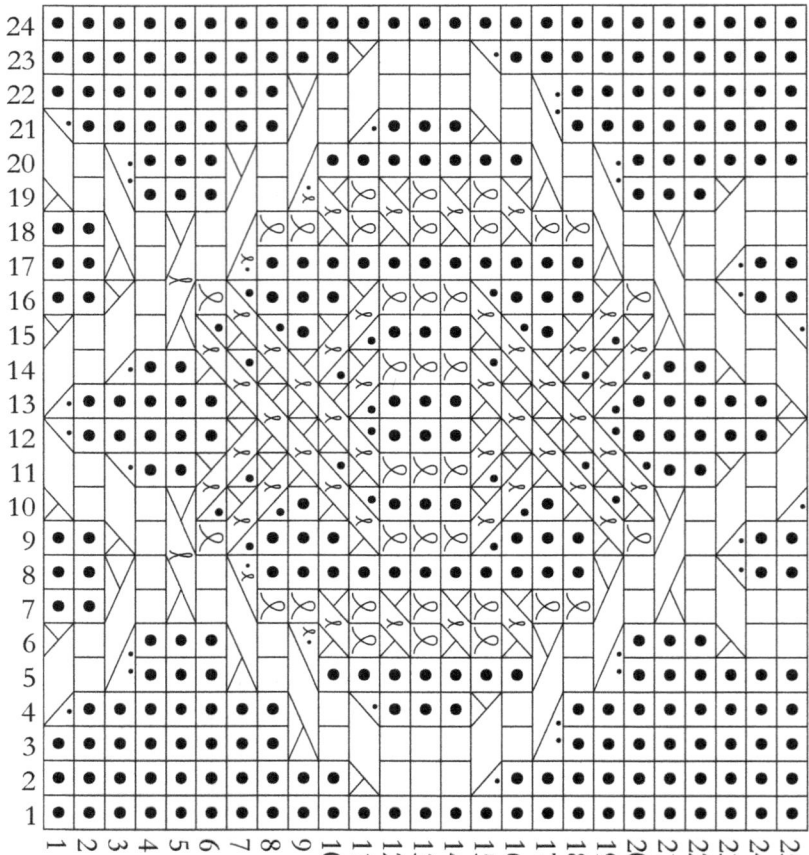

Twisted Loop

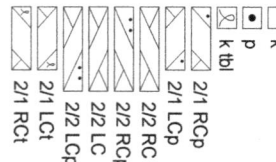

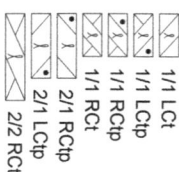

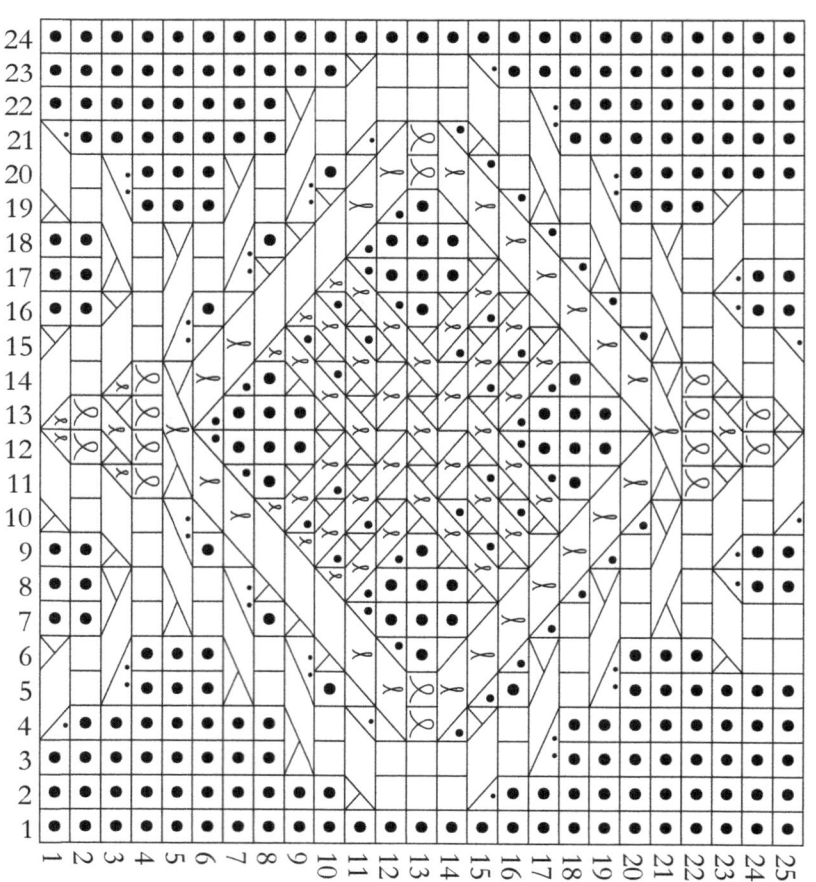

Twisted X

Riviera Nights Stole

Brenda Castiel

SIZE

One size

FINISHED MEASUREMENTS

Length: 60" / 152.5cm
Width: 22" / 56cm

MATERIALS

Knit Picks Andean Treasure Sport Weight (100% baby alpaca; 110 yds / 100m per 50g skein)

- [Color A] Meringue Heather; 4 skeins
- [Color B] Mystery Heather; 4 skeins

32-inch US #6 / 4mm circular needle, or size needed to obtain gauge

Yarn needle

GAUGE

17 sts and 24 rows = 4" / 10cm in St st
Gauge is not critical in this pattern, but a different gauge will affect yardage and size of finished item.

REQUIRED SKILLS

Increases/decreases; i-cord; simple intarsia

PATTERN NOTES

This stole can easily be made larger or smaller simply by casting on more or fewer stitches.

STITCHES AND TECHNIQUES

Applied I-cord: On circular needle, CO 4 sts. *Slide the sts to the opposite end of the needle. K3, sl 1 purlwise. With left hand tip, pick up a st on edge of stole. Slip the last st on right needle tip back onto left tip. K2tog. Repeat from * until all sts on stole edge are worked, changing from color A to color B to match the body of the stole.

Twist: When changing colors, hold the yarn you're stopping over to the left and then bring the new yarn up from under it, towards the right. This will twist it. To start the first st of the new color, you just knit that st with the new color.

PATTERN

First Half

CO 90 sts in color A.
Row 1 (WS): Purl.
Row 2 (RS): Knit to last 4 sts, k2tog, k1, attach color B, twist, kfb in color B.

Row 3: Purl, working sts in same color as row below, twisting 2 colors tog at color change.

Row 4: K1, p1, knit until 3 sts remain in color A, k2tog, k1, twist, change to color B, k1, LLI.

This stole can be worn over a strapless evening dress or a tailored day dress. The black-and-white color scheme is simple and dramatic. It's a look that Grace Kelly as Francie might have worn in To Catch a Thief *for those Riviera nights with a hint of chill.*

The stole is comprised of two rectangles, each bisected into a black and a white triangle, using intarsia to create the design. Increases and decreases keep the intarsia border straight and even. Applied i-cord provides an elegant, smooth edging. A little bit of ribbing at the edges adds stability and helps prevent curling. For versatile modern usage, this piece could be worn as a scarf or wrap to accent a simple dress or jacket.

Row 5: Purl to last 2 sts, working sts in same color as row below, k1, p1.

Row 6: K1, p1, knit until 3 sts remain in color A, k2tog k1, twist, change to color B, k2, LLI.

Row 7: Purl to last 2 sts, working sts in same color as row below, k1, p1.

Row 8: [K1, p1] twice, knit until 3 sts remain in color A, k2tog, k1, twist, change to color B, k2, LLI, k1.

Row 9: Purl to last 4 sts, working sts in same color as row below, [k1, p1] twice.

Row 10: [K1, p1] twice, knit until 3 sts remain in color A, k2tog, k1, twist, change to color B, k2, LLI, knit to end.

Row 11: Purl to last 4 sts, working sts in same color as row below, [k1, p1] twice.

Row 12: [K1, p1] twice, knit until 3 sts remain in color A, k2tog, k1, twist, change to color B, k2, LLI, knit to end.

Row 13: Purl to last 4 sts, working sts in same color as row below, [k1, p1] twice.

Row 14: [K1, p1] twice, knit until 3 sts remain in color A, k2tog, k1, twist, change to color B, k2, LLI, k2, p1, k1.

Row 15: P1, k1, purl to last 4 sts, working sts in same color as row below, [k1, p1] twice.

Row 16: [K1, p1] twice, knit until 3 sts remain in color A, k2tog, k1, twist, change to color B, k2, LLI, knit to last 4 sts, [p1, k1] twice.

Row 17: [P1, k1] twice, purl to last 4 sts, [k1, p1] twice, working sts in same color as row below.

Repeat Rows 16 & 17 until 7 sts remain in color A.

Row 168: K1, p1, knit until 3 sts remain in color A, k2tog, k1, twist, change to color B, k2, LLI, knit to last 4 sts, [p1, k1] twice.

Row 169: [P1, k1] twice, purl to last 2 sts, k1, p1, working sts in same color as row below.

Row 170: Knit until 3 sts remain in color A, k2tog, k1, twist, change to color B, k2, LLI, knit to last 4 sts, [p1, k1] twice.

Row 171: [P1, k1] twice, purl to end, working sts in same color as row below.

Row 172: Knit until 3 sts remain in color A, k2tog, k1, twist, change to color B, k2, LLI, knit to last 4 sts, [p1, k1] twice.

Row 173: [P1, k1] twice, purl to end, working sts in same color as row below.

Row 174: Knit until 3 sts remain in color A, k2tog, k1, twist, change to color B, k2, LLI, knit to last 4 sts, [p1, k1] twice.

Row 175: [P1, k1] twice, purl to end, working sts in same color as row below.

Row 176: K2tog, k1, twist, change to color B, k2, LLI, knit to last 4 sts, [p1, k1] twice.

Row 177: [P1, k1] twice, purl to end, working sts in same color as row below.

Row 178: K2tog, twist, change to color B, k2, LLI, knit to last 4 sts, [p1, k1] twice.

Row 179: [P1, k1] twice, purl to end, working sts in same color as row below.

Row 180: With color B, k2tog (color B and color A sts tog), k2, LLI, knit to last 4 sts, [p1, k1] twice.

Second Half

Switch to color A.
Row 1 (WS): Purl.

Row 2 (RS): K1 in color B, twist, knit to end in color A.

Row 3: Purl, working sts in same color as row below, twisting 2 colors tog at color change.

Row 4: RLI, k1 in color B, twist, change to color A, k1, ssk, knit to last 2 sts, p1, k1.

Row 5: P1, k1, purl to end, working sts in same color as row below.

Row 6: K1, RLI, k1 in color B, twist, change to color A, k1, ssk, knit to last 2 sts, p1, k1.

Row 7: P1, k1, purl to end, working sts in same color as row below.

Row 8: Knit until 2 sts remain in color B, RLI, k2 in color B, twist, change to color A, k1, ssk, knit to last 4 sts, [p1, k1] twice.

Row 9: [P1, k1] twice, purl to end, working sts in same color as row below.

Row 10: K1, p1, knit until 2 sts remain in color B, RLI, k2 in color B, twist, change to color A, k1, ssk, knit to last 4 sts, [p1, k1] twice.

Row 11: [P1, k1] twice, purl to last 2 sts, k1, p1, working sts in same color as row below.

Row 12: K1, p1, knit until 2 sts remain in color B, RLI, k2 in color B, twist, change to color A, k1, ssk, knit to last 4 sts, [p1, k1] twice.

Row 13: [P1, k1] twice, purl to last 2 sts, k1, p1, working sts in same color as row below.

Row 14: K1, p1, knit until 2 sts remain in color B, RLI, k2 in color B, twist, change to color A, k1, ssk, knit to last 4 sts, [p1, k1] twice.

Row 15: [P1, k1] twice, purl to last 2 sts, k1, p1, working sts in same color as row below.

Row 16 [K1, p1] twice, knit until 2 sts remain in color B, RLI, k2 in color B, twist, change to color A, k1, ssk, knit to last 4 sts, [p1, k1] twice.

Row 17 [P1, k1] twice, purl to last 4 sts, [k1, p1] twice, working sts in same color as row below.

Repeat Rows 16 & 17 until 7 sts remain in color A.

Row 168: [K1, p1] twice, knit until 2 sts remain in color B, RLI, k2 in color B, twist, change to color A, k1, ssk, k2, p1, k1.

Row 169: P1, k1, purl to last 4 sts, [k1, p1] twice, working sts in same color as row below.

Row 170: [K1, p1] twice, knit until 2 sts remain in color B, RLI, k2 in color B, twist, change to color A, k1, ssk, k1, p1, k1.

Row 171: P1, k1, purl to last 4 sts, [k1, p1] twice, working sts in same color as row below.

Row 172: [K1, p1] twice, knit until 2 sts remain in color B, RLI, k2 in color B, twist, change to color A, k1, ssk, k2.

Row 173: Purl to last 4 sts, [k1, p1] twice, working sts in same color as row below.

Row 174: [K1, p1] twice, knit until 2 sts remain in color B, RLI, k2 in color B, twist, change to color A, k1, ssk, k1.

Row 175: Purl to last 4 sts, [k1, p1] twice, working sts in same color as row below.

Row 176: K1, p1, knit until 2 sts remain in color B, RLI, k2 in color B, twist, change to color A, k1, ssk.

Row 177: Purl to last 2 sts, k1, p1, working sts in same color as row below.

Row 178: K1, p1, knit until 2 sts remain in color B, RLI, k2 in color B, twist, change to color A, ssk.

Row 179: Purl to last 2 sts, k1, p1, working sts in same color as row below.

Row 180: K1, p1, knit until 2 sts remain in color B, RLI, k1 in color B, ssk (color B and color A tog).

Row 181: Purl.
Do not bind off. Leave sts live for applied i-cord.

Finishing

Starting with the live sts, and color B, work applied i-cord all around the stole, changing colors so that i-cord matches the color of the stole. Weave in ends. Block stole.

Not Your Gal Friday Sweater

Jennette Cross

SIZES

Women's XS (S, M, L, 1X, 2X, 3X, 4X); shown in size L
Intended to be worn with approx 2" / 5cm of positive
ease.

FINISHED MEASUREMENTS

Bust: 32.25 (34.75, 39.75, 44.25, 47.25, 52.75, 55.5,
60.25)" / 82 (63, 101, 112.5, 120, 134, 141, 153)cm

MATERIALS

Old Maiden Aunt Superwash Merino / Cashmere
/ Nylon (80% superwash merino, 10% cashmere,
10% nylon sock; 400 yds / 366m per 100g skein)

- ⟩ [MC] Red Velvet; 2 (2, 3, 3, 4, 4, 5, 5) skeins
- ⟩ [CC] Army & Navy; 1 skein

32-inch US #3 / 3.25mm circular needle, or size
needed to obtain gauge
32-inch US #2 / 2.75mm circular needle
1 set US #3 / 3.25mm double-point needles or
circular needle for magic loop
1 set US #2 / 2.75mm double-point needles or
circular needle for magic loop
US size F / 3.75mm crochet hook

8 removable stitch markers
1 × ½" / 13mm button
Stitch holder or waste yarn
Yarn needle

GAUGE

28 sts and 40 rows = 4" / 10cm in St st, on larger
needle

REQUIRED SKILLS

Knitting in the round; knitting with double-
pointed needles or magic loop; increases/decreases;
backward loop cast on; sewn bind off; knowledge of
basic sweater construction; picking up stitches; basic
crochet stitches; sewing on buttons

PATTERN NOTES

This sweater is worked from the top down. It is
worked flat to the end of the keyhole, then joined to
work in the round to the sleeve divide. The sleeves
are put on holders or waste yarn while the body is
worked down to the hem, then the sleeves are picked
up and worked. When working flat in the keyhole
section, the slip at the beginning of each row is
worked with yarn in front as if to purl.

STITCHES AND TECHNIQUES

Stripe Section
Round 1: Switch to CC, knit to end of round.
Round 2: K1 into st below, knit to end of round.
Round 3: Switch to MC, knit to end of round.
Round 4: K1 into st below, knit to end of round.
Rounds 5–8: Rep Rounds 3 & 4 twice more.

Ribbing Round
K1, [p2, k2] to last 3 sts, p2, k1.

PATTERN

Ribbing and Set Up

With smaller needles and MC, CO 136 (152, 168, 184,
204, 220, 236, 252) sts using backward-loop cast on.

*Rear Window is by far my favorite Hitchcock movie, and I love Lisa. When she and Jeff have that little
conversation about how she's his Gal Friday and he points out that the hero never marries Friday, I always
want to smack him. How many other women would climb a fire escape to snoop around in a suspected
murderer's apartment wearing a dress and heels? The Not Your Gal Friday Sweater is a little less formal for
your own personal breaking and entering, but still stylish and fun.*

Row 1 (RS): Knit to end.
Row 2 (WS): Sl1, p2, [k2, p2] to last st, k1.
Row 3: Sl1, k2 [p2, k2] to last st, k1.
Rep Rows 2 & 3 until work measures 1.25" / 3cm from cast on, ending with a RS Row.

Switch to larger needles and work Row 4, placing markers as follows:

> XS: Sl1, p22, pm, p1, pm, p20, pm, p1, pm, p46, pm, p1, pm, p20, pm, p1, pm, p22, k1.

> S: Sl1, p25, pm, p1, pm, p21, pm, p1, pm, p54, pm, p1, pm, p21, pm, p1, pm, p25, k1.

> M: Sl1, p29, pm, p1, pm, p22, pm, p1, pm, p60, pm, p1, pm, p22, pm, p1, pm, p29, k1.

> L: Sl1, p32, pm, p1, pm, p24, pm, p1, pm, p66, pm, p1, pm, p24, pm, p1, pm, p32, k1.

> 1X: Sl1, p36, pm, p1, pm, p26, pm, p1, pm, p74, pm, p1, pm, p26, pm, p1, pm, p36, k1.

> 2X: Sl1, p40, pm, p1, pm, p26, pm, p1, pm, p82, pm, p1, pm, p26, pm, p1, pm, p40, k1.

> 3X: Sl1, p43, pm, p1, pm, p27, pm, p1, pm, p90, pm, p1, pm, p27, pm, p1, pm, p43, k1.

> 4X: Sl1, p47, pm, p1, pm, p28, pm, p1, pm, p96, pm, p1, pm, p28, pm, p1, pm, p47, k1.

Yoke

Join CC. This point marks the beginning of the stripes. The first 2 rows are worked in CC; the next 6 rows are worked in MC. After working flat in the stripe pattern for 22 (22, 28, 30, 30, 36, 36, 38) rows, the yarn is broken and a new starting point is set in order to help mitigate the jog that forms when striping in the round.

Row 1 (RS): Sl1, [Knit to marker, m1R, sm, k1, sm, m1L] 4 times, knit to end of row.

Row 2 (and all WS rows): Sl1, purl to last st, k1.

Rep Rows 1 & 2 another 10 (10, 14, 14, 14, 18, 18, 18) times. 224 (240, 288, 304, 324, 372, 388, 404) sts; 35 (38, 46, 49, 53, 61, 64, 68) each front, 70 (78, 92, 98, 106, 122, 130, 136) in back, 42 (43, 52, 54, 56, 64, 65, 66) each sleeve. Single sts between markers eventually become part of the front or back.

Set up for working in the round: Break both yarns, Sl 77 (81, 98, 103, 109, 125, 129, 134) sts.

The first st of the round is now the st between the increases for the back and the left sleeve. Join MC.

Round 1: [K1, sm, m1L, knit to marker, m1R, sm] twice, k1, sm, m1L, knit to Keyhole break, CO 2 sts using backward loop method, knit to marker, m1L, sm, k1, sm, m1R, knit to marker, m1L, sm. 234 (250, 298, 314, 334, 382, 398, 414) sts; 74 (80, 96, 102, 110, 126, 132, 140) in front, 72 (80, 94, 100, 108, 124, 132, 138) in back, 44 (45, 54, 56, 58, 66, 67, 68) each sleeve.

Round 2: Knit to end of round.

Round 3: Join / switch to CC, [k1, sm, m1L, knit to marker, m1R, sm] 4 times.

Round 4: K1 into st below, knit to end of round.

Round 5: Switch to MC, [k1, sm, m1L, knit to marker, m1R, sm] 4 times.

Round 6: K1 into st below, knit to end of round.

Round 7: [K1, sm, m1L, knit to marker, m1R, sm] 4 times.

Round 8: Knit to end of round.

Rounds 9–10: Rep Rounds 7 & 8 once more. 266 (282, 330, 346, 366, 414, 430, 446) sts; 82 (88, 104, 110, 118, 134, 140, 148) in front, 80 (88, 102, 108, 116, 132, 140, 146) in back, 52 (53, 62, 64, 66, 74, 75, 76) each sleeve. The previous 8 rounds (Rounds 3–10) establish the stripe pattern for the rest of the Yoke.

Work 14 (14, 14, 22, 14, 14, 14, 14) more rounds in established stripe pattern, ending with a Round 8. 322 (338, 386, 434, 422, 470, 486, 502) sts; 96 (102, 118, 132, 132, 148, 154, 162) in front, 94 (102, 116, 130, 130, 146, 154, 160) in back, 66 (67, 76, 86, 80, 88, 89, 90) in each sleeve.

Size 1X only:

Work Rounds 9, 10, 3, and 4 of previous section once more. 438 sts; 136 in front, 134 in back, 84 in each sleeve.

Round 1: Switch to MC, knit to end of round.
Round 2: K1 into st below, knit to end of round.
Round 3: [K1, sm, m1L, knit to marker, m1R, sm] 4 times.
Rounds 4–6: Knit to end of round.
Round 7: Switch to CC, [k1, sm, m1L, knit to marker, m1R, sm] 4 times.
Round 8: K1 into st below, knit to end of round.

Work Rounds 1–4 of this section once more. 462 sts; 142 in front, 140 in back, 90 in each sleeve.

Sizes 2X (3X, 4X) only:

Rounds 1–2: Knit to end of round.
Round 3: Switch to CC, [k1, sm, m1L, knit to marker, m1R, sm] 4 times.
Round 4: K1 into st below, knit to end of round.
Round 5: Switch to MC, knit to end of round.
Round 6: K1 into st below, knit to end of round.
Round 7: [K1, sm, m1L, knit to marker, m1R, sm] 4 times.
Round 8: Knit to end of round.

Rep Rounds 1–8 another 1 (2, 3) times. 502 (534, 566) sts; 156 (166, 178) in front, 154 (166, 176) in back, 96 (101, 106) in each sleeve.

Divide for Armholes (all sizes)

With MC, [k1, sm, knit to marker, sm, k1, sm, sl 66 (67, 76, 86, 90, 96, 101, 106) sleeve sts to holder, CO 18 (20, 22, 24, 26, 30, 32, 34)] twice. 226 (244, 278, 310, 334, 370, 396, 422) body sts.

Knit 1 more round, removing all markers. Break both yarns.

Lower Body

The End of Round now needs to move a few sts back so it is located on the side seam. Sl 9 (10, 11, 12, 13, 15, 16, 17) sts from right needle to left needle. Pm to indicate new End of Round. Join CC.

Work 8 rounds of Stripe Section until the work measures 11.5 (11.5, 11.25, 11, 10.75, 10.5, 10.5, 10)" / 29 (29, 28.5, 28, 27.5, 26.5, 26.5, 25.5)cm from underarm, ending with a Round 6. On last round, stop 12 (6, 12, 30, 17, 0, 27, 32) sts before End of Round. Break CC.

Decrease Round:

- XS: *[K3, k2tog] 5 times, [k2, k2tog] 22 times,
- S: *[K4, k2tog] twice, [k3, k2tog] 22 times,
- M: *[K4, k2tog] 4 times, [k3, k2tog] 23 times,
- L: *[K4, k2tog] 10 times, [k3, k2tog] 19 times,
- 1X: *[K5, k2tog] 5 times, [k4, k2tog] 22 times,
- 2X: *K3, k2tog, [k4, k2tog] 30 times,
- 3X: *[K7, k2tog] 6 times, [K6, k2tog] 18 times,
- 4X: *[K6, k2tog] 8 times, [k5, k2tog] 21 times,

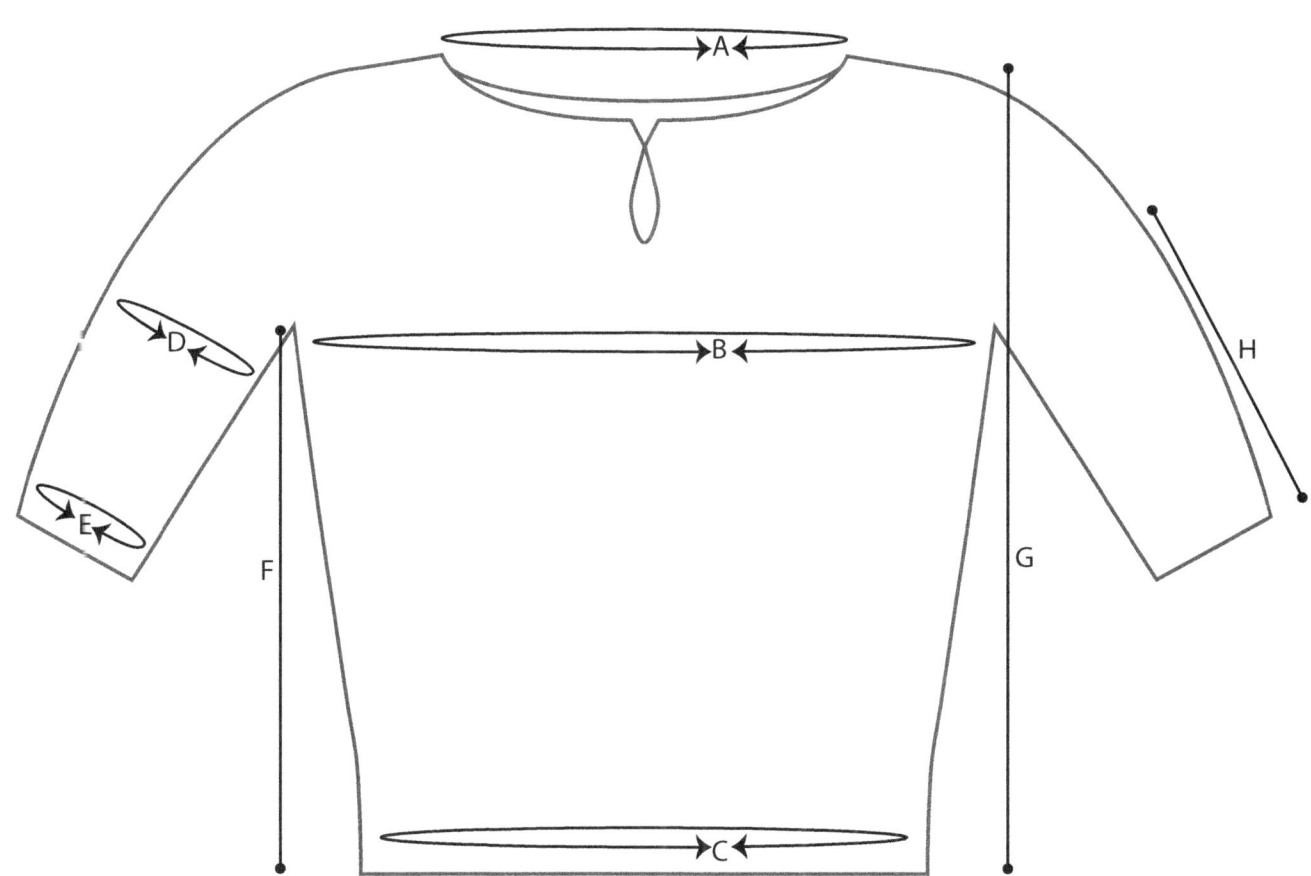

A: 19.5 (21.75, 24, 26.25, 29.25, 31.5, 33.75, 36)"
B: 32.25 (34.75, 39.75, 44.25, 47.75, 52.75, 56.5, 60.25)"
C: 24.5 (27.75, 32, 36, 40, 44, 49.75, 52)"
D: 12.5 (13, 14.5, 16.25, 17.25, 18.5, 19.5, 20.5)"
E: 8 (8.5, 10.25, 12, 13.25, 14.25, 15.5, 16)"
F: 15.5 (15.5, 15.25, 15, 15.25, 15, 15.5, 15)"
G: 21.5 (21.5, 22, 22.5, 22, 22.5, 23, 22.5)"
H: 8 (8.5, 8.5, 9, 9, 9.5, 9.5, 10)"

All sizes: Rep from * once more, knit to end of round. 172 (196, 224, 252, 280, 308, 348, 364) sts.

Switch to smaller needles.

Work Ribbing Round (see Stitches and Techniques section) for 4 (4, 4, 4, 4.5, 4.5, 5, 5)" / 10 (10, 10, 10, 11.5, 11.5, 12.5, 12.5)cm.

Turn work, and with WS facing, work a sewn bind off (see Abbreviations and Techniques).

Sleeves

With RS facing and starting in the middle of the cast-on sts at underarm, use larger needles to pick up and knit 9 (10, 11, 12, 13, 15, 16, 17) of the cast-on sts, pick up and knit 2 sts from the corner, k1 from the sts on hold, pm, knit 64 (65, 74, 84, 88, 94, 99, 104) sts from the sts on hold, pm, k1, pick up and knit 2 sts from the corner, pick up and knit 9 (10, 11, 12, 13, 15, 16, 17) of the cast-on sts, pm to indicate End of Round. 88 (91, 102, 114, 120, 130, 137, 144) sts.

Decrease Round: Knit to 3 sts before marker, k3tog, remove marker, knit to marker, remove marker, sssk, knit to end of round. 84 (87, 98, 110, 116, 126, 133, 140) sts.

Join CC and work 8 rounds of Stripe Section until sleeve measures 5 (5.5, 5.5, 6, 5.5, 6, 5.5, 6)" / 12.5 (14, 14, 15, 14, 15, 14, 15)cm from underarm, ending with a Round 6. On last round, stop 0 (21, 21, 27, 18, 18, 44, 0) sts before End of Round. Break CC.

Decrease Round:

- ➤ XS: [K1, k2tog] 28 times.
- ➤ S: [K1, k2tog, k2, k2tog] 6 times, [k1, k2tog] 15 times.

- ➤ M: [K2, k2tog, k1, k2tog] 6 times, [k2, k2tog] 14 times.
- ➤ L: [K2, k2tog, k3, k2tog] 6 times, [[k2, k2tog] 14 times.
- ➤ 1X: [K3, k2tog, k2, k2tog] 4 times, [k3, k2tog] 16 times.
- ➤ 2X: [K3, k2tog, k2, k2tog] 4 times, [k3, k2tog] 18 times.
- ➤ 3X: [K3, k2tog, k4, k2tog] 8 times, [k3, k2tog] 9 times.
- ➤ 4X: [K3, k2tog] 28 times.

All sizes: Knit to end of round. 56 (60, 72, 84, 92, 100, 108, 112) sts.

Switch to smaller needles.

Work Ribbing Round (see Stitches and Techniques section) for 3 (3, 3, 3, 3.5, 3.5, 4, 4)" / 7.5 (7.5, 7.5, 7.5, 9, 9, 10, 10)cm.

Turn work, and with WS facing, work a sewn bind off (see Abbreviations and Techniques).

Finishing

On the right side of the keyhole, mark one of the V's at the point where the neckline ribbing switches to stockinette.

Starting on the left side of the keyhole and with Right Side facing, join MC with the crochet hook.

Work a sc into each V down the left side of the keyhole, into the each of the 2 cast-on sts at the bottom of the keyhole, and up to the marked st on the Right Side, ch3, work a sc up the rest of the right side of the keyhole.

Break yarn and weave in all ends. Sew button opposite chained loop.

Wet block.

Francie Scarf

Triona Murphy

SIZE

One size

FINISHED MEASUREMENTS

Length: 33" / 84cm
Width: 33" / 84cm

MATERIALS

Tactile Fiber Arts Studio Larkspur Lace (70% baby alpaca, 30% silk; 650 yds / 594m per 100g skein); color: Pomegranate; 2 skeins

32-inch US #4 / 3.5mm circular needle, or size needed to obtain gauge

2 stitch markers
Yarn needle
Pins for blocking
Blocking wires (recommended)

GAUGE

24 sts and 20 rows in Lace Pattern (blocked) = 4" / 10cm wide × 3" / 7.5cm tall

Gauge is not critical in this pattern, but a different gauge will affect yardage and size of finished item.

REQUIRED SKILLS

Increases/decreases; working simple/intricate lace from chart or written instructions

PATTERN NOTES

This lace pattern expands a lot with blocking, particularly lengthwise. Make sure to knit a gauge swatch and block it in the same way you plan to block the finished piece, so you will know if you need to work a few more or less rows of the main pattern to make the finished scarf block into a square.

STITCHES AND TECHNIQUES

Double Moss Stitch

Worked flat over an odd number of sts.
Row 1 (RS): K1, [p1, k1] to end.
Row 2 (WS): P1, [k1, p1] to end.
Row 3: P1, [k1, p1] to end.
Row 4: K1, [p1, k1] to end.
Repeat Rows 1–4 for Double Moss Stitch.

Lace Pattern

Worked flat over a multiple of 6 sts plus 2. Also shown in the chart on the next page.
Row 1 (RS): K1, [k4, k2tog, yo] to last st, k1.
Row 2 (WS): P1, [yo, p1, p2tog, p3] to last st, p1.
Row 3: K1, [k2, k2tog, k2, yo] to last st, k1.
Row 4: P1, [yo, p3, p2tog, p1] to last st, p1.
Row 5: K1, [k2tog, k4, yo] to last st, k1.
Row 6: P2, [p4, yo, p2tog] to end.
Row 7: K1, [k1, yo, k3, k2tog] to last st, k1.
Row 8: P1, [p2tog, p2, yo, p2] to last st, p1.
Row 9: K1, [k3, yo, k1, k2tog] to last st, k1.
Row 10: P1, [p2tog, yo, p4] to last st, p1.
Repeat Rows 1–10 for Lace Pattern.

This square scarf was inspired by the incomparable Grace Kelly in To Catch a Thief. *The piece is wispy enough to be tied around the neck with very little bulk, but also substantial enough (and large enough) to wrap attractively around the head in one of Ms. Kelly's preferred styles. A tutorial for wearing the scarf in this manner is provided at the end of the pattern.*

PATTERN

CO 211 sts.
Work in Double Moss Stitch for 12 rows.

Setup Rows

Next Row (RS): Work 11 sts in Double Moss Stitch, pm, k2tog, knit to last 11 sts, pm, work last 11 sts in Double Moss Stitch. 210 sts.

Next Row (WS): Work 11 sts in Double Moss Stitch, sm, purl to second marker, sm, work last 11 sts in Double Moss Stitch.

Main Pattern

Row 1 (RS): Work 11 sts in Double Moss Stitch, sm, work Row 1 of Lace Pattern to second marker, sm, work 11 sts in Double Moss Stitch.

Continue working Rows 1–10 of Lace Pattern between markers and all sts before the first marker and after the second marker in Double Moss Stitch until the Lace Pattern has been worked a total of 20 times (or for the number of rows needed so your piece will be a square after blocking—see Pattern Notes).

Next Row (RS): Work 11 sts in Double Moss Stitch, sm, m1L, knit to second marker, sm, work 11 sts in Double Moss Stitch. 211 sts.

Next Row (WS): Work 11 sts in Double Moss Stitch, remove m, purl to second marker, remove m, work 11 sts in Double Moss Stitch.

Work all sts in Double Moss Stitch for 12 rows.

BO loosely in patt (as you would work the next row of Double Moss Stitch).

Finishing

Soak scarf in cold water. Squeeze out excess moisture by rolling in a towel. Stretch and pin out scarf into a square. The use of blocking wires is recommended to ensure straight edges.

Allow scarf to dry completely before unpinning.

Weave in ends.

Lace Pattern Chart

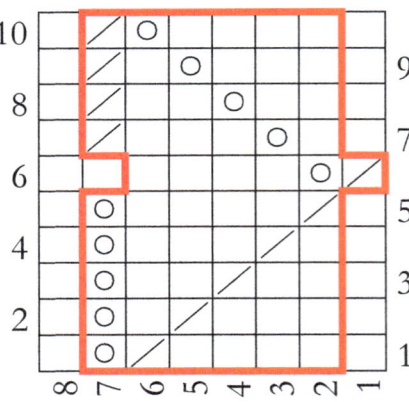

☐	RS: k; WS: p
○	yo
◢	RS: k2tog; WS: p2tog

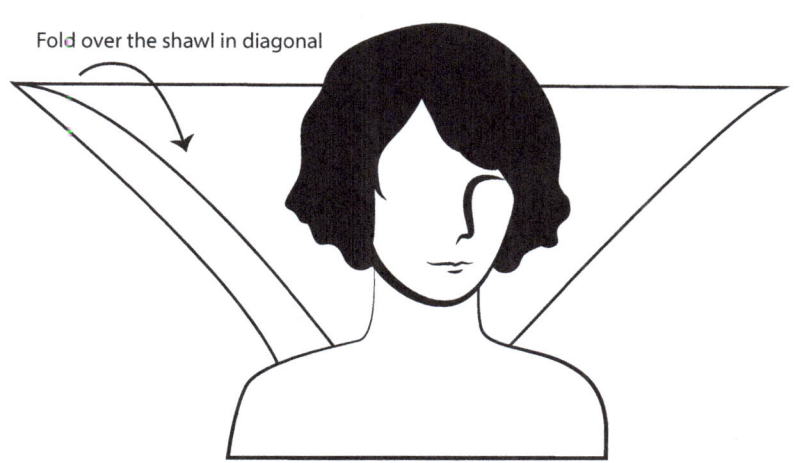

Fold over the shawl in diagonal

Wear It Like Grace Kelly

Step 1: Fold the scarf along the diagonal, with the RS facing out.

Step 2: Place the scarf over your head, with the folded side to the front.

Step 3: Cross the folded points under your chin and bring around your neck.

Step 4: Tie the points behind your neck.

Miss Fremont Shawl

Jaala Spiro

SIZE

One size

FINISHED MEASUREMENTS

Wingspan: 56" / 142cm
Radius: 26" / 66cm

MATERIALS

Blue Sky Alpacas Sport Weight [100% baby alpaca; 110 yds / 100m per 50g skein]

- ☙ [Color A] Light Gray #507; 1 skein
- ☙ [Color B] Medium Gray #508; 2 skeins
- ☙ [Color C] Dark Gray #509; 4 skeins

32-inch US #7 / 4.5mm circular needle, or size needed to obtain gauge

16 removable stitch markers
Yarn needle

GAUGE

18 sts and 26 rows = 4" / 10cm in St st

Gauge is not critical in this pattern, but a different gauge will affect yardage and size of finished item.

REQUIRED SKILLS

Increases/decreases; working intricate lace from chart or written instructions; garter tab cast on (see Pattern Notes below)

PATTERN NOTES

A garter tab is used to start this shawl: you knit a small square of garter stitch, then pick up stitches around it to create a crescent shape. The tab will disappear into the garter stitch shawl edging as you work.

Work garter tab as follows:

- ☙ CO 3 sts.
- ☙ Knit 6 rows.
- ☙ Turn work 90 degrees. Pick up and knit 3 sts along garter ridged edge. 6 sts.
- ☙ Turn work 90 degrees again. Pick up and knit 3 sts evenly to CO st. 9 sts.

For a photo tutorial, see this downloadable pdf: <knitcircus.com/pdfs/newsletter/2012_May_15_Garter_Tab.pdf>

Borders

Knit the 3 sts (Border sts) at the beginning and end of every row. The stitches between the Border sts are the Body sts. You'll work increases in the Body section to shape the shawl.

STITCHES AND TECHNIQUES

Daisy Lace Pattern Stitch Repeat

(Worked flat over 12 sts)
All even rows 2–24: Purl.
Row 1: K1, yo, k3, k2tog, k1, ssk, k3, yo.
Row 3: K2, yo, k2, k2tog, k1, ssk, k2, yo, k1.
Row 5: K1, k2tog, yo, k1, k2tog, yo, [k1, yo, ssk] twice.
Row 7: Sk2p, yo, k1, k2tog, yo, k3, yo, ssk, k1, yo.
Row 9: K2, [k2tog, yo] twice, k1, [yo, ssk] twice, k1.

Inspired by Grace Kelly's Rear Window *dress with its dramatic flowers radiating from the waist, this shawl flows outward like a circle skirt. With each shawl tier the colors gradually darken, a nod to the way that Hitchcock exposed the shadier side of human nature.*

Row 11: K1, [k2tog, yo] twice, k3, [yo, ssk] twice.
Row 13: K1, ssk, k3, yo, k1, yo, k3, k2tog.
Row 15: K1, ssk, k2, yo, k3, yo, k2, k2tog.
Row 17: [K1, yo, ssk] twice, [k1, k2tog, yo] twice.
Row 19: K2, yo, ssk, k1, yo, sk2p, yo, k1, k2tog, yo, k1.
Row 21: K1, [yo, ssk] twice, k3, [k2tog, yo] twice.
Row 23: K2, [yo, ssk] twice, k1, [k2tog, yo] twice, k1.

PATTERN

Set Up

Using Color A, work Garter Tab as in Pattern Notes above. 9 sts.

First Tier

Row 1 (RS): Using Color A, k3 (Border sts), [k1, yo] three times (Body sts), k3 (Border sts). 12 sts.

Row 2 and all WS Rows: Purl all Body sts; knit all Border sts.

Row 3 (inc row): K3, [k1, yo] 6 times, k3. 18 sts.

Row 5: Knit.

Row 7 (inc row): K3, [k1, yo] 12 times, k3. 30 sts.

RS Rows 9–13: Knit.

Row 15 (inc row): K3, [k1, yo] 24 times, k3. 54 sts.

Row 17 (inc row): K3, yo, [k4, yo] 12 times, k3. 67 sts.

Row 19: K4, ssk, k3, yo, [Row 1 of Daisy Lace patt] 4 times, k1, yo, k3, k2tog, k4.

Row 21: K4, ssk, k2, yo, k1, [Row 3 of Daisy Lace patt] 4 times, k2, yo, k2, k2tog, k1.

Row 23: K4, yo, ssk, k1, yo, ssk, [Row 5 of Daisy Lace patt] 4 times, [k1, k2tog, yo] twice, k4.

Row 25: K5, yo, ssk, k1, yo, [Row 7 of Daisy Lace patt] 4 times, sk2p, yo, k1, k2tog, yo, k5.

Row 27: K4, [yo, ssk] twice, k1, [Row 9 of Daisy Lace patt] 4 times, k2, [k2tog, yo] twice, k4.

Row 29: K5, [yo, ssk] twice, [Row 11 of Daisy Lace patt] 4 times, k1, [k2tog, yo] twice, k5.

Row 31: K4, yo, k3, k2tog, [Row 13 of Daisy Lace patt] 4 times, k1, ssk, k3, yo, k4.

Row 33: K5, yo, k2, k2tog, [Row 15 of Daisy Lace patt] 4 times, k1, ssk, k2, yo, k5.

Row 35: K4, k2tog, yo, k1, k2tog, yo, [Row 17 of Daisy Lace patt] 4 times, [k1, yo, ssk] twice, k4.

Row 37: K3, [k2tog, yo, k1] twice, [Row 19 of Daisy Lace patt] 4 times, k2, yo, ssk, k1, yo, ssk, k3.

Row 39: K5, [k2tog, yo] twice, [Row 21 of Daisy Lace patt] 4 times, k1, [yo, ssk] twice, k5.

Row 41: K4, [k2tog, yo] twice, k1, [Row 23 of Daisy Lace patt] 4 times, k2, [yo, ssk] twice, k4.

Row 43 (inc row): K3, [k1, yo] 60 times, k4. 127 sts.

Second Tier

Change to Color B.
RS Rows 45–69: Knit all sts.

Rows 71–93: Work as for Rows 19–41 above, working Daisy Lace pattern 9 times.

Row 95 (inc row): K9, [k1, yo] 108 times, k10. 235 sts.

Third Tier

Change to Color C.
RS Rows 97–135: Knit all sts.

Rows 137–161: Work as for Rows 19–41 above, working Daisy Lace pattern 18 times.

Row 163 (inc row): K3 (border), yo, k6, yo, k1, yo, [k11, yo, k1, yo] 18 times, yo, k6, yo, k3 (border). 276 sts.

Garter Edging

Rows 164–169: Knit all sts.

Finishing

BO all sts loosely or use Jeny's Surprisingly Stretchy Bind Off (see Abbreviations and Techniques).

Weave in all ends.
Wet block.

Daisy Lace Chart

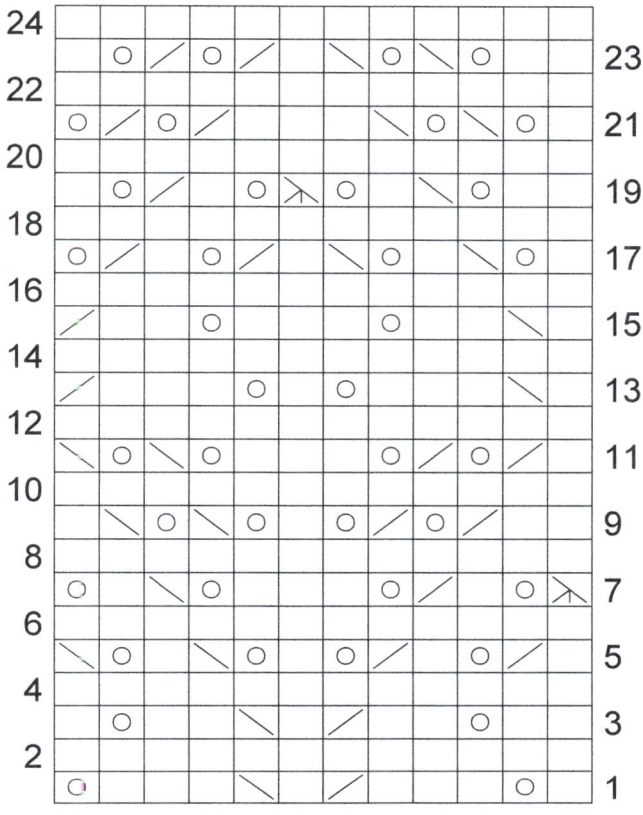

		RS: k; WS: p
	○	yo
	╱	k2tog
	╲	ssk
	⋏	sk2p

Robie Sweater

Christina Wall

SIZES

To fit chest circumferences: 34 (36, 38, 40, 42, 44, 46, 48, 50, 52)" / 86.5 (91.5, 96.5, 101.5, 106.5, 111.5, 117, 122, 127, 132)cm; shown in 44" / 111.5cm. Intended to be worn with 2" / 5cm positive ease.

FINISHED MEASUREMENTS

Chest: 36 (38, 40, 42, 44, 46, 48, 50, 52, 54)" / 91.5 (96.5, 101.5, 106.5, 111.5, 117, 122, 127, 132, 137)cm

MATERIALS

Springtree Road Julep Sock (80% merino, 10% cashmere, 10% nylon, 434 yds / 396m per 100g skein)

> [MC] Jenny Linsky; 4 (4, 4, 4, 4, 4, 5, 5, 5, 6) skeins
> [CC1] Silver Screen; 1 skein
> [CC2] Red Delicious; 1 skein

32-inch US #3 / 3.25mm circular needle or size needed to obtain gauge
16-inch US #3 / 3.25mm circular needle or size used to obtain gauge
1 set US #3 / 3.25mm double-point needles or size used to obtain gauge
32-inch US #1 / 2.25mm circular needle
16-inch US #1 / 2.25mm circular needle

4 removable stitch markers

Separating zipper: 26 (26, 28, 28, 30, 30, 30, 30, 32, 32)" / 66 (66, 71, 71, 76, 76, 76, 76, 81, 81)cm

> Please note this is an approximation. If you change the body length of the garment you will need a different length of zipper. It is safest to measure your garment after blocking and then purchase an appropriately sized zipper.

2 stitch holders or waste yarn
Yarn needle
Contrasting yarn for basting zipper in place
Wool thread (tapestry wool) for sewing zipper into place.

GAUGE

24 sts and 38 rows = 4" / 10cm in St st on larger needles

REQUIRED SKILLS

Increases/decreases; long-tail cast on; picking up stitches; knitted-on i-cord; sewing in zippers

PATTERN NOTES

Instructions are given to cut MC and CC1 at the end of Rows 5 and 6 of stripe sequence and to leave a 3–4" / 7.5–10cm tail for weaving in later. Please note that it is important to do so. Carrying your yarn along will distort the edge of your garment.

The Robie Sweater is a modern twist on the turtleneck pullover Cary Grant wore in the opening scenes of To Catch a Thief. I loved how comfortable Cary Grant looked in his pullover. Despite the fact that he is running away from the police, leaping over market stalls, and riding the waves in a speed boat, he looks at ease and relaxed in his striped pullover. May the modern man in your life find this top-down, zippered cardigan just as easy and effortless to wear.

STITCHES AND TECHNIQUES

Stripe Sequence

Row 1 (RS): Knit in MC.
Row 2 (WS): Purl in MC.
Row 3: Knit in MC.
Row 4: Purl in MC.
Row 5: Knit in MC. At end of row, cut MC leaving a 3–4" / 7.5–10cm tail.
Row 6: Purl in CC1. At end of row, cut CC1 leaving a 3–4" / 7.5–10cm tail.

PATTERN

Yoke

With MC and larger needle, using the long-tail cast on, CO 2, pm, CO 8 (8, 9, 9, 10, 10, 11, 11, 12, 12), pm, CO 20 (20, 26, 26, 30, 30, 40, 40, 44, 44), pm, CO 8 (8, 9, 9, 10, 10, 11, 11, 12, 12), pm, CO 2. 40 (40, 48, 48, 54, 54, 66, 66, 72, 72) sts.

Purl 1 row.

Work raglan yoke as follows:
Row 1 (RS): With MC [knit to 2 sts before m, kfb, k1, sm, kfb] 4 times, knit to end of row. 8 sts increased.
Row 2 (WS): With MC purl.
Row 3: Repeat Row 1. 8 sts increased.
Row 4: Repeat Row 2.
Row 5: Repeat Row 1. At end of row cut MC leaving a 3–4" / 7.5–10cm tail. 8 sts increased.
Row 6: With CC1 purl. At end of row, cut CC1 leaving a 3–4" / 7.5–10cm tail.
Row 7: With MC CO 12 (12, 14, 14, 16, 16, 18, 18, 18, 18) sts, [knit to 2 sts before m, kfb, k1, sm, kfb] 4 times, knit to end of row, CO 12 (12, 14, 14, 16, 16, 18, 18, 18, 18) sts. 96 (96, 108, 108, 118, 118, 134, 134, 140, 140) sts.

Repeat Rows 1–6 another 13 (13, 14, 14, 15, 15, 15, 16, 16) times. You will now have 408 (408, 444, 444, 478, 478, 494, 494, 524, 524) total sts divided by section as:

> Fronts: 57 (57, 62, 62, 67, 67, 69, 69, 72, 72) sts.

> Sleeves: 94 (94, 101, 101, 108, 108, 109, 109, 116, 116) sts.

> Back: 106 (106, 118, 118, 128, 128, 138, 138, 148, 148) sts.

Divide sleeves from body:

On RS with MC knit to 1st m, rm, slip all sleeve sts between 1st m and 2nd m onto a stitch holder, remove 2nd m, CO – (3, –, 6, –, 6, 4, 9, 3, 10), knit to 3rd m, remove 3rd m, slip all sleeve sts between 3rd and 4th m onto a stitch holder, remove 4th m, CO – (3, –, 6, –, 6, 4, 9, 3, 10) sts, knit to end.

> Body: 220 (226, 242, 254, 262, 274, 284, 294, 298, 312) sts.

> Sleeves: 94 (94, 101, 101, 108, 108, 109, 109, 116, 116) sts.

Lower Body

Using MC work in St st until piece measures 13 (13, 13.5, 13.5, 14, 14, 14.5, 14.5, 15, 15)" / 33 (33, 34.5, 34.5, 35.5, 35.5, 37, 37, 38, 38)cm from underarm to needles, or desired body length minus 4" / 10cm. End by working a RS row.

Bottom stripes:

Row 1 (WS): With CC1 purl.
Rows 2, 4, 6 (RS): With MC knit.
Rows 3 & 5: With MC purl.
Repeat Rows 1–6 another 5 times.
End by working a RS row.

Body hem:

Row 1 (WS): With MC knit.
Row 2 (RS): With MC knit.
Row 3: With CC2 purl.
Row 4: With CC2 knit.

Repeat Rows 3 & 4 another times. Repeat Row 3 once more. End by working a WS row.

BO loosely knitwise.

Sleeves

Place sts from stitch holder onto larger 16" circular needle or dpns. Pm for beginning of round. Using MC pick up and knit 2 (5, 2, 8, 2, 8, 6, 11, 5, 12) sts at underarm, pm, knit to end of round. Please note you are picking up 2 more sts than you cast on at the underarms. If you did not cast on any sts at underarms, you will pick up 2 sts. This closes any gaps that may have occurred. 96 (99, 103, 109, 110, 116, 115, 120, 121, 128) sts.

Underarm decreases
Round 1: With MC knit to marker, sm, ssk, knit to 2 sts before end of round, k2tog.
Repeat Round 1, – (1, –, 3, –, 3, 2, 3, 1, 3) more times. 94 (95, 101, 101, 108, 108, 109, 112, 117, 120) sts.
Remove markers and place 1 marker at center of underarm on sleeve sts to indicate beginning of round.

Sleeve decreases:

Rounds 1–4: With MC knit.
Round 5: Knit to 2 sts bfore m, ssk, sm, k1, k2tog.

Work Rounds 1–5 a total of 22 (21, 23, 22, 25, 23, 23, 22, 25, 23) times. 50 (53, 55, 57, 58, 62, 63, 68, 67, 74) sts.

Work even until sleeve measures 18 (18.5, 18.5, 19.5, 19.5, 20, 20, 20.5, 20.5, 21)" / 45.5 (47, 47, 49.5, 49.5, 51, 51, 52, 52, 53.5)cm from underarm to needles, or desired length. Please note that if you began on a 16" circular needle you will need to change to dpns or preferred method of small circular knitting as you decrease.

Sleeve hem:

Round 1: With MC, purl.
Round 2: With MC, knit.
Rounds 3–10: With CC2, knit.
With CC2, BO loosely knitwise.

Repeat for second sleeve.

Neck Edging

Using smaller 16" circular needle and MC, with RS facing and starting at right front neckline corner, pick up and knit 72 (72, 84, 84, 94, 94, 110, 110, 116, 116) sts along neck edge.

Rows 1, 3, 5, 7, 9 (WS): Purl.
Rows 2, 4, 6, 8, 10 (RS): Knit.
Row 11: Knit.
Row 12: Knit.
Rows 13, 15, 17, 19: With CC2 purl.
Rows 14, 16, 18: With CC2 knit.
With CC2 BO loosely knitwise.

Front Bands

Using smaller 32" circular needle and MC, with RS facing and starting at right front hem corner, pick up and knit 2 sts for every 3 rows.

Rows 1–9: Knit.
BO purlwise very loosely.
Repeat for second band, starting the pickup and knit at the left front neckline corner.

Finishing

With tapestry needle and CC2 fold body hem to the inside and whipstitch to body along bound off edge.
Repeat for sleeve and neck hems.
Weave in all ends.
Wet block, being very careful not to overstretch garment.

Zipper

Using a tapestry needle and contrasting yarn, baste front bands together.
Pin zipper to front bands and then baste each zipper side into place.
With tapestry needle and matching thread to MC sew zipper into garment by hand. (See tutorial on following page.)

How to sew in the zipper

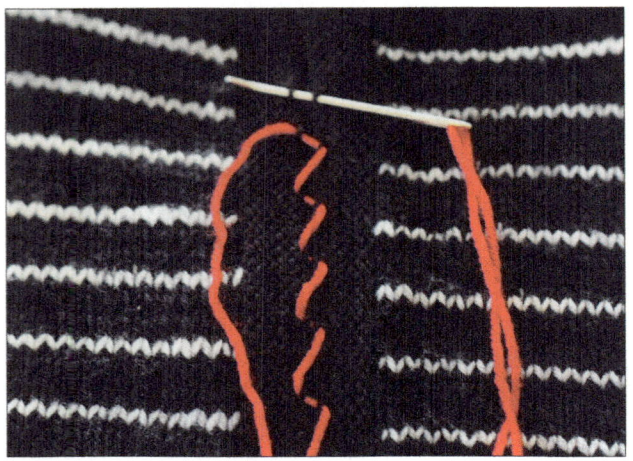

1: Using an embroidery needle and contrasting yarn, baste front bands together.

2: Turn sweater inside out and pin zipper to front bands.

3: With embroidery needle and contrasting yarn baste each side of zipper to corresponding sides of front bands.

4: Turn sweater right side out. Thread an embroidery needle with a yarn that matches MC. Use a running stitch or seam stitch between garter ridges to sew zipper into garment by hand.

5: Turn garment inside out and with matching yarn to MC whip stitch outer edge of zipper to garment.

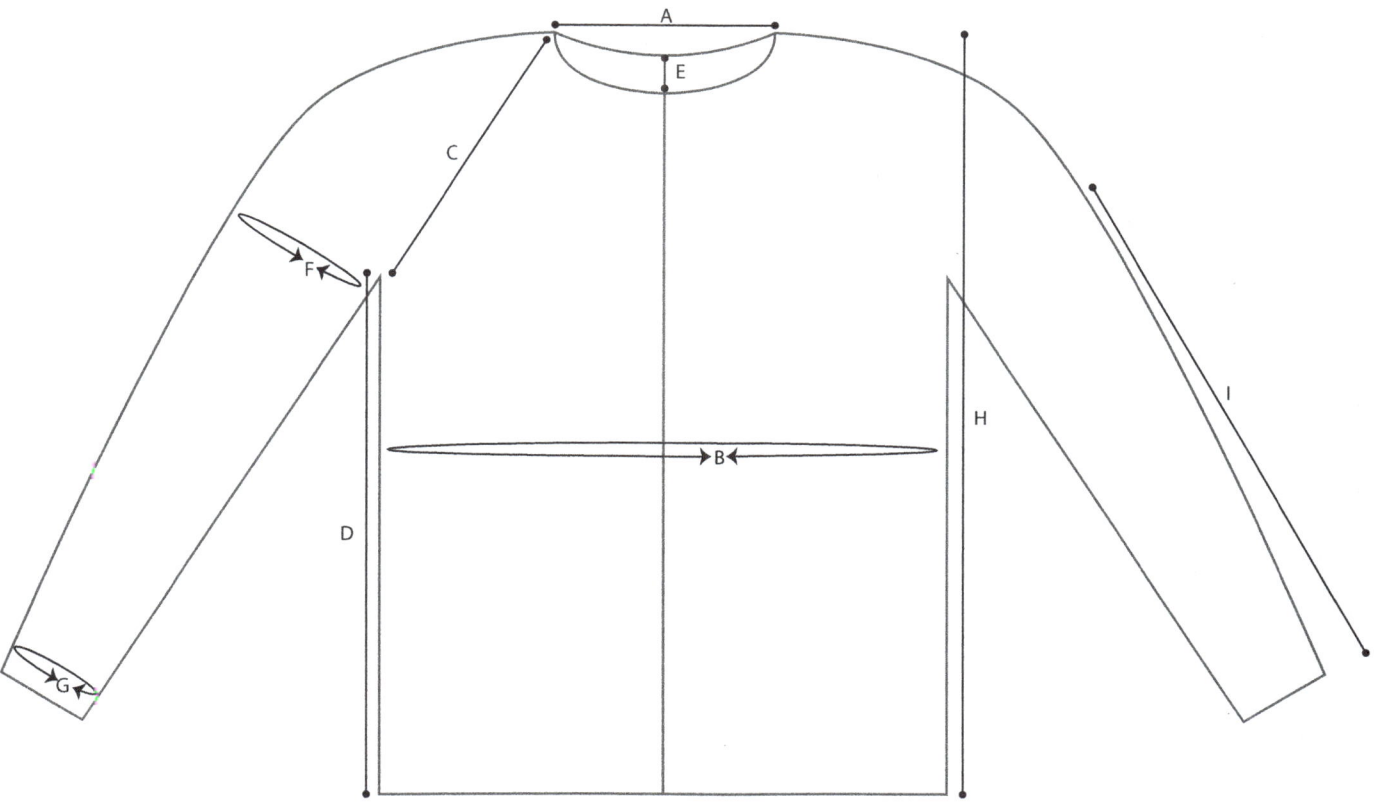

A: 6.5 (7, 7.25, 7.5, 7.75, 8, 8.25, 8.5, 8.75, 9)"
B: 36 (38, 40, 42, 44, 46, 48, 50, 52, 54)"
C: 11.5 (11.5, 12, 12, 13, 13, 13, 13, 14, 14)"
D: 17 (17, 17.5, 17.5, 18, 18, 18.5, 18.5, 19, 19)"
E: 1" all sizes
F: 15.5 (16.25, 16.75, 18, 18, 19, 19, 20, 20, 21.25)"
G: 7 (7, 7.5, 7.5, 8, 8, 8.5, 8.5, 9, 9)"
H: 25.75 (25.75, 27, 27, 28.25, 28.25, 28.5, 28.5, 29.75, 29.75)"
I: 18 (18.5, 18.5, 19.5, 19.5, 20, 20, 20.5, 20.5, 21)"

Ambrose Chapel Capelet

Luise O'Neill

SIZE

One size

FINISHED MEASUREMENTS

Back length: 15" / 38cm
Hem (tip to tip): 86" / 218.5cm

MATERIALS

Indigodragonfly MCS Worsted (75% merino, 15% cashmere, 10% silk; 190 yds / 174m per 115g skein); color: Only the Exact Phrase I Used Was, "Don't" (Inara); 4 skeins

48-inch US #8 / 5mm circular needle, or size needed to obtain gauge
1 set US #8 / 5mm double-point needles

2 stitch markers
1 removable stitch marker or waste yarn
Waste yarn for provisional cast on
Stitch holder
Yarn needle

GAUGE

18 sts and 25 rows = 4" / 10cm in St st

REQUIRED SKILLS

Knitting in the round; increases/decreases; provisional cast on; short rows; working ribbed cables from written instructions; slipped stitches; knit-on edging; picking up stitches; kitchener stitch (grafting)

PATTERN NOTES

This capelet is worked flat, beginning with a provisionally cast on (PCO) tab at the back of the neck. Stitches are then picked up along one long edge of the tab; the PCO stitches are transferred to the needles at the same time. The edgings are worked in a garter stitch edged ribbed cable, while the main portion of the capelet is worked in slipped garter stitch.

The side edgings are turned at the bottom corners using short rows and are then expanded into a larger ribbed cable edging that is worked across the bottom of the shawl, incorporating the live shawl stitches.

The bottom edging meets at the center back where the edging stitches are grafted using a double-sided grafting technique.

SPECIAL STITCHES

4/4 LRC: Sl 4 to cn, hold in front. [P1, k1] twice; [p1, k1] twice from cn.

4/4 RRC: Sl 4 to cn, hold in back. [K1, p1] twice; [k1, p1] twice from cn.

6/6 LRC: Sl 6 to cn, hold in front. [P1, k1] 3 times; [p1, k1] 3 times from cn.

6/6 RRC: Sl 6 to cn, hold in back. [K1, p1] 3 times; [k1, p1] 3 times from cn.

In 1956, Doris Day won the best song Oscar for her performance of Que Sera, Sera *in Alfred Hitchcock's* The Man Who Knew Too Much. *The wardrobe for her role as Jo McKenna in this film was designed by the talented Edith Head; the Ambrose Chapel Capelet was inspired by one of her creations. The capelet is edged with a reversible ribbed cable and is constructed to hug the shoulders. The pattern stitch presents a pleasant face on both right and wrong side, allowing for two completely different looks from this one pattern.*

PATTERN

Initial rows are worked using double-pointed needles; change to the circular needle as required. The instructions use the stitch markers as reference points; be sure to keep stitch markers in their proper position when changing needles.

Using dpns and waste yarn, provisionally CO 14 sts.

Row 1 (RS): Sl 1 wyif, k2, p2, [k1, p1] 4 times, k1.
Row 2 (WS): [P1, k1] 4 times, p1, k5.
Repeat Rows 1 & 2 four more times.

Row 11: Sl 1 wyif, k2, p1, 4/4 LRC, p1, pm, k1.

Using second dpn, pick up and knit 8 sts along left side of work, pm; transfer 13 sts from the provisional cast on onto third dpn; use fourth dpn to work sts on third dpn as follows: P1, 4/4 RRC, p1, k3. 35 sts.

Row 12 (WS): Sl 1 wyif, k4, [p1, k1] 4 times, sm, k9, sm, [k1, p1] 4 times, k5.

Row 13 (inc): Sl 1 wyif, k2, p2, [k1, p1] 4 times, sm, kfb 9 times, sm, [p1, k1] 4 times, p2, k3. 44 sts.

Row 14: Sl 1 wyif, k4, [p1, k1] 4 times, knit to next marker, [k1, p1] 4 times, k5.

Row 15: Sl 1 wyif, k2, p2, [k1, p1] 4 times, knit to next marker, [p1, k1] 4 times, p2, k3.

Row 16: Repeat Row 14.

Row 17 (inc): Sl 1 wyif, k2, p1, 4/4 LRC, p1, sm, kfb to 1 st before next marker, k1, sm, p1, 4/4 RRC, p1, k3. 61 sts.

Row 18: Repeat Row 14.

Row 19: Sl 1 wyif, k2, p2, [k1, p1] 4 times, sm, [k1, sl 1 wyib] to 1 st before next marker, k1, sm, [p1, k1] 4 times, p2, k3.

Row 20: Sl 1 wyif, k4, [p1, k1] 4 times, sm, [k1, sl 1 wyif] to 1 st before next marker, k1, sm, [k1, p1] 4 times, k5.

Row 21: Repeat Row 15.
Row 22: Repeat Row 14.

Row 23: Sl 1 wyif, k2, p2, [k1, p1] 4 times, sm, k2, sl 1 wyib, [k1, sl 1 wyib] to 2 sts before next marker, k2, sm, [p1, k1] 4 times, p2, k3.

Row 24: Sl 1 wyif, k4, [p1, k1] 4 times, sm, k2, sl 1 wyif, [k1, sl 1 wyif] to 2 sts before next marker, k2, sm, [p1, k1] 4 times, k5.

Row 25 (inc): Repeat Row 17. 95 sts.
Row 26: Repeat Row 14.
Row 27: Repeat Row 19.
Row 28: Repeat Row 20.
Row 29: Repeat Row 15.
Row 30: Repeat Row 14.
Row 31: Repeat Row 23.
Row 32: Repeat Row 24.

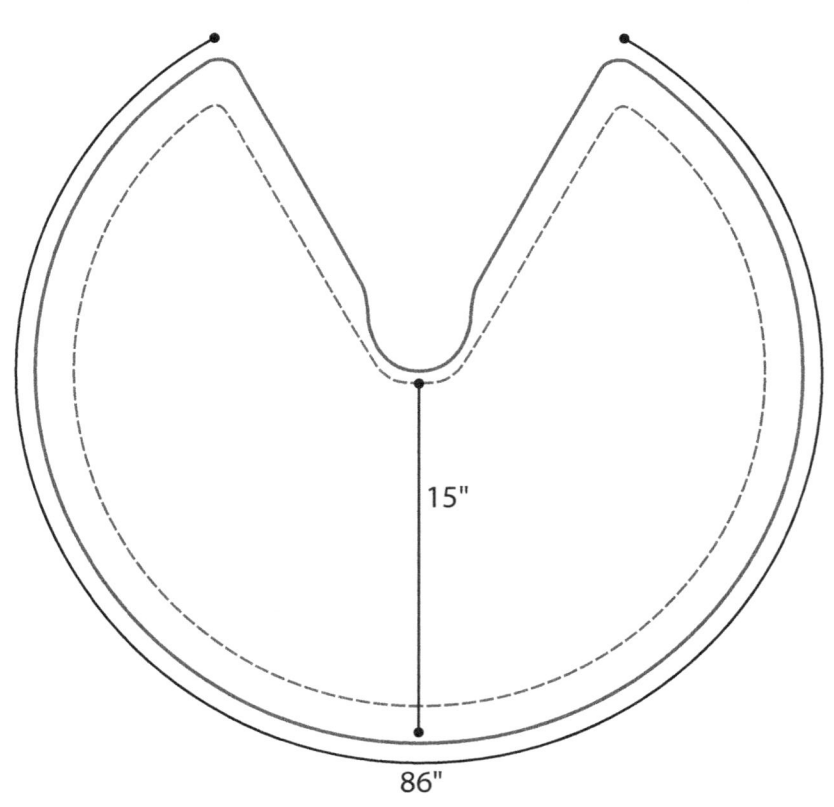

15"

86"

Row 33: Sl 1 wyif, k2, p1, 4/4 LRC, p1, knit to next marker, p1, 4/4 RRC, p1, k3.

Rows 34–40: Repeat Rows 26–32.

Row 41 (inc): Sl 1 wyif, k2, p1, 4/4 LRC, p1, sm, k7, kfb to 3 sts before next marker, k6, sm, p1, 4/4 RRC, p1, k3. 151 sts.

Rows 42–49: Repeat Rows 26–33.
Rows 50–56: Repeat Rows 26–32.

Row 57 (inc): Sl 1 wyif, k2, p1, 4/4 LRC, p1, sm, k13, [kfb, k1] to 12 sts before next marker, k12, sm, p1, 4/4 RRC, p1, k3. 201 sts.

Rows 58–65: Repeat Rows 26–33.
Rows 66–72: Repeat Rows 26–32.

Row 73 (inc): Sl 1 wyif, k2, p1, 4/4 LRC, p1, sm, k13, [kfb, k2] to 12 sts before next marker, k12, sm, p1, 4/4 RRC, p1, k3. 251 sts.

Row 74 Repeat Row 14.
Row 75 Repeat Row 19.
Row 76 Repeat Row 20.

Row 77 (inc): Sl 1 wyif, k2, p2, [k1, p1] 4 times, sm, kfb twice, knit to 2 sts before next marker, kfb twice, sm, [p1, k1] 4 times, p2, k3. 255 sts.

Row 78: Repeat Row 14.
Row 79: Repeat Row 23.
Row 80: Repeat Row 24.

Row 81 (inc): Sl 1 wyif, k2, p1, 4/4 LRC, p1, sm, kfb twice, knit to 2 sts before next marker, kfb twice, sm, p1, 4/4 RRC, p1, k3. 259 sts.

Rows 82–113: Repeat Rows 74–81 four times. 291 sts.
Row 114: Repeat Row 14.

Bottom Edging

The bottom cable edging is worked from both sides toward the center back where the sts are grafted. There are 265 sts between the stitch markers; mark the center st (the 133rd st) with a removable stitch marker or piece of waste yarn as a visual reminder of this center point.

Left Corner

The following rows are worked as short rows. Turn work at the end of each of the following rows.

Row 1 (RS): Sl 1 wyif, k2.
Row 2 (WS): Sl 1 wyib, k2.
Row 3: Sl 1 wyif, k2, p1.
Row 4: Sl 1 wyib, k3.
Row 5: Sl 1 wyif, k2, p2.
Row 6: Sl 1 wyib, k4.
Row 7: Sl 1 wyif, k2, p2, k1.
Row 8: Sl 1 wyif, k5.

Row 9: Sl 1 wyif, k2, p2, k1, p1.
Row 10: Sl 1 wyib, p1, k5.
Row 11: Sl 1 wyif, k2, p2, k1, p1, k1.
Row 12: Sl 1 wyif, k1, p1, k5.
Row 13: Sl 1 wyif, k2, p2, [k1, p1] twice.
Row 14: Sl 1 wyib, p1, k1, p1, k5.
Row 15: Sl 1 wyif, k2, p2, k1, [p1, k1] twice.
Row 16: Sl 1 wyif, [k1, p1] twice, k5.
Row 17: Sl 1 wyif, k2, p2, [k1, p1] 3 times.
Row 18: Sl 1 wyib, p1, [k1, p1] twice, k5.
Row 19: Sl 1 wyif, k2, p2, [k1, p1] 3 times, k1.
Row 20: Sl 1 wyif, [k1, p1] 3 times, k5.
Row 21 (inc): Sl 1 wyif, k2, p1, sl 4 to cn and hold in front, pfbf, k1, p1, k1; [pfbf, k1, p1, k1] from cn; p1. Remove stitch marker. Turn.
Row 22: Sl 1 wyib, [p1, k1] 6 times, k4.

Attach Edge to Shawl

Turn at the end of every row.

Row 1 (RS, inc): Sl 1 wyif, k2, p2, [k1, p1] 5 times, k1, M1P, p2tog (1 edge st + 1 shawl st).

Row 2 (WS): K2, [p1, k1] 6 times, k4.
Row 3: Sl 1 wyif, k2, p2, [k1, p1] 6 times, p2tog.

Row 4: Repeat Row 2.
Row 5: Repeat Row 3.
Row 6: Repeat Row 2.

Row 7: Sl 1 wyif, k2, p1, 6/6 LRC, p1, p3tog (1 edge st + 2 shawl sts).

Row 8: Repeat Row 2.
Row 9: Repeat Row 3.
Row 10: Repeat Row 2.
Row 11: Repeat Row 3.
Row 12: Repeat Row 2.
Repeat Rows 3–12 another 20 times.
Next Row: Repeat Row 3.

Repeat Rows 2–3 four more times. Final row ends at shawl, having incorporated the last shawl st before the marked center point st.

Cut yarn, leaving a 24" / 60cm tail. Place 18 edging sts on a stitch holder.

Right Corner

With WS facing, push sts to tip of circular needle to work the next row. Attach yarn.

Setup Row (WS): Sl 1 wyif, k2.
Row 1 (RS): Sl 1 wyib, k2.
Row 2: Sl 1 wyif, k3.
Row 3: Sl 1 wyif, k3.
Row 4: Sl 1 wyif, k4.
Row 5: Sl 1 wyif, p1, k3.
Row 6: Sl 1 wyif, k4, p1.
Row 7: Sl 1 wyib, p2, k3.
Row 8: Sl 1 wyif, k4, p1, k1.

Row 9: Sl 1 wyif, k1, p2, k3.
Row 10: Sl 1 wyif, k4, p1, k1, p1.
Row 11: Sl 1 wyib, p1, k1, p2, k3.
Row 12: Sl 1 wyif, k4, [p1, k1] twice.
Row 13: Sl 1 wyif, [k1, p1] twice, p1, k3.
Row 14: Sl 1 wyif, k4, p1, [k1, p1] twice.
Row 15: Sl 1 wyib, [p1, k1] twice, p2, k3.
Row 16: Sl 1 wyif, k4, [p1, k1] 3 times.
Row 17: Sl 1 wyif, [k1, p1] 3 times, p1, k3.
Row 18: Sl 1 wyif, k4, p1, [k1, p1] 3 times.
Row 19: Sl 1 wyib, [p1, k1] 3 times, p2, k3.
Row 20: Sl 1 wyif, k4, [p1, k1] 4 times. Remove stitch marker. Turn.
Row 21 (inc): Sl 1 wyif, sl 4 to cn and hold in back, k1, p1, k1, pfbf; [k1, p1, k1, pfbf] from cn; p1, k3.

Attach Edge to Shawl

Edging sts are attached to shawl on WS rows. Turn at the end of every row.

Setup Row (WS)(inc): Sl 1 wyif, k4, [p1, k1] 5 times, p1, M1, k2tog tbl (1 edge st + 1 shawl st).

Row 1 (RS): P2, [k1, p1] 6 times, p1, k3.
Row 2: Sl 1 wyif, k4, [p1, k1] 6 times, k2tog tbl.
Row 3: Repeat Row 1.
Row 4: Repeat Row 2.
Row 5: Repeat Row 1.

Row 6: Sl 1 wyif, k4, [p1, k1] 6 times, k3tog tbl (1 edge st + 2 shawl sts).
Row 7: P2, 6/6 RRC, p1, k3.
Row 8: Repeat Row 2.
Row 9: Repeat Row 1.
Row 10: Repeat Row 2.
Row 11: Repeat Row 1.

Repeat Rows 2–11 twenty more times.
Next Row: Repeat Row 2.
Repeat Rows 1–2 three more times.
Repeat Row 1.
Repeat Row 6. All shawl sts have been incorporated into the edging.

Cut yarn, leaving a 24" / 60cm tail.

Finishing

Graft bottom edging: Separating the sts as described in the following sections creates two separate sets of knit sts, one on the RS of the work and one on the WS of the work. The grafting is done in two stages, one with the RS facing and the second with the WS facing; however, because of the initial stitch separation, all of the grafting is done on knit sts.

Separate knit and purl stitches on the right edging: With RS facing and using one dpn for knit sts and the second dpn for purl sts, slip sts onto their respective dpns, always keeping the needle holding the purl sts to the back of the work and needle holding the knit sts to the front of the work. The last st is included with the sts on the purl (back) needle. 6 sts on knit (front) needle; 12 sts on purl (back) needle.

Separate knit and purl stitches on the left edging: Keep yarn tail attached to this section to the WS of the work. With RS facing and using two more dpn, slip first 5 sts onto one needle and hold to back of the work. Separate remaining sts as for Right Edging, slipping purl sts onto the back needle and knit sts onto the dpn held to the front of the work. 6 sts on knit (front) needle; 12 sts on purl (back) needle.

Graft the edging (RS): Carefully turn the work over to have the RS facing up and the shawl to the knitter's right. Lay the two dpns holding 6 sts each parallel to each other. Thread the yarn tail attached to the Left Edging onto a tapestry needle; the yarn tail is attached to the upper needle, furthest away from the knitter. Graft sts.

Weave in all ends. Block.

Graft the edging (WS): Carefully turn the work over to have the WS facing up and the shawl to the knitter's right. Bring the two dpns holding the 12 sts each to the WS, laying them parallel to each other. Thread the yarn tail attached to the Right Edging onto a tapestry needle; the yarn tail is attached to the upper needle, furthest away from the knitter. Graft sts.

Madeleine Gloves

Rebecca Blair

SIZES

S (M, L) to fit hands of 7 (8, 9)" / 18 (10.5, 23)cm circumference, measured above the thumb; shown in M.

MATERIALS

Cephalopod Yarns Skinny Bugga! (80% superwash Merino wool, 10% cashmere, 10% nylon; 424 yds / 387m per 113g skein); color: Rose Weevil; 1 skein

1 set US #2 /2.75mm double-point needles
US size C /2.75mm crochet hook

5 removable stitch markers
6 × ¼" / 6mm buttons
Waste yarn
Yarn needle

GAUGE

32 sts and 44 rounds = 4" / 10cm in St st
30 sts and 42 rows = 4" / 10cm in cuff pattern stitch (Chart 1 or Chart 3)

REQUIRED SKILLS

Knitting in the round; increases/decreases; backward loop cast on; working simple lace from chart or written instructions; picking up stitches; sewing on buttons; basic crochet stitches

PATTERN NOTES

These gloves begin with split cuffs worked back and forth, which are then joined to knit in the round toward the fingers.

Charts 1 and 3 are worked back and forth; every uncharted wrong side (even-numbered) row is purled. Charts 2 and 4 are worked in the round; every uncharted even-numbered row is knitted.

PATTERN—RIGHT GLOVE

Cuff

CO 56 (64, 72) sts. Do not join into the round.
Next row (WS): Purl.

Next row (RS): K0 (1, 2), work Row 1 of Chart 1 across to last 0 (1, 2) sts, k0 (1, 2).
Next row: Purl.

Continue following Chart 1 until all rows of chart have been completed, ending with Row 19 (RS). Divide sts between needles for working in the round.

Join for working in the round. Pm to mark beginning of round.

Next round: Knit.
Next round: K14 (17, 20), pm, work Round 1 of Chart 2 across next 22 sts, pm, knit to end of round.
Next round: Knit.

Continue following Chart 2 until 4 more rounds have been completed.

These sleek gloves were inspired by a pair from the 1950s, adorned with a lace cuff and lace inset detail on the back of each hand. The short split cuff is an elegant detail and an opportunity to show off a few precious small buttons, and a very narrow crocheted finish allows the lace to flow all the way to the edge of the cuff. The springy cashmere blend yarn blooms with blocking to produce a smooth stockinette fabric and stretchy lace.

Thumb Gusset

Setup round: Knit to first marker, work next round of Chart 2 to next marker, k7 (11, 13), pm, m1R, k1, m1L, pm, knit to end of round. 2 sts increased.

Rounds 1–2: Knit to first marker, work next round of Chart 2 to next marker, knit to end.

Round 3 (inc round): Knit to first marker, work next round of Chart 2 to next marker, knit to next marker, sm, m1R, knit to next marker, m1L, sm, knit to end of round. 2 sts increased.

Repeat last 3 rounds 5 (6, 7) more times, then work Rounds 1–2 once more. 70 (80, 90) sts.

Next round: Knit to first marker, work next round of Chart 2 to next marker, knit to next marker, remove marker, sl next 15 (17, 19) sts to scrap yarn, CO 1 st using the backward loop method, remove marker, knit to end of round. 56 (64, 72) sts.

Hand

Next round: Knit to first marker, work next round of Chart 2 to next marker, knit to end of round.

Repeat last round until all rounds of Chart 2 have been completed, then remove markers and knit every round until work measures 1 (1.25, 1.5)" / 2.5 (3, 4)cm above thumb hole, or desired length to base of little finger.

Next round: K8 (9, 10), sl next 12 (14, 16) sts to scrap yarn, CO 2 sts using the backward loop method, knit to end of round. 46 (52, 58) sts. (Little finger will be worked last.)

Knit 3 (3, 4) rounds, or until the glove reaches the base of the ring finger when tried on. At end of last round, shift marker 1 st to the right as foll: knit to 1 st before end, sl st to RH needle, remove marker, sl st back to left needle, replace marker.

Ring finger

K16 (18, 20). Transfer remaining sts in round to scrap yarn and divide knitted sts between needles for working in the round. CO 2 sts using backward loop method, pm, and join in the round. 18 (20, 22) sts. Knit every round until finger measures 2 (2.25, 2.5)" / 5 (5.5, 6.5)cm, or desired finished length.

*

Size M only:
Next round: [K2, k2tog] around. 15 sts.

Size L only:
Next round: K2, k3tog, [k2, k2tog] to last 5 sts, k2, k3tog. 15 sts.

All sizes:
Next round: [K1, k2tog] around.
Next round: K2tog around.

Break yarn, thread through remaining sts, and fasten off.

Middle finger

Place next 7 (8, 9) sts from each side onto needles. Join yarn at cast-on edge of ring finger. Pick up and knit 4 sts from cast-on edge, k7 (8, 9), CO 2 sts using backward loop method, k7 (8, 9), pm. 20 (22, 24) sts.

Next round: K2tog, ssk, knit to end of round. 18 (20, 22) sts.

Knit every round until finger measures 2.25 (2.5, 2.75)" / 5.5 (6.5, 7)cm, or desired finished length.

Finish as for ring finger from *.

Index finger

Transfer remaining held sts to needles. Join yarn at cast-on edge of middle finger. Pick up and knit 4 sts from cast-on edge, knit across remaining sts, pm. 20 (22, 24) sts.

Next round: K2tog, ssk, knit to end of round. 18 (20, 22) sts.

Knit every round until finger measures 2 (2.25, 2.5)" / 5 (5.5, 6.5)cm, or desired finished length.

Finish as for ring finger from *.

Little finger

Transfer 12 (14, 16) held sts to needles. Join yarn at adjacent cast-on edge. Pick up and knit 4 sts from cast-on edge, knit across remaining sts, pm. 16 (18, 20) sts.

Knit every round until finger measures 1.5 (1.75, 2)" / 4 (4.5, 5)cm, or desired finished length.

Size M only: [K7, k2tog] twice. 16 sts.

Next round: [K2, k2tog] around.
Next round: [K1, k2tog] around.
Next round: K2tog around.

Break yarn, thread through remaining sts, and fasten off.

Thumb

Transfer 15 (17, 19) held sts to needles. Join yarn at adjacent cast-on edge. Pick up and knit 3 sts from cast-on edge, knit across remaining sts, pm. 18 (20, 22) sts.

Knit every round until thumb measures 1.75 (2, 2.25)" / 4.5 (5, 5.5)cm, or desired finished length.

Finish as for ring finger from *.

LEFT GLOVE

Cuff

CO 56 (64, 72) sts. Do not join.
Next row (WS): Purl.

Next row (RS): K0 (1, 2), work Row 1 of Chart 3 across to last 0 (1, 2) sts, k0 (1, 2).
Next row (WS): Purl.

Continue following Chart 3 until all rows of chart have been completed, ending with Row 19 (RS). Divide sts between needles for working in the round.

Join for working in the round and pm to mark beg of round.

Next round: Knit.
Next round: K19 (24, 31), pm, work Round 1 of Chart 4 across next 22 sts, pm, knit to end of round.
Next round: Knit.

Continue following Chart 4 until 4 more rounds have been completed.

Thumb Gusset

Setup round: K12 (13, 16), pm, m1R, k1, m1L, pm, work in est patt to end of round. 2 sts increased.

Rounds 1–2: Knit to third marker, work next round of Chart 2 to next marker, knit to end.

Round 3 (inc round): Knit to first marker, sl marker, m1R, knit to next marker, m1L, sl marker, knit to next marker, work next round of Chart 2 to next marker, knit to end of round. 2 sts increased.

Repeat last 3 rounds 5 (6, 7) more times, then work Rounds 1–2 one more time. 70 (80, 90) sts.

Next round: Knit to first marker, remove marker, sl next 15 (17, 19) sts to scrap yarn, CO 1 st using backward loop method, remove marker, knit to next marker, work next round of Chart 2 to next marker, knit to end of round. 56 (64, 72) sts.

Hand

Next round: Knit to first marker, work next round of Chart 2 to next marker, knit to end of round.

Repeat last round until all rounds of Chart 2 have been completed, then remove markers and knit

every round until work measures 1 (1.25, 1.5)" / 2.5 (3, 4)cm above thumb hole, or desired length to base of little finger.

Next round: K36 (41, 46), sl next 12 (14, 16) sts to scrap yarn, CO 2 sts using backward loop method, knit to end of round. 46 (52, 58) sts.

K 3 (3, 4) rounds, or until the glove reaches the base of the ring finger when tried on.

Next round: Remove end-of-round marker, k29 (33, 37).

Work all fingers as for right glove.

Finishing

Right glove:

With crochet hook, join yarn at apex of cuff slit and ch 1. Working from right to left, sc into each bar between garter ridges along adjacent side of cuff slit to last bar; 2 sc in last bar. 2 sc in first V from cast-on edge, sc into each V across cast-on edge until 1 remains, 2 sc into it. 2 sc into next bar between garter ridges, 1 sc into next bar, *ch 5, sl st into same space as last sc, sc into next bar between garter ridges 3 times; repeat from * twice more; 1 sc into apex of cuff slit, sl st into first sc. Break yarn and fasten off.

Left glove:

With crochet hook, join yarn at apex of cuff slit and ch 1. Working from right to left, *sc into next bar between garter ridges 3 times, ch 5, sl st into same space as last sc; repeat from * twice more, 2 sc into last bar between garter ridges. 2 sc in first V from cast-on edge, sc into each V across cast-on edge until 1 remains, 2 sc into it. 2 sc into next bar between garter ridges, sc into each remaining bar, 1 sc into apex of cuff slit, sl st into first sc. Break yarn and fasten off.

Both gloves:

Sew three buttons to each cuff slit opposite the button loops. Weave in all ends, using the end at the base of each finger to mend any holes in the area if necessary. Block gloves by soaking in lukewarm water, squeezing out excess water in a towel, and laying flat to dry.

Chart 1

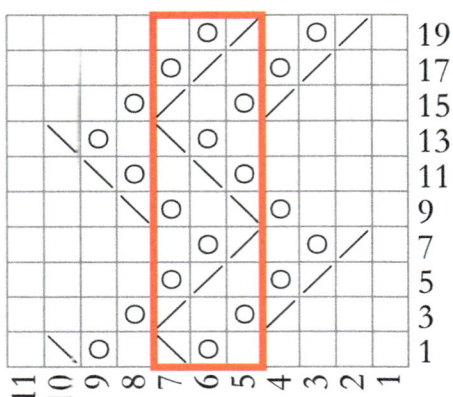

Chart 2

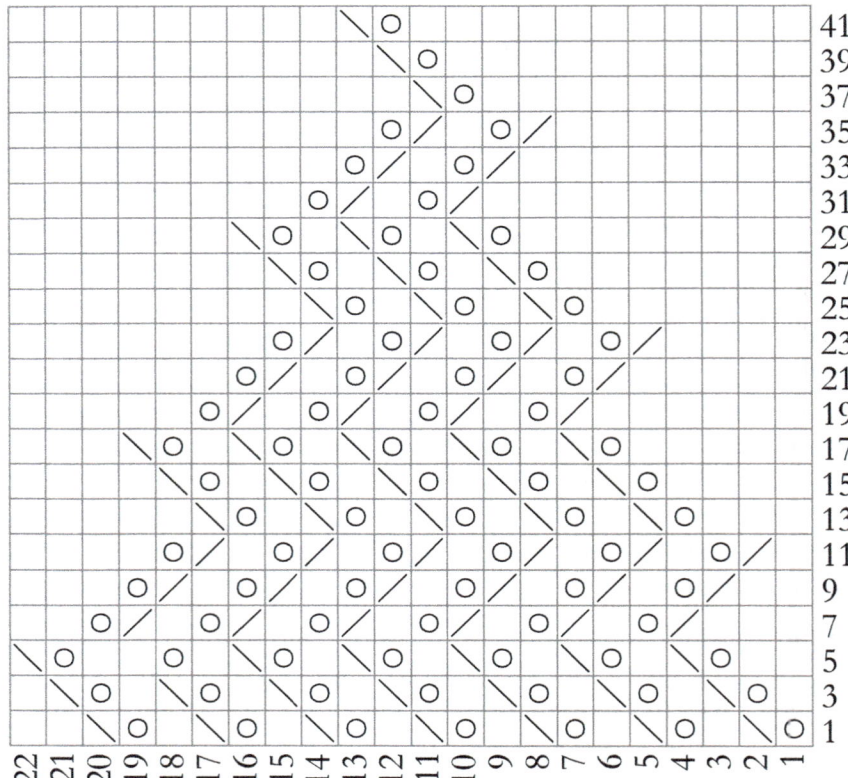

k
yo
k2tog
ssk

Chart 3

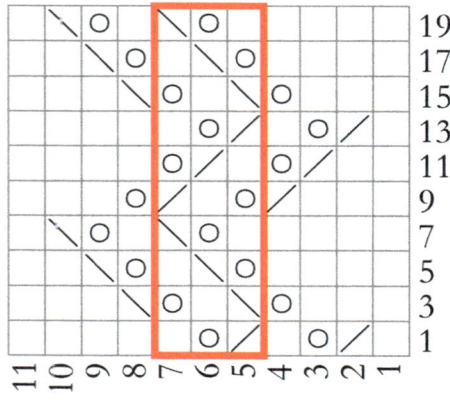

Chart 4

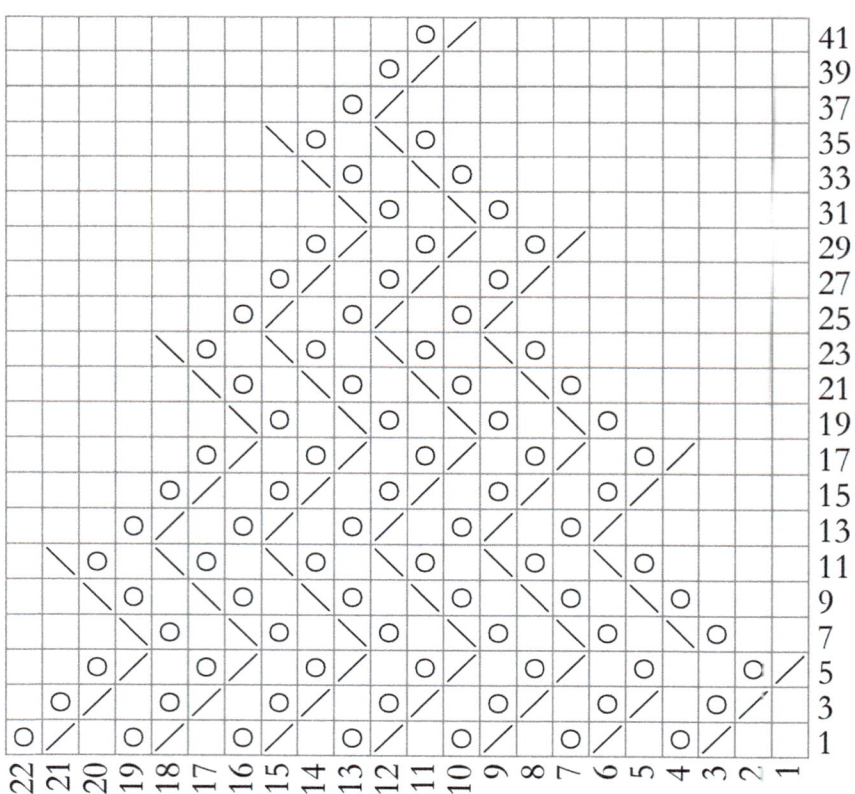

San Juan Bautista Shawl

Elizabeth Green Musselman

SIZE

Adjustable

FINISHED MEASUREMENTS

Wingspan (measured around outside edge): 78" / 198cm

Width (along the short, straight edge): 20" / 51cm

MATERIALS

Shibui Knits Staccato (70% superwash merino, 30% silk; 191 yds / 175m per 50g skein)

- [Color A] Ash; 1 skein
- [Color B] Redwood; 1 skein

32-inch (or longer) US #6 / 4mm circular needle, or size needed to obtain gauge

Yarn needle

GAUGE

14 sts and 46 rows = 4" / 10cm in pattern stitch, after blocking

Gauge is not critical in this pattern, and the shawl stretches dramatically (that is, the number of sts per inch drops dramatically) during blocking. Note, however, that a different gauge will affect the yardage and size of finished item.

REQUIRED SKILLS

Knitted cast on; lace knitting, either from chart or written instruction; Jeny's Surprisingly Stretchy Bind Off

PATTERN NOTES

This shawl begins at the narrow tip and builds diagonally, as shown in the schematic. This construction allows you to use as much of your yarn as you can. The sample was knit until only 6" / 15cm remained of color A. Work as many repeats of the stitch pattern as you like, using the instructions to determine where in the stitch pattern to stop.

As with most lace patterns, using needles that have pointy tips is recommended.

When Alfred Hitchcock first saw the San Juan Bautista Mission south of San Francisco, he knew he had found the perfect location for the climactic scenes in Vertigo *(1958). The Spanish mission, built in the eighteenth century, projected just the right ominous air for his main character's confrontation with death and acrophobia.*

The famous tower from that film, however, like Madeleine's apparent suicide from its top, is—spoiler alert!— entirely fabricated. The mission's steeple had burned in a fire years before, so Hitchcock used scale models, studio sets, and trick photography to create the illusion of a tower.

Taking a cue from Hitchcock, this shawl creates its own illusion, using a very simple lace pattern to reproduce the graphic look of Vertigo's *striking movie poster. This is easy knitting that won't make you want to jump from a steeple.*

STITCHES AND TECHNIQUES

Diagonal Ridge Pattern

Each time you finish the first row of color A, you will CO 5 sts. Rows 11–20 are the same as Rows 1–10, but with the color scheme reversed.

Row 1 (RS): With color A, k2tog, yo, [k3, k2tog, yo] to last 5 sts, k5. Turn work and CO 5 sts using knitted cast on (KCO; see Abbreviations & Techniques).

Row 2 (WS): With color A, p2, [k3, p2] to end.

Row 3: With color B, k4, k2tog, yo, [k3, k2tog, yo] to last st, k1.

Row 4: With color B, k1, [p2, k3] to last st, p1.

Row 5: With color A, [k3, k2tog, yo] to last 2 sts, k2. Turn work and CO 5 sts using KCO.

Row 6: With color A, k2, [p2, k3] to end.

Row 7: With color B, k2, [k2tog, yo, k3] to end.

Row 8: With color B, [k3, p2] to last 2 sts, k2.

Row 9: With color A, k1, k2tog, yo, [k3, k2tog, yo] to last 4 sts, k4. Turn work and CO 5 sts using KCO.

Row 10: With color A, p1, [k3, p2] to last st, k1.

Row 11: With color B, k2tog, yo, [k3, k2tog, yo] to last 5 sts, k5.

Row 12: With color B, p2, [k3, p2] to end.

Row 13: With color A, k4, k2tog, yo, [k3, k2tog, yo] to last st, k1. Turn work and CO 5 sts using KCO.

Row 14: With color A, k1, [p2, k3] to last st, p1.

Row 15: With color B, [k3, k2tog, yo] to last 2 sts, k2.

Row 16: With color B, k2, [p2, k3] to end.

Row 17: With color A, k2, [k2tog, yo, k3] to end. Turn work and CO 5 sts using KCO.

Row 18: With color A, [k3, p2] to last 2 sts, k2.

Row 19: With color B, k1, k2tog, yo, [k3, k2tog, yo] to last 4 sts, k4.

Row 20: With color B, p1, [k3, p2] to last st, k1.

PATTERN

With color A, CO 7 sts.

Set-up Row 1: Knit.
Set-up Row 2: Knit all sts; turn work and CO 5 sts, using KCO. 12 sts.

Work Diagonal Ridge Pattern, following either written instructions above or chart on next page. Begin on Row 2 of pattern.

Continue working pattern until there are 212 sts on the needle, or desired size is reached. End with a color A RS row (that is, a Row 1, 5, 9, 13, or 17), making sure to CO 5 sts at the end of that row if it is called for.

Using Jeny's Surprisingly Stretchy Bind Off (see Abbreviations and Techniques), BO in patt according to the next WS row. (BO knitwise for knit sts and purlwise for purl sts.)

Finishing

Wet block shawl to dimensions and shape shown in schematic.

Weave in ends.

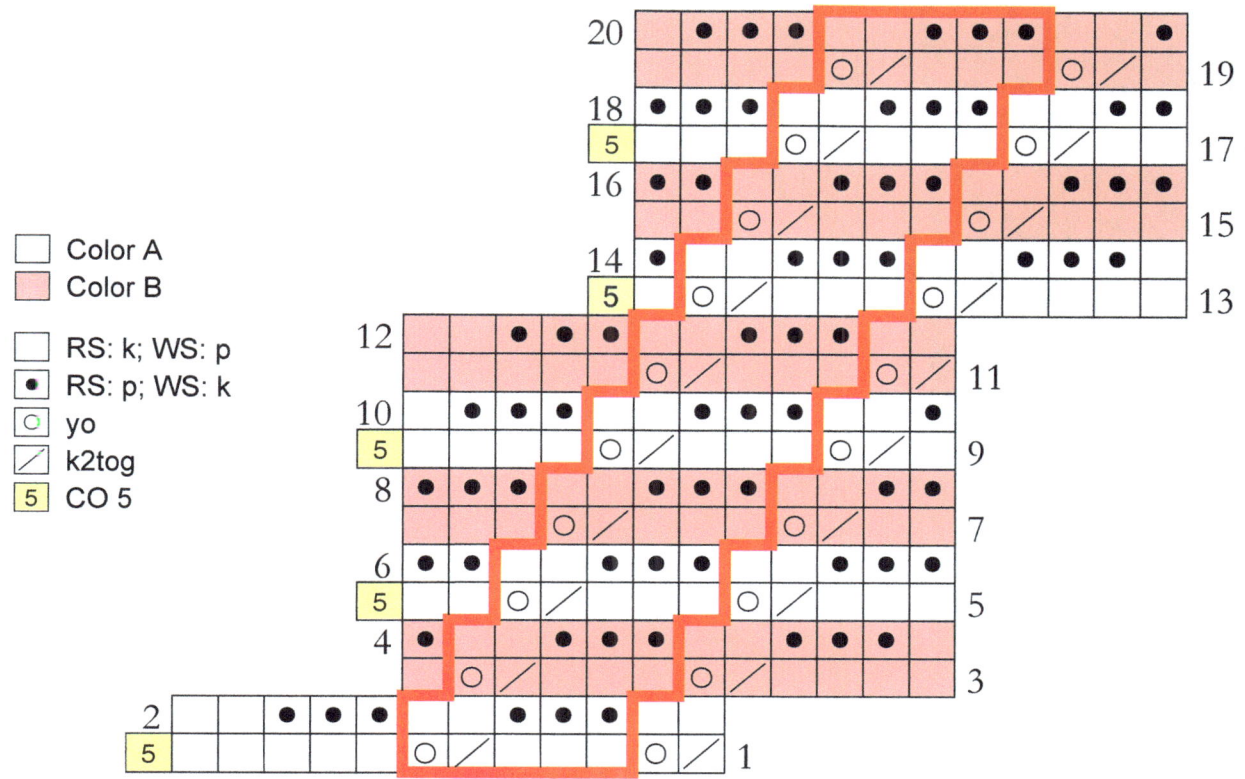

Color A
Color B

RS: k; WS: p
RS: p; WS: k
yo
k2tog
CO 5

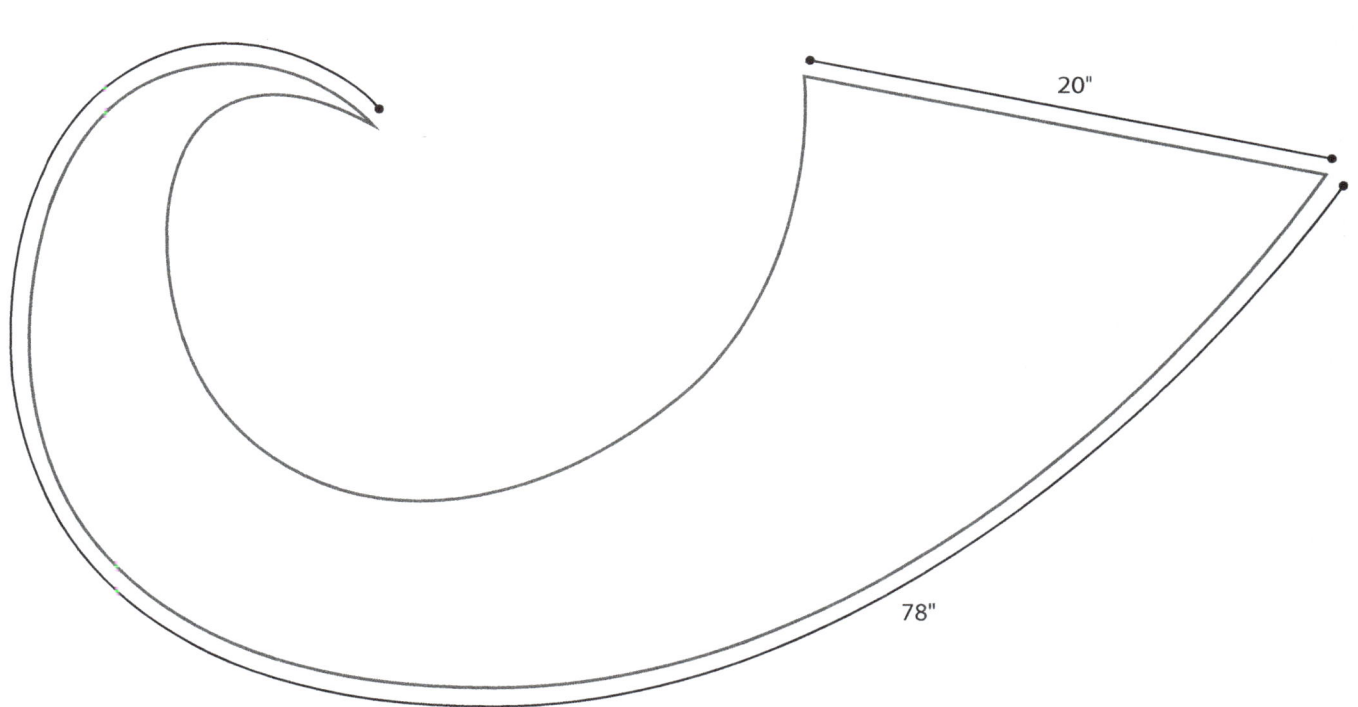

20"

78"

Souvenir of a Killing Beret

Kristen Hanley Cardozo

SIZES

Women's S (M, L); shown in size L (slouch version)

FINISHED MEASUREMENTS

Band circumference: 16.5 (17.75, 20)" / 42 (45, 51)cm
Length: 8 (8, 8.25)" / 20.5 (20.5, 21)cm for beret;
8.75 (9, 9)" / 22 (23, 23)cm for slouch

MATERIALS

Sincere Sheep Equity Sport (100% Rambouillet wool; 200 yds / 183m per 56g skein)

> [MC] Natural; 1 (1, 1) skein

> [CC] Undyed Dark Grey; 1 (1, 1) skein

16-inch US #3 / 3.25mm circular needle
16-inch US #5 / 3.75mm circular needle
1 set US #5 / 3.75 mm double-point needles OR
32-inch or longer US #5 / 3.75mm circular needle for magic loop

Stitch marker
Yarn needle

GAUGE

24 sts and 36 rounds = 4" / 10cm in St st, on larger needle

REQUIRED SKILLS

Knitting in the round; knitting with double-pointed needles or magic loop; increases/decreases

PATTERN NOTES

Souvenir of a Killing is knit simply, using only one color per row, to create a bold chevron pattern. The stitch pattern used to create the chevrons in this hat is a very simple one, but it does result in different stitch counts on every row by using increase and decrease rows to create the zig zags, so attention is necessary.

STITCHES AND TECHNIQUES

M2: [K1, yo, k] into a single st.

PATTERN

Brim

Using smaller needles and MC, CO 104 (112, 120) sts, pm, and join to work in the round.

Round 1: [K tbl, p1] to end of round.
Repeat Round 1 until brim measures 1 (1, 1.5)" / 2.5 (2.5, 4)cm.

Inc Round: [K2, M1] to end of round. 156 (168, 180) sts.

Body

Switch to larger needles.
Set-up Round: Knit.

Round 1: Using CC, remove marker and sl 1 st from RH needle to LH needle. [S2kp, k9] to end of round. 130 (140, 150) sts.

Round 2: Using CC, k5, [M2, k9] to last 5 sts, M2, k4. 156 (168, 180) sts.

Vertigo remains iconic in my mind, helped in part by the stark, graphic posters and opening titles by Saul Bass. With the Souvenir of a Killing beret, I sought to capture some of that stark, graphic element. Bass used Lissajous spirals to portray dizziness; I used gray and white chevrons. In the film, Scottie tells Judy that she shouldn't have kept "souvenirs of a killing." He's referring to a necklace, but it could as easily refer to himself and his vertigo.

Round 3: Using MC, remove marker and sl 1 st from RH needle to LH needle. [S2kp, k9] to end of round. 130 (140, 150) sts.

Round 4: Using MC, k5, [M2, k9] to last 5 sts, M2, k4. 156 (168, 180) sts.

Repeat Rounds 1–4 (ending on Round 4), until hat measures approx 5 (5, 5.25)" / 12.5 (12.5, 13.5)cm from cast-on edge for a beret, and 5.75 (6, 6)" / 14.5 (15, 15)cm from cast-on edge for a slouchy hat.

Begin Decreases

Switch to dpns or long circular needle for magic loop when necessary.

Round 1: Using CC, remove marker and sl 1 st from RH needle to LH needle. [S2kp, k9] to end of round. 130 (140, 150) sts.

Round 2: Using CC, knit to end.

Round 3: Using MC, remove marker and sl 1 st from RH needle to LH needle. [S2kp, k7] to end of round. 104 (112, 120) sts.

Round 4: Using MC, k4, [M2, k7] to last 4 sts, M2, k3. 130 (140, 150) sts.

Round 5: Using CC, remove marker and sl 1 st from RH needle to LH needle. [S2kp, k7] to end of round. 104 (112, 120) sts.

Round 6: Using CC, k4, [M2, k7] to last 4 sts, M2, k3. 130 (140, 150) sts.

Round 7: Using MC, remove marker and sl 1 st from RH needle to LH needle. [S2kp, k7] to end of round. 104 (112, 120) sts.

Round 8: Using MC, k4, [M2, k7] to last 4 sts, M2, k3. 130 (140, 150) sts.

Round 9: Using CC, remove marker and sl 1 st from RH needle to LH needle. [S2kp, k7] to end of round. 104 (112, 120) sts.

Round 10: Using CC, knit to end of round.

Round 11: Using MC, remove marker and sl 1 st from RH needle to LH needle. [S2kp, k5] to end of round. 78 (84, 90) sts.

Round 12: Using MC, k3, [M2, k5] to last 3 sts, M2, k2. 104 (112, 120) sts.

Round 13: Using CC, remove marker and sl 1 st from RH needle to LH needle. [S2kp, k5] to end of round. 78 (84, 90) sts.

Round 14: Using CC, k3, [M2, k5] to last 3 sts, M2, k2. 104 (112, 120) sts.

Round 15: Using MC, remove marker and sl 1 st from RH needle to LH needle. [S2kp, k5] to end of round. 78 (84, 90) sts.

Round 16: Using MC, k3, [M2, k5] to last 3 sts, M2, k2. 104 (112, 120) sts.

Round 17: Using CC, remove marker and sl 1 st from RH needle to LH needle. [S2kp, k5] to end of round. 78 (84, 90) sts.

Round 18: Using CC, knit to end of round.

Round 19: Using MC, remove marker and sl 1 st from RH needle to LH needle. [S2kp, k3] to end of round. 52 (56, 60) sts

Round 20: Using MC, k2, [M2, k3] to last 2 sts, M2, k1. 78 (84, 90) sts.

Round 21: Using CC, remove marker and sl 1 st from RH needle to LH needle. [S2kp, k3] to end of round. 52 (56, 60) sts.

Round 22: Using CC, knit to end of round.

Round 23: Using MC, remove marker and sl 1 st from RH needle to LH needle. [S2kp, k1] to end of round. 26 (28, 30) sts.

Round 24: Using MC, [K2, M1] to end of round. 39 (42, 45) sts.

Round 25: Using CC, remove marker and sl 1 st from RH needle to LH needle. S2kp to end of round. 13 (14, 15) sts.

Round 26: Using CC, knit to end of round. Break yarn, leaving a long tail to weave in later.

Round 27: Using MC, knit to end of round.

Finishing

Leaving a long tail, break yarn. Using a yarn needle, thread yarn through remaining sts twice and pull tightly to close hole.

Block hat. To achieve a beret shape, squeeze most water out of hat, then allow it to dry stretched over a 10 inch dinner plate.

Weave in all ends after hat is dry.

Cypress Point Sweater

Glenna C.

SIZES

Women's XS (S, M, L, XL, 2XL); shown in size S. Intended to be worn with 0–2" / 0–5cm of ease at bust.

FINISHED MEASUREMENTS

Bust: 35 (38, 41, 44, 47, 50)" / 89 (96.5, 104, 111.5, 119.5, 127)cm when worn closed.

At bust, front of garment measures slightly larger than back, with the use of darts shaping for bust.

MATERIALS

Verdant Gryphon Traveller [100% superwash merino wool, 280 yds per 4 oz skein], color: The South Pole; 5 (5, 6, 6, 7, 8) skeins

US #5 / 3.75mm needles, or size required to obtain gauge
US #4 / 3.5mm needles, or one size smaller than that required to obtain gauge
32-inch US #4 / 3.5mm circular needle (for finishing collar and neckband)

2 stitch markers
Yarn needle
6 × ¾" / 19mm buttons

GAUGE

21 sts and 32 rows = 4" / 10cm in St st, on larger needle

REQUIRED SKILLS

Knowledge of basic sweater construction; increases/decreases; seaming; sewing on buttons; 3-needle bind off or kitchener stitch (grafting)

PATTERN NOTES

This sweater is worked in pieces from the bottom up. Stitch markers are placed for dart shaping decreases (for hips) and increases (for bust). All pieces are seamed together in finishing.

PATTERN

Back

With smaller needles, CO 102 (110, 118, 122, 132, 136) sts.

Work in garter stitch for 6 rows, ending by working a WS row.

Next, work garter ridges as follows:
Row 1 (RS): Knit.
Row 2 (WS): Purl.
Rows 3 & 4: Knit.
Repeat Rows 1–4 another 3 times. This works a garter ridge every 4th row, 4 times.

Change to larger needles. Work even in St st until work measures 3.5" / 9cm from cast-on edge, ending by working a RS row.

Next WS Row: P34 (35, 39, 42, 44, 46), pm, purl to 34 (35, 39, 42, 44, 46) from end of row, pm, purl to end of row.

This fitted buttoned cardigan conforms to the style of a ladies' cardigan jacket. It features a folded lapel collar and darts for hip and bust shaping. Add a stylish belt for extra flair, or wear on its own for elegant comfort. Just like the mid-20th-century style of Hitchcock's leading lady Kim Novak, you'll be ready for whatever intrigue awaits you about town.

Work decreases as follows:
Row 1 (RS): Knit to 2 sts before first marker, ssk, sm, knit to second marker, sm, k2tog, knit to end of row.
Rows 2–4: Work even in St st.

Repeat Rows 1–4 another 7 (9, 10, 9, 10, 9) times. 86 (90, 96, 102, 110, 116) sts for waist.

Work even in St st for 12 (12, 10, 10, 10, 10) more rows.

Work increases for back as follows:
Row 1 (RS): Knit to 1 st before first marker, m1R, k1, sm, knit to 1 st after second marker, k1, m1L, knit to end of row.
Rows 2–8: Work even in St st.

Repeat Rows 1–8 twice more (all sizes). 92 (96, 102, 108, 116, 122) sts for bust at back.

Work even, removing markers as you come to them, until back measures 16 (16, 16, 16, 15.5, 15.5)" / 40.5 (40.5, 40.5, 40.5, 39.5, 39.5)cm from cast-on edge, ending by working a WS row.

Next 2 rows: BO 4 (5, 5, 6, 6, 7) sts at beginning of next 2 rows. 84 (86, 92, 96, 104, 108) sts

Next RS row: K2, k2tog, knit to 4 before end, ssk, k2.
Next WS row: Purl.
Repeat these last 2 rows 4 (4, 5, 5, 5, 5) more times. 74 (76, 80, 84, 92, 96) sts remain across shoulders.

Work even until armhole measures 7.5 (8, 8.5, 9, 9.5, 10)" / 19 (20.5, 21.5, 23, 24, 25.5)cm from cast-on edge, ending by working a WS row.

Shape shoulders as follows: BO 6 (6, 6, 6, 7, 7) sts at beginning of next 2 rows, then 6 (6, 7, 7, 7, 7) sts at beginning of following 2 rows, then finally BO 6 (6, 7, 7, 8, 8) sts at beginning of following 2 rows.

BO remaining sts.

Left Front

With smaller needles, CO 54 (58, 62, 66, 70, 74) sts. Work in garter stitch for 6 rows.

Work garter ridges as follows:
Row 1 (RS): Knit.
Row 2 (WS): Purl.
Row 3 & 4: Knit.
Repeat Rows 1–4 another 3 times. This works a garter ridge every 4th row, 4 times.

Change to larger needles. Work even in St st until work measures 3.5" / 9cm from cast-on edge, ending by working a RS row.

Next WS row: P6, pm for buttonband, p19 (23, 25, 27, 29, 31), pm for dart, purl to end. From this point forward, work these 6 sts in garter ridge pattern as

for hem, working a garter ridge every 4th row, AT THE SAME TIME as all subsequent instructions.

Work decreases as follows:
Row 1 (RS): Knit to 2 sts before dart marker, ssk, sm, knit to end.
Rows 2–4: Work even in St st.
Repeat Rows 1–4 another 7 (9, 10, 9, 10, 9) times. 46 (48, 51, 56, 59, 64) sts remaining at waist.

Work even in St st for 12 (12, 10, 10, 10, 10) more rows.

Work increases for bust as follows:
Row 1 (RS): Knit to dart marker, m1R, sm, knit to end of row.
Rows 2–4: Work even in St st.

Repeat Rows 1–4 another 6 (7, 8, 8, 8, 8) times. 53 (56, 60, 65, 68, 73) sts total at bust.

Work even until Left Front measures 16 (16, 16, 16, 15.5, 15.5)" / 40.5 (40.5, 40.5, 40.5, 39.5, 39.5)cm from beg, ending with a WS row.

Next RS row: BO 4 (5, 5, 6, 6, 7) sts at beginning of row, work to end. 49 (51, 55, 59, 62, 66) sts.

Work next row even, removing both markers as you come to them.

From this point forward, armhole shaping AND V-neck and collar shaping will be worked AT THE SAME TIME. Begin both on next RS row, working armhole shaping at beginning of row and V-neck shaping at end. Armhole shaping will be completed well before the V-neck / collar work.

Armhole shaping:

Row 1 (RS): K2, k2tog, work to end.
Row 2 (WS): Work even.
Repeat Rows 1–2, 4 (4, 5, 5, 5, 5) more times.

V-neck / collar shaping:

Row 1 (RS): Work to 5 sts from end of row, k2tog, pm, kfb, pm, kfb, p1.*

Row 2 (WS): Knit to first marker, sm, purl to second marker, sm, p2tog, purl to end of row.

Row 3 (RS): Work to 2 sts before first marker, k2tog, sm, kfb, knit to 1 st before second marker, kfb, sm, pfb twice, p1.

Row 4 (WS): Knit to first marker, purl to second marker, p2tog, purl to end of row.

(3 sts each increased for collar and lapel, 4 sts decreased at V-neck.)

*When viewed with RS facing, sts between the two markers are for collar, sts to the left of the markers are for the lapel which will later be folded back, and sts to the right of the marker are for the body.

Repeat the last 2 rows 2 more times. (7 sts each increased for collar and lapel, 6 sts decreased for V-neck.)

Row 5 (RS): Work to 2 sts before first marker, k2tog, sm, kfb, knit to 1 st before next marker, kfb, sm, k1, kfb, knit to 2 sts from end, kfb, k1. This row creates a garter ridge on the lapel sts, and works a V-neck decrease.

Row 6 (WS): Knit to first marker, purl to second marker, purl to end of row.

Row 7 (RS): Work to 2 sts before first marker, k2tog, sm, knit to second marker, sm, purl to end. (Decreases 1 st at V-neck.)

Row 8 (WS): Knit to knit to first marker, purl to second marker, purl to end of row.

Repeat Rows 5–8 until there are 15 sts between each pair of markers. Then, repeat Rows 5–8 while only working the increases on the lapel sts (no increases in collar), until there are 21 (21, 21, 23, 23, 25) sts for the lapel.

Cease V-neck decreases when 18 (18, 20, 20, 22, 22) sts remain in body.

Work all sts even, maintaining garter ridges on lapel, until armhole measures 6.5 (7, 7.5, 8, 8.5, 9)" / 16.5 (17.5, 19, 20.5, 21,5, 23)cm from beginning of armhole, ending by working a RS row, then continue to work even in body while working decreases for lapel slope by binding off 7 (7, 7, 8, 8, 8) sts at beginning of next 2 WS rows, then binding off 7 (7, 7, 7, 7, 9) sts at beginning of following WS row. 33 (33, 35, 35, 37, 37) sts remain.

Work 2 rows even, then shape shoulders by continuing to work even and binding off

BO 6 (6, 6, 6, 7, 7) sts at beginning of RS row, 6 (6, 7, 7, 7, 7) sts at beginning of following RS row, then finally BO 6 (6, 7, 7, 8, 8) sts at beginning of following RS row. 15 sts remain (all sizes).

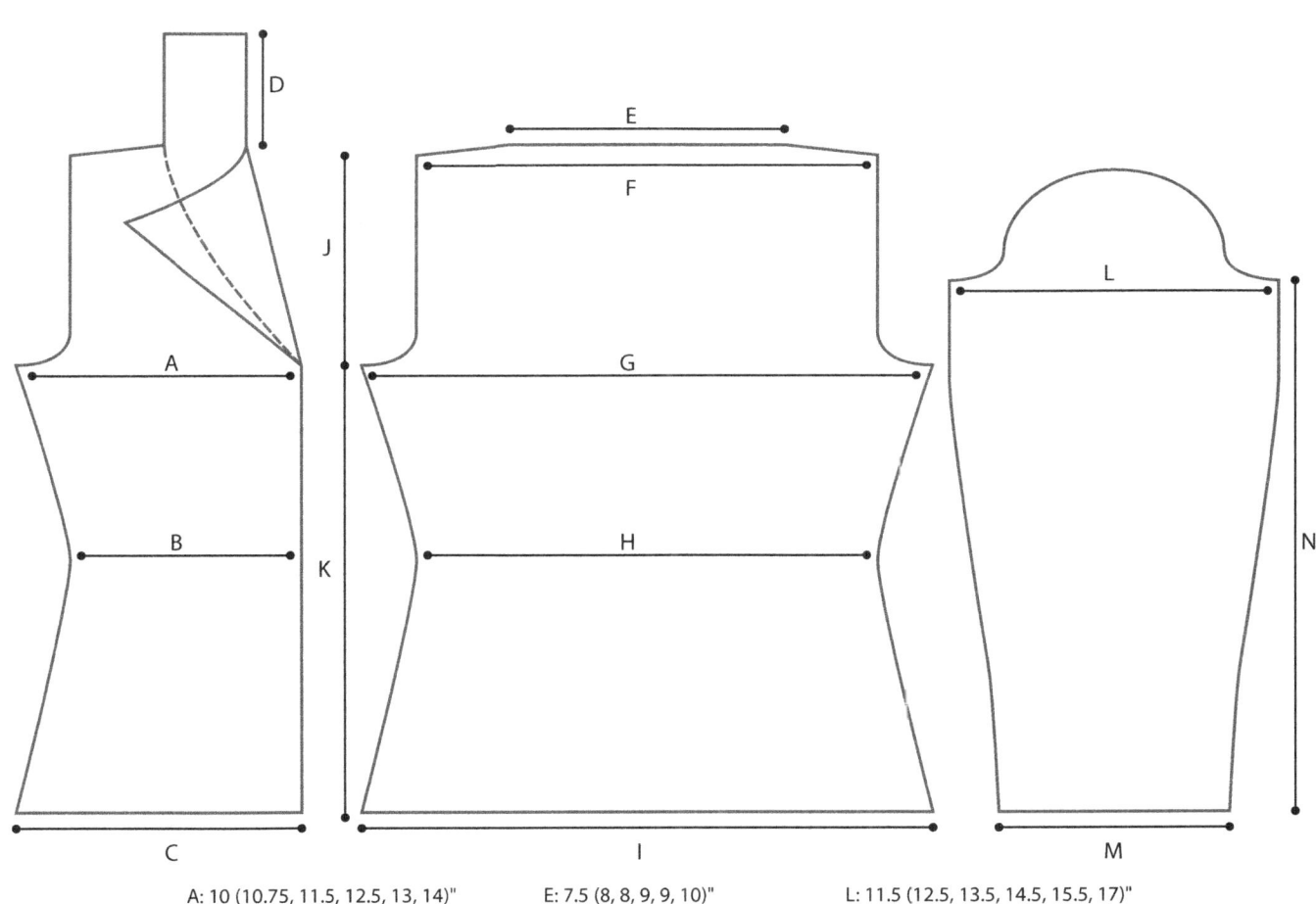

A: 10 (10.75, 11.5, 12.5, 13, 14)"
B: 8 (8.5, 9.25, 10, 10.75, 11.5)"
C: 9.75 (10.5, 11.25, 12, 12.75, 13.5)"
D: 3 (3, 3, 3.5, 4.25, 4.25)"

E: 7.5 (8, 8, 9, 9, 10)"
F: 14.5 (15, 16, 17, 17.5, 18)"
G: 17.5 (18, 19.5, 20.5, 22, 23)"
H: 16 (17, 18.5, 20, 21.5, 22)"
I: 19.5 (21, 22.5, 24, 25.5, 27)"
J: 7.5 (8, 8.5, 9, 9.5, 10)"
K: 16 (16, 16, 16, 15.5, 15.5)"

L: 11.5 (12.5, 13.5, 14.5, 15.5, 17)"
M: 8.5 (9.25, 10, 10.75, 10.75, 11.5)"
N: 17.5 (18, 18.5, 19, 19, 20)"

Work remaining 15 sts for collar even in St st until collar measures 3 (3, 3, 3.5, 4.25, 4.25)" / 7.5 (7.5, 7.5, 9, 11, 11)cm from beginning of collar, then slip all sts to a stitch holder or waste yarn.

Along button-band edge of Left Front, mark placement of 6 buttons, evenly spaced between bottom edge and beginning of V-neck. These will be used as reference for placement of buttonholes along Right Front.

Right Front

With smaller needles, CO 54 (58, 62, 66, 70, 74) sts. Work in garter stitch for 6 rows.

While following instructions below, AT THE SAME TIME remember to place a 4-st buttonhole on corresponding rows from marked places on Left Front.

Work buttonholes at beginning of RS row as follows: K1, sl1 wyif, sl1 wyib, pass first slipped st over second. Slip 3 more sts in this manner. Turn work, CO 5 new sts over gap. Turn work, k1, pass final cast-on st over k1. Continue with rest of row according to pattern.

Work garter ridges as follows:
Row 1 (RS): Knit.
Row 2 (WS): Purl.
Rows 3 & 4: Knit.
Repeat Rows 1–4 three more times. This works a garter ridge every 4th row, 4 times.

Change to larger needles. Work even in St st until work measures 3.5" / 9cm from beg, ending by working a RS row.

Next WS row: P27 (29, 31, 33, 35, 37), pm for dart, purl to 6 sts before end, pm for buttonhole band, purl to end. From this point forward, work these 6 sts in garter ridge pattern as for hem, working as garter ridge every 4th row, AT THE SAME TIME as all subsequent instructions.

Work decreases as follows:
Row 1 (RS): Knit to dart marker, sm, k2tog, knit to end.
Rows 2–4: Work even in St st.
Repeat Rows 1–4 another 7 (9, 10, 9, 10, 9) times. 46 (48, 51, 56, 59, 64) sts remain at waist.

Work even in St st for 12 (12, 10, 10, 10, 10) more rows.

Work increases for bust as follows:
Row 1: Knit to dart marker, sm, m1L, knit to end of row.
Rows 2–4: Work even in St st.
Repeat Rows 1–4 another 6 (7, 8, 8, 8, 8) times. 53 (56, 60, 65, 68, 73) sts total at bust.

Work even until Right Front measures 16 (16, 16, 16, 15.5, 15.5)" / 40.5 (40.5, 40.5, 40.5, 39.5, 39.5)cm from cast-on edge, ending with a RS row.

Next WS Row: BO 4 (5, 5, 6, 6, 7) sts at beginning of row, work to end of row, removing both markers as you come to them. 49 (51, 55, 59, 62, 66) sts remain.

From this point forward, armhole shaping and V-neck and collar shaping will be worked AT THE SAME TIME. Begin both on next RS row, working V-neck shaping at beginning of row and armhole shaping at end. Armhole shaping will be completed well before the V-neck / collar work.

Armhole shaping:

Row 1 (RS): Work to 4 sts from end of row, ssk, k2.
Row 2 (WS): Work even.
Repeat Rows 1–2 another 4 (4, 5, 5, 5, 5) times.

V-neck / collar shaping:

Row 1 (RS): P1, kfb, pm, kfb, pm, ssk, knit to end of row.*

Row 2 (WS): Purl to 2 sts before first marker, ssp, sm, purl to second marker, sm, knit to end of row.

Row 3: P1, pfb, pfb, sm, k1, kfb, kfb, sm, ssk, knit to end of row.

Row 4: Purl to 2 sts before first marker, ssp, sm, purl to second marker, sm, knit to knit to end of row.

(3 sts increased each for collar and lapel, 4 sts decreased for V-neck.)

*When viewed with RS facing, sts between the two markers are for collar, sts to the right of the markers are for the lapel which will later be folded back, and sts to the left of the markers are for the body.

Repeat the last 2 rows 2 more times. (7 sts each increased for collar and lapel, 6 sts decreased for V-neck.)

Row 5 (RS): K1, kfb, knit to 1 st before first marker, kfb, sm, k1, kfb, knit to 1 st before second marker, kfb, sm, ssk, knit to end of row. This row creates a garter ridge on the lapel sts, and works a V-neck decrease.

Row 6 (WS): Purl to second marker, sm, knit to end of row.

Row 7 (RS): Purl to first marker, sm, knit to second marker, sm, ssk, knit to end. (Decreases 1 st at V-neck.)

Row 8 (WS): Purl to second marker, sm, knit to end of row.

Repeat Rows 5–8 until there are 15 sts between each pair of markers. Then, repeat Rows 5–8 while only working the increases on the lapel sts (no increases in collar), until there are 21 (21, 21, 23, 23, 25) sts for the lapel.

Cease V-neck decreases when 18 (18, 20, 20, 22, 22) sts remain in body.

Work all sts even, maintaining garter ridges on lapel, until armhole measures 6.5 (7, 7.5, 8, 8.5, 9)" / 16.5 (17.5, 19, 20.5, 21.5, 23)cm from beginning of armhole, ending by working a WS row, then continue to work even in body while working decreases for lapel slope by binding off 7 (7, 7, 8, 8, 8) sts at beginning of next 2 RS rows, then binding off 7 (7, 7, 7, 7, 9) sts at beginning of following RS row. 33 (33, 35, 35, 37, 37) sts remain.

Work 2 rows even, then shape shoulders by continuing to work even and binding off

6 (6, 6, 6, 7, 7) sts at beginning of next WS row, 6 (6, 7, 7, 7, 7) sts at beginning of following WS row, then finally binding off 6 (6, 7, 7, 8, 8) sts at beginning of following WS row. 15 sts remain (all sizes).

Work remaining 15 sts for collar even in stockinette until collar measures 3 (3, 3, 3.5, 4.25, 4.25)" / 7.5 (7.5, 7.5, 9, 11, 11)cm from beginning of collar, then slip all sts to a stitch holder or waste yarn.

Sleeve

With smaller needles, CO 44 (48, 52, 56, 56, 60) sts. Work in garter stitch for 4 rows.

Next, work garter ridges as follows:
Row 1 (RS): Knit.
Row 2 (WS): Purl.
Rows 3 & 4: Knit.
Repeat Rows 1–4 five more times. This works a garter ridge every 4th row, 6 times.

Change to larger needles. Work 2 rows in St st.

Begin increases for sleeve shaping as follows:
Row 1 (RS): K2, m1, knit to 2 sts from end of row, m1, k2. (2 sts increased).
Rows 2–8: Work even in St st.

Repeat Rows 1–6 –(–, –, –, –, 3) more times.

Repeat Rows 1–8 another 8 (8, 9, 10, 12, 11) times. 62 (66, 72, 78, 82, 90) sts total for sleeve at upper arm.

Work even in St st until sleeve measures 17.5 (18, 18.5, 19, 19, 20)" / 44.5 (45.5, 47, 48, 48, 51)cm from cast-on edge, or to desired length of sleeve before sleeve cap.

BO 4 (5, 5, 6, 6, 7) sts at beginning of next 2 rows. 54 (56, 62, 66, 70, 76) sts remain.

Dec 1 st each end of each row, 1 (–, –, 1, –, 1) time. 52 (56, 62, 64, 70, 74) sts remain.

Dec 1 st each end of each RS row, 13 (14, 17, 17, 20, 21) times. 26 (28, 28, 30, 30, 32) sts remain.

BO 2 sts at beginning of next 2 rows. 22 (24, 24, 26, 26, 28) sts remain.
BO 3 sts at beginning of next 2 rows.
BO remaining 16 (18, 18, 20, 20, 22) sts.

Finishing

Block pieces to measurements. Sew shoulder seams.

Collar:

Using 3-needle bind off or Kitchener stitch, attach ends of each collar edge to each other, ensuring any seam is only visible on the WS of work.
Next, sew down edge of collar to back of neck along back piece.

Lapel and button bands:

With RS facing, using long circular needle in smaller size, and starting at bottom hem of Right Front buttonhole band, pick up 2 sts for every 3 rows along edge.
Work next 3 rows in garter stitch.
BO all sts knitwise.

Sew sleeves into armholes. Sew sleeve seams. Sew side seams.

Wash and block completed garment according to fiber content and yarn label instructions.

Judy Henley

Carolyn Noyes

SIZES

Women's size XS (S, M, L, XL, 2X, 3X); shown in size M

Intended to be worn with 1–2" / 2.5–5cm of positive ease in bodice; little or no ease in ribbing.

FINISHED MEASUREMENTS

Bust: 32 (36, 40, 44.5, 48.5, 53, 57)" / 81.5 (91.5, 101.5, 113, 123, 134.5, 144.5)cm

MATERIALS

Quince & Co. Lark (100% wool; 134 yds / 123m per 50g skein); color: Winesap; 8 (9, 10, 10, 12, 13, 13) skeins

32-inch US #6 / 4mm circular needle, or size needed to obtain gauge
32-inch US #5 / 3.75mm circular needle

3 removable stitch markers
8 × ½" / 13mm buttons
Stitch holder or waste yarn
Yarn needle

GAUGE

18 sts and 28 rows = 4" / 10cm in pattern stitch, on larger needle

20 sts and 28 rows = 4" / 10cm in St st, on larger needle

16 rows = 2" / 5cm = 1 point in Zigzag Buttonhole Placket on smaller needle

REQUIRED SKILLS

Knowledge of basic sweater construction; increases/decreases; backward loop cast on; provisional cast on; working simple stitch pattern from written instructions; slipped stitches; picking up stitches; seaming; sewing on buttons

PATTERN NOTES

All pieces are worked flat and seamed in finishing.

Sleeves are provisionally cast on and worked bottom up to cap; then cast-on stitches are placed on the needle to work down for the cuff and placket.

Be sure to realign Zigzag Stitch pattern at beg of each RS row as stitch count changes during armhole decs.

For the Zigzag Buttonhole Placket, row gauge is more important than stitch gauge; the Placket's finished measurement must be 8" / 20.5cm, as the places to beg armhole shaping and to divide the Front piece are based on it. (If you are altering the Front's hem-to-armhole length or the armhole depth, be aware that it may affect placket placement). Adjust needle size if necessary to obtain stated row gauge for the placket.

When picking up sts for the neckband, the first 4 sts should occur halfway down the sloped edge of the Placket's first point to prevent any gap between the Right and Left Front bands.

With a nod to the classic styles of the 1950s, this design was inspired as much by one of Hitchcock's female leads (Kim Novak playing both Judy and Madeleine) as the film in which she appears, Vertigo.

From the bodice's garter zigzag stitch pattern that recalls that jagged feeling of true vertigo to the fitted ribbings and rich red colorway, the Zigzag Henley blends vintage elements with a contemporary silhouette for a sweater with everyday and work-worthy appeal.

Slipstitch Rib
(Worked flat over multiple of 5 sts plus 2)
Row 1 (WS): K2, [p3, k2] to end.
Row 2 (RS): P2, [sl wyib, k1, sl wyib, p2] to end.
Repeat Rows 1 & 2 to desired measurement.

Zigzag Garter Stitch
(Worked flat over multiple of 6 sts and 12 rows)
Row 1 and all WS rows: Purl.
Row 2 (RS): [K3, p3] to end.
Row 4: P1, [k3, p3] to last 2 sts, p2.
Row 6: P2, [k3, p3] to last st, p1.
Row 8: [P3, k3] to end.
Row 10: P2, [k3, p3] to last st, p1.
Row 12: P1, [k3, p3] to last 2 sts, p2.

Zigzag Buttonhole Placket
(16 rows = 1 point)
Row 1: K1, kfb, k1.
Row 2: K1, kfb, k2.
Row 3: K3, kfb, k1.
Row 4: K1, kfb, k4.
Row 5: K5, kfb, k1.
Row 6: K1, kfb, k6.
Row 7: K7, kfb, k1.
Row 8 (buttonhole row): K1, kfb, k1, yo, k2tog, k5.
11 sts.
Row 9: K8, k2tog, k1.
Row 10: K1, k2tog, k7.
Row 11: K6, k2tog, k1.
Row 12: K1, k2tog, k5.
Row 13: K4, k2tog, k1.
Row 14: K1, k2tog, k3.
Row 15: K2, k2tog, k1.
Row 16: K1, k2tog, k1.

PATTERN

Back

With larger needle, CO 67 (77, 87, 97, 107, 117, 127) sts. Work in Slipstitch Rib for 5.5 (5.5, 6, 6, 6, 6, 6)" / 14 (14, 15, 15, 15, 15, 15)cm, ending by working a WS row.

Next row (RS): Knit all the previously slipped sts while inc 5 (7, 9, 5, 7, 3, 5) sts evenly across row. 72 (84, 96, 102, 114, 120, 132) sts.

Change to Zigzag Garter Stitch and work until piece measures 14 (14, 14.5, 14.5, 14.75, 14.75, 14.75)" / 35.5 (35.5, 37, 37, 37.5, 37.5, 37.5)cm, ending by working a RS row.

Shape armhole:

BO 4 (4, 5, 5, 6, 6, 7) sts at beg of next 2 rows. 64 (76, 86, 92, 102, 108, 118) sts.

Dec 1 st each end every other row 1 (5, 7, 8, 11, 11, 14) times. 62 (66, 72, 76, 80, 86, 90) sts.

Beg and end each RS row with k1, work even for 7 (7.5, 8.25, 8.5, 9, 9.75, 10.25)" / 17.5 (19, 21, 21.5, 22.5, 24.5, 26)cm, ending by working a RS row.

Shape neck and shoulders:

Work 21 (22, 25, 26, 27, 29, 31) sts, drop yarn, sl 20 (22, 22, 24, 26, 28, 28) sts to a stitch holder. With a second ball of yarn, work rem 21 (22, 25, 26, 27, 29, 31) sts.

Next row: Working both sides at once, dec 1 st each neck edge every row 1 (2, 2, 3, 3, 2, 3) times. AT THE SAME TIME, BO 6 (6, 7, 7, 8, 9, 10) sts in patt each armhole edge, then BO 7 (7, 8, 8, 8, 9, 9) sts at each edge, twice.

Buttonhole placket:

With smaller needle, CO 3 sts. Setup row: knit. Work Zigzag Buttonhole Placket 4 times total. Knit 1 row. BO knitwise. Lightly block and measure length. Use as a reference when working Front.

Front—Sizes XS (S, M, L, XL)

Work as for Back until piece measures 11.25 (11.5, 12.5, 12.5, 13.25)" / 28.5 (29, 31.5, 31.5, 33.5)cm, ending by working a WS row. 72 (84, 96, 102, 114) sts.

Divide front:

Next RS row: Work in patt for 37 (43, 49, 52, 58) sts, BO3, work in patt to end. Left Front 37 (43, 49, 52, 58) sts; Right Front 32 (38, 44, 47, 53) sts.

Next WS row: Working both Fronts at once, purl across Right Front, drop yarn when reaching bound-off sts. With another ball of yarn, using the backward loop method, CO 2 sts to left needle; purl these and all sts of Left Front to end. Left Front 39 (45, 51, 54, 60) sts.

Next RS row: Pm 2 sts in from each Front placket edge; work these placket sts in garter stitch.

AT THE SAME TIME, when Fronts measure 14 (14, 14.5, 14.5, 14.75)" / 35.5 (35.5, 37, 37, 37.5)cm, beg armhole shaping:

Next WS row: Working both Fronts at once, BO 4 (4, 5, 5, 6) sts at beg of next 2 rows. Left Front 35 (41, 46, 49, 54) sts; Right Front 28 (34, 39, 42, 47) sts.

Purl 1 row.

Next RS row: Dec 1 st each armhole edge every RS row 1 (5, 7, 8, 11) total times. Left Front 34 (36, 39, 41, 43) sts; Right Front 27 (29, 32, 34, 36) sts.

Continuing to work the 2 placket sts on each Front in garter stitch, work even until placket opening measures 8" / 20.5cm, ending by working a RS row.

Place Right Front sts on holder. Continue to Left Front.

Front—Sizes 2X (3X)

Work as for Back until piece measures 14.75" / 37.5cm, ending by working a WS row. Beg armhole shaping. BO 6 (7) sts at beg of next 2 rows. 108 (118) sts.

Next RS row: Dec 1 st each end every RS row 1 (3) total times. 106 (112) sts.

Work 1 row even.

Divide front:

Next RS row: K1, ssk, work in patt for 51 (54) sts, BO 3, work in patt to last 3 sts, k2tog, k1. Left Front 53 (56) sts; Right Front 48 (51) sts.

Next WS row: Working both Fronts at once, purl across Right Front, drop yarn when reaching the bound off sts. With another ball of yarn, using the backward loop method, CO 2 sts to left needle, purl these and all sts of Left Front to end. Left Front 55 (58) sts.

Pm 2 sts in from each Front placket edge; work these placket sts in garter st.

Next RS row: Dec 1 st each armhole edge every RS row 9 (10) total times. Left Front 46 (48) sts; Right Front 39 (41) sts.

Continuing to work the 2 placket sts on each Front in garter stitch, work even until placket opening measures 8" / 20.5cm, ending by working a RS row.

Place Right Front sts on holder.

Left Front

Shape neckline:

With WS facing, BO 9 (9, 10, 10, 10, 10, 10) sts at neck edge, work in patt to end. 25 (27, 29, 31, 33, 36, 38) sts.

Next rows: Dec 1 st at neck edge every row 5 (7, 6, 8, 9, 9, 10) total times. 20 (20, 23, 23, 24, 27, 28) sts.

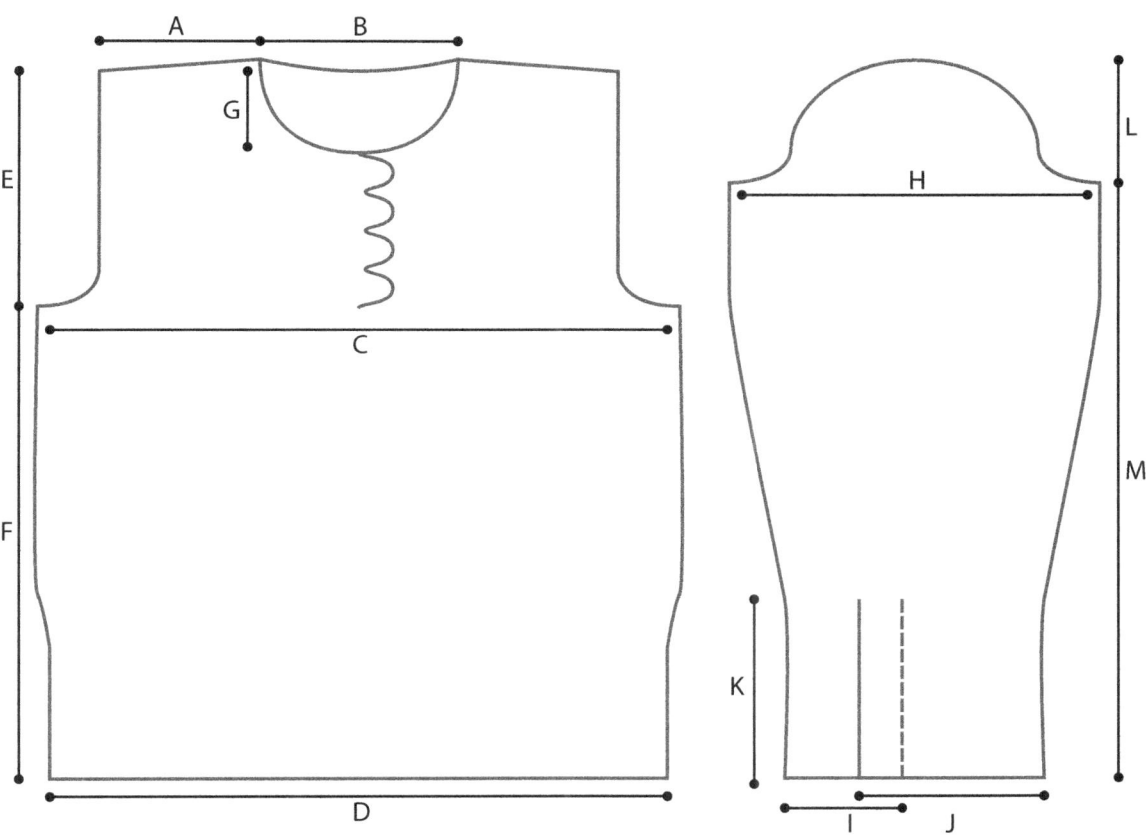

A: 4.5 (4.5, 5, 5, 5.25, 6, 6)"
B: 4.5 (4.5, 5, 6, 6.25, 6.25, 6.5)"
C: 16 (18, 20.25, 22, 24.25, 26.5, 28.5)"
D: 15 (17, 19.5, 21.5, 23.5, 26, 28)"
E: 7 (7.5, 8.25, 8.5, 9, 9.75, 10.25)"
F: 14 (14, 14.5, 14.5, 14.75, 14.75, 14.75)"
G: 2 (2, 2.25, 2.5, 2.5, 2.5, 2.5)"

H: 11.25 (12.5, 13.25, 14.75, 16, 17.5, 18.5)"
I: 3.5 (3.5, 4.5, 4.5, 5.5, 5.5, 6.5)"
J: 5.75 (5.75, 6.25, 6.25, 7.25, 7.25, 8.25)"
K: 3" (all sizes)
L: 5.75 (6.25, 6.75, 6.75, 7.25, 7, 7.25)"
M: 12.5 (12.5, 13, 13, 13, 13, 13)"

Work even until armhole measures 7 (7.5, 8.25, 8.5, 9, 9.75, 10.25)" / 17.5 (19, 21, 21.5, 22.5, 24.5, 26)cm, ending by working a WS row.

Shape shoulder:

Next row: BO 6 (6, 7, 7, 8, 9, 10) sts at armhole edge, work in patt to end.

Work 1 row as est.

Next row: BO 7 (7, 8, 8, 8, 9, 9) sts at armhole edge. Repeat last 2 rows.

Right Front

Shape neckline:

With WS facing, place sts back on needle and work 1 row as est.

Next row: BO 3 (3, 4, 4, 4, 4, 4) sts at neck edge, work in patt as established to end. 24 (26, 28, 30, 32, 35, 37) sts.

Next rows: Dec 1 st at neck edge every row 4 (6, 5, 7, 8, 8, 9) total times. 20 (20, 23, 23, 24, 27, 28) sts.

Work even until armhole measures 7 (7.5, 8.25, 8.5, 9, 9.75, 10.25)" / 17.5 (19, 21, 21.5, 22.5, 24.5, 26)cm, ending by working a RS row.

Shape shoulder:

Work as for Left Front.

Sleeves

With larger needle, using a provisional method, CO 42 (42, 48, 54, 58, 62, 66) sts and purl 1 row. Next RS row: Inc 1 st each end this and every 8 (6, 7, 6, 6, 5, 5) rows 7 (10, 9, 10, 11, 13, 13) total times. 56 (62, 66, 74, 80, 88, 92) sts.

Work even until piece measures 9.5 (9.5, 10, 10, 10, 10, 10)" / 23 (23. 25.5, 25.5, 25.5, 25.5, 25.5)cm.

Shape cap:

BO 4 (4, 5, 5, 6, 6, 7) sts at beg of next 2 rows. Dec 1 st each end every 2nd (2nd, 2nd, 2nd, 2nd, 1, 1) row, 5 (9, 7, 22, 23, 4, 3) times, then every 3rd (3rd, 3rd, –, 1, 2nd, 2nd) row, 6 (2, 6, –, 1, 19, 22) times, then every 2nd (2nd, 2nd, –, –, 1, 1) row, 5 (8, 6, –, –, 4, 3) times. BO rem 16 (16, 18, 20, 20, 22, 22) sts loosely.

Left cuff:

With RS facing, place live sts from provisional CO onto larger needle. Join a ball of yarn to right edge, k25 (25, 27, 32, 32, 37, 37), pm, using backward loop method CO 4 sts to right needle to make placket. Drop yarn. Join another ball of yarn to first st on left needle. Using backward loop method, CO – (–, 1, –, 1, 2, 3) sts. Knit across new sts and rem 17 (17, 21, 22, 26, 25, 29) sts. Right Side 29 (29, 31, 36, 36, 41, 41) sts; Left Side 17 (17, 22, 22, 27, 27, 32) sts.

Sizes XS and S only:

Next WS row: Work Row 1 of Slipstitch Rib, drop yarn. With other yarn strand work 4 placket sts in St st, sm, work in Slipstitch Rib starting with p3 and ending with k2.

All other sizes:

Next WS row: Work Row 1 of Slipstitch Rib, drop yarn. With other yarn strand, work 4 placket sts in St st, sm, work in Slipstitch Rib to end.

All sizes:

Next rows: Working both sides at once, and slipping first st of placket wyif on WS rows, work as established until cuff measures 1.25" / 3cm, ending by working a WS row.

Next RS row: Work as established to m, sm. Make buttonhole on 4-st placket edge: k2tog, yo, k2. Work other side in patt to end. Work 7 rows in Slipstitch Rib and St st placket, ending by working a WS row.

Next row: Repeat buttonhole row.

Work 3 rows in Slipstitch Rib, ending by working a WS. BO in patt, knitting all previously slipped sts.

Right cuff:

With RS facing, place live sts from provisional cast on onto larger needle. Join a ball of yarn to right edge k17 (17, 21, 22, 26, 25, 29), then using backward loop method CO – (–, 1, –, 1, 2, 3) sts to right needle. Drop yarn. Join another ball of yarn to first st on left needle and, using backward loop method, CO 4 sts to make placket. Knit across new sts, pm, k25 (25, 27, 32, 32, 37, 37) sts. Right Side 17

(17, 22, 22, 27, 27, 32) sts; Left Side 29 (29, 31, 36, 36, 41, 41) sts.

Sizes XS and S only:

Next WS row: Beginning with p3 and ending with k2, work Row 1 of Slipstitch Rib to m, sm, work 4 placket sts in St st, drop yarn. With other yarn strand, work in Slipstitch Rib to end.

All other sizes:

Next WS row: Work Row 1 of Slipstitch Rib to m, sm, work 4 placket sts in St st, drop yarn. With other yarn strand, work in Slipstitch Rib to end.

All sizes:

Next rows: Working both sides at once and slipping first st of placket wyib on RS rows, work as established until cuff measures 1.25" / 3cm, ending by working a WS row.

Next row: Work right side of cuff in patt to end. Make buttonhole on 4-st placket edge: Sl 1, k1, yo, k2tog, sm, work in Slipstitch Rib to end. Work 7 rows in Slipstitch Rib and St st placket, ending by working a WS row.

Next RS row: Repeat buttonhole row.

Work 3 rows in Slipstitch Rib, ending by working a WS. BO in patt, knitting all previously slipped sts.

Finishing

Block bodice ribbing aggressively to measurement; lightly block other pieces. Sew bottom of Buttonhole Placket to the 3-st bind off edge of Right Front; sew straight edge of Buttonhole Placket to Right Front opening. Sew buttons onto Left Front. Sew shoulder seams.

With smaller needle and RS facing, beg at top edge of Zigzag Placket, pick up 12 (12, 12, 12, 12, 12, 12) sts across right front, 2 (4, 4, 5, 6, 6, 6) sts along sloped edge of right front, 7 (6, 7, 7, 6, 6, 6) sts to right shoulder seam, 3 (3, 4, 4, 4, 4, 5) sts to meet back neck sts, knit across 20 (21, 22, 24, 26, 28, 28) sts from holder, pick up 3 (3, 4, 4, 4, 4, 5) sts to back left shoulder seam, 7 (6, 7, 7, 6, 6, 6) sts along straight edge of left front, 2 (4, 4, 5, 6, 6, 6) sts along sloped edge of left front, 8 (8, 9, 9, 9, 10, 10) sts to end. 60 (63, 69, 73, 75, 78, 80) sts.

Next WS row: Knit.
Next RS row: Purl.
Repeat these 2 rows 1 more time. BO knitwise.

Sew horizontal edge of cuff placket to cuff; sew on buttons. Sew sleeve into armhole, easing to fit. Sew side and sleeve seams. Weave in ends.

Stolen Jewels Mitts

Stephannie Tallent

SIZES

Women's S (M, L); shown in size M

FINISHED MEASUREMENTS

Palm circumference: 6.5 (7, 7.75)" / 16.5 (18, 20)cm

MATERIALS

Shibui Staccato (70% superwash merino, 30% silk; 191 yds /175m per 50g skein); color: Abyss; 1 skein

US #1 / 2.25mm needles, or size to obtain gauge
US #0 / 2.0mm, or one size smaller than main needle

- For both needle sizes, your choice of magic loop, 2 circulars or dpns for circular knitting.

Crochet hook for beading (I used a Chiao Goo #14 / 0.8mm hook)

3 stitch markers
Waste yarn or extra circular needle for provisional cast on
Yarn needle

Beads (Size 6/0)

- [Color A] 110 beads
- [Color B] 26 beads

GAUGE

30 sts and 48 rounds = 4" / 10cm in St st, on larger needle

REQUIRED SKILLS

Knitting in the round; beading; provisional cast on; working bead placement from chart; sewn hem

STITCHES AND TECHNIQUES

How to Hook Beads

- Work up to the stitch that will have a bead.
- Place the bead onto the crochet hook.
- Grab the stitch on the left hand needle with the hook. I pull tightly so that the yarn is as snug as possible against the crochet hook.
- Pull the bead over the yarn. You should have a loop of yarn – the stitch – sticking out of the bead.
- Replace the stitch onto the left hand needle. The bead is sitting below the knitting needle.
- Knit the stitch.

PATTERN

Picot Hem

With smaller needles, provisionally CO 46 (50, 56) sts. Join in the round, being careful not to twist. Pm for beginning of round. Knit 6 rounds.

Note: if it's easier for you, knit 1 row, purl 1 row, knit 1 row, join in the round, knit 3 more rounds (6 rows/rounds total), then proceed to the picot round. You can simply seam the edges when finishing the cuff.

Change to larger needles.
Picot round: [Yo, k2tog] to end.

Work 6 more rounds in St st.

Hem round: Place sts from provisional cast on onto a spare needle. Fold hem with wrong sides together,

These lovely fingerless mitts have just enough bling to suit Kim Novak as Madeleine in Vertigo. *I can't get that image of her in that white coat with the black gloves out of my mind, but I wanted to make something a little easier to wear.*

spare needle behind working needle. [K1 from front needle tog with 1 st from back needle] to end.

Next round: K15, rli, knit to end. 47 (51, 57) sts.

Cuff

Rounds 1–29: Work chart over 31 sts, knit to end.

Beading is completed; the remainder of the mitt is worked in St st.

Body of Mitt

Right mitt: K28 (29, 32) sts, pm for gusset, k2, pm for gusset, knit to end.

Left mitt: K1 (0, 55) sts, pm for gusset, k2, pm for gusset, knit to end.
Note: this placement of the left thumb gusset mirrors the placement of the right. For size M mitt, beginning-of-round marker can double as the beginning-of-gusset marker. For size L mitt, beginning-of-round marker can double as the end-of-gusset marker.

Both mitts:

Round 1: Work to 1st thumb gusset marker, sm, rli, knit to 2nd thumb gusset marker, lli, sm. Knit to end of round.

Rounds 2 & 3: Work in established pattern, knitting sts between gusset markers.

Repeat above 3 rounds until you have 18 (18, 20) sts between gusset markers, finishing on a Round 3.

Next round: Knit to thumb gusset marker, remove gusset marker, k1, place 16 (16, 18) thumb sts on waste yarn, CO 2 sts using backward loop method, k1, remove next gusset marker, knit to end. 49 (53, 59) sts.

Knit 15 rounds.

Top Cuff

Work 7 rounds of garter stitch, beginning with a purl round.

BO knitwise.

Thumb

Place held sts on larger needles. Pick up 4 sts along cast on. Join to work in the round, pm. 20 (20, 22) sts.

Knit 3 rounds.
Work 5 rounds of garter stitch, beginning with a purl round.

BO knitwise.

Finishing

Weave in loose ends. Block.

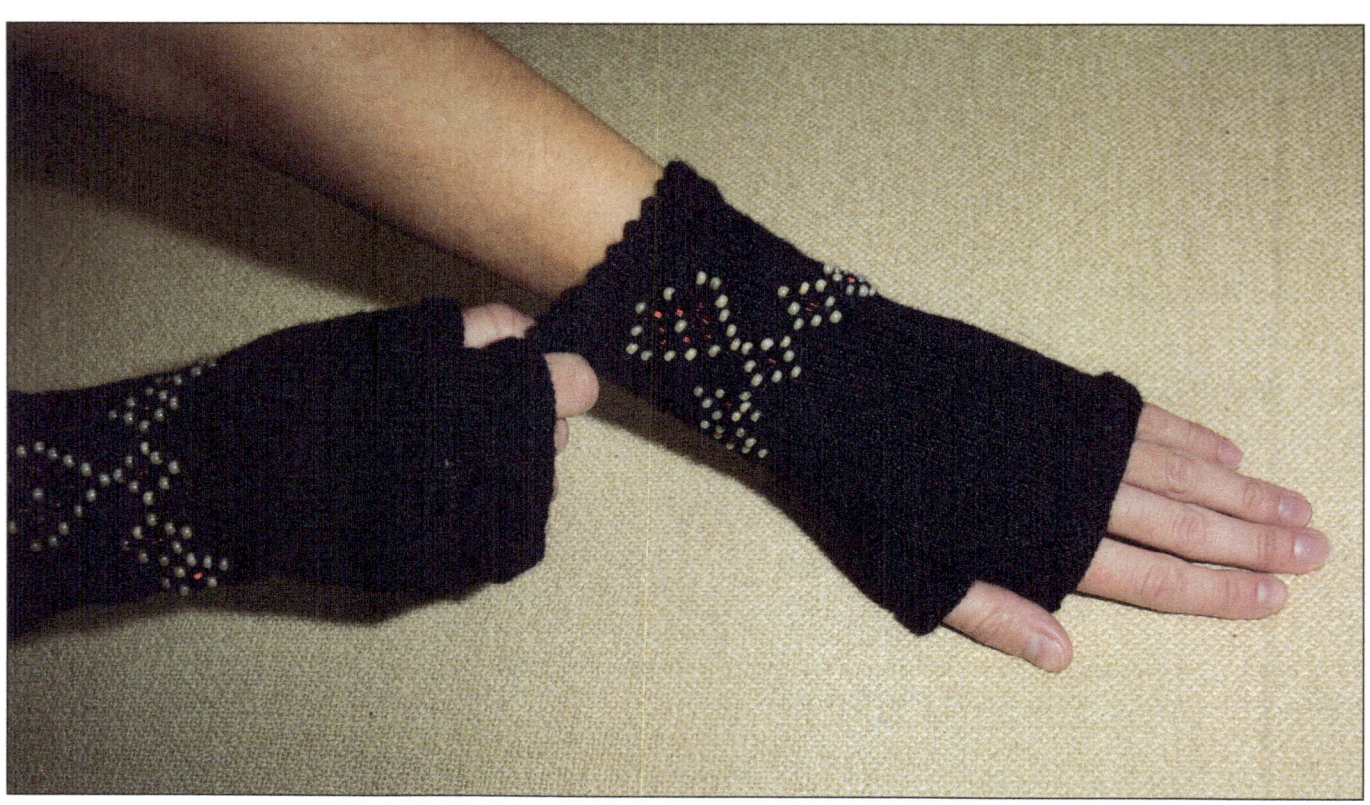

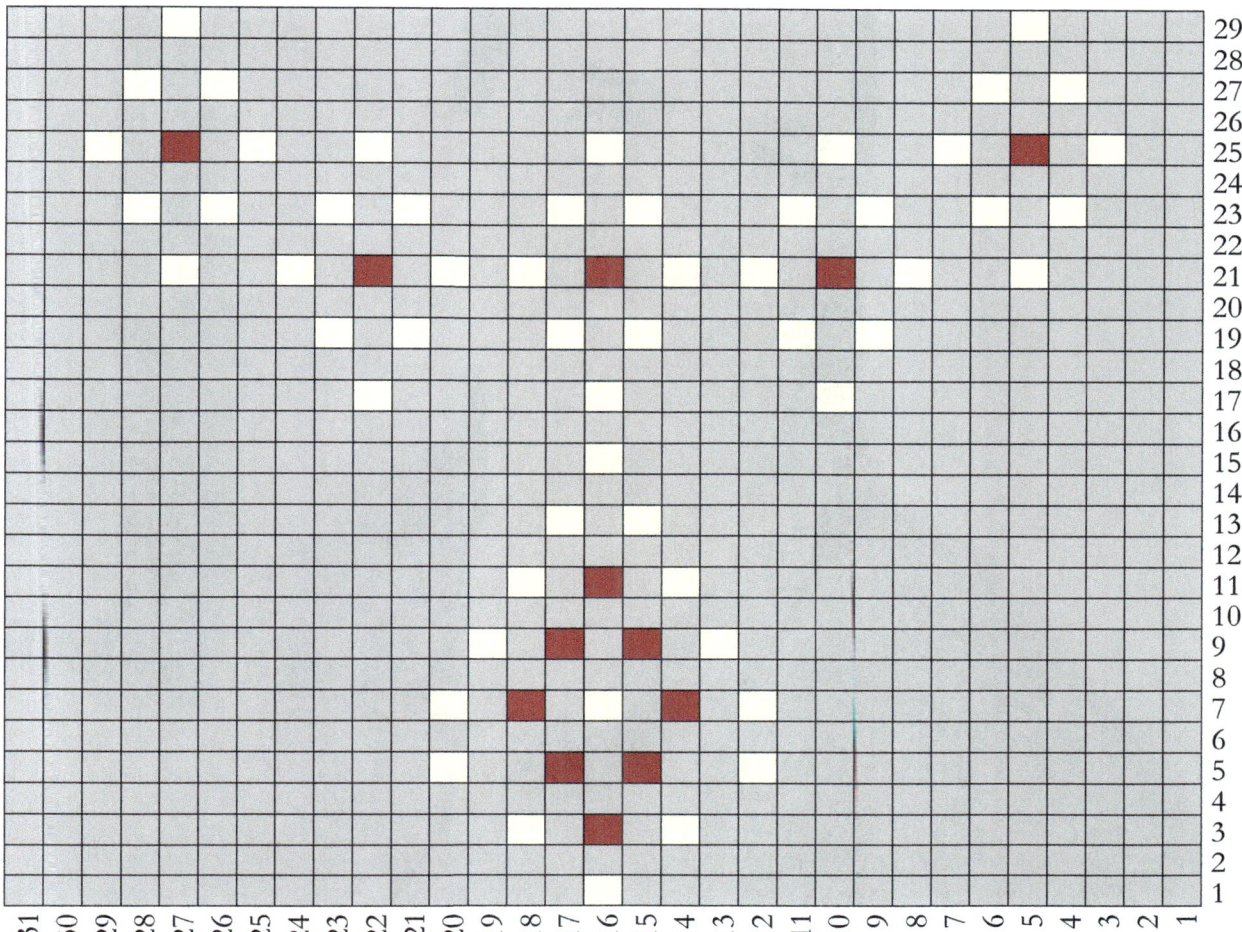

Yarn color: Abyss
Place bead: Color A
Place bead: Color B

Our Gal Midge Sweater

Karin Wilmoth

SIZES

Women's XS (S, M, L, XL, 2X, 3X); shown in size M
Garment designed to be worn with 3" / 7.5cm
positive ease.

FINISHED MEASUREMENTS

Bust: 33.5 (37.75, 41, 45, 49.25, 52.75, 56.75)" /
85 (96, 104, 114.5, 125, 134, 144)cm

Length: 20.75 (20.75, 21, 21.25, 21.75, 22.5, 23)" /
52.5 (52.5, 53.5, 54, 55, 57, 58.5)cm

MATERIALS

The Woolen Rabbit Opal Light Sport weight (75%
merino / 15% silk / 10% cashmere; 400 yds / 373.5m
per 115g skein); color: Grey Goose; 3 (3, 4, 4, 4, 5, 5)
skeins or 1025 (1150, 1350, 1500, 1650, 1825, 2000)
yds / 940 (1050, 1235, 1375, 1510, 1670, 1830)m

32-inch US 4 / 3.5mm circular needle; or size needed
to obtain gauge
1 set US 4 / 3.5mm dpns (or 9-inch circular needle)
32-inch US 3 / 3.25mm circular needle
1 set US 3 / 3.25mm dpns (or 9-inch circular needle)

6 stitch markers
8 × ½" / 13mm buttons
Waste yarn for holding sleeve stitches
Yarn needle

Strip of contrasting fabric, measuring 13.75 (13.75,
13.75, 14, 14.5, 14.75, 15.25)" × 2" / 34.5 (34.5, 34.5,
35.5, 37, 37.5, 38.5)cm × 5cm

Sewing thread to match fabric
Sewing needle

GAUGE

26 sts and 32 rows = 4" / 10cm (gauge for shoulder
rows only: 28 rows = 4" / 10cm) in St st, on larger
needle

REQUIRED SKILLS

Knitting in the round; increases/decreases; knitted
cast on; picking up stitches; sewing on buttons

PATTERN

Yoke

Using larger needles, CO 42 (42, 45, 47, 52, 57, 62)
sts.

Setup row: P1 (left front sts), pm (left front marker),
p2 (shoulder sts), pm (shoulder marker), p6, pm
(back shaping marker), p24 (24, 27, 29, 34, 39,
44), pm (back shaping marker), p6, pm (shoulder
marker), p2 (shoulder sts), pm (right front marker),
p1 (right front sts).

Begin shoulder shaping:

Row 1: Knit to 1 st before m, kfb, sm, k2, sm, kfb,
knit to back shaping marker, sm, kfb, knit to 1 st
before back shaping marker, kfb, sm, knit to 1 st
before next marker, kfb, sm, k2, sm, kfb, knit to end.

In Vertigo, *Barbara Bel Geddes plays the part of Midge, the gal-next-door. Her intelligent, comfortable
manner inspired this one-piece, top-down, three-quarter-sleeve polo shirt.*

*Worked in DK-weight yarn, this everyday-wear sweater has an unusual construction—the Contiguous method.
With this method you increase at the top of the shoulder every row until the desired shoulder width is reached,
giving the perfect fit. This also creates the look of a set-in sleeve without seaming. A strip of fabric on the
button band adds a pop of color, while glass buttons add a bit of drama to an otherwise simple sweater.*

Row 2: Purl to 1 st before m, pbf, sm, p2, sm, pbf, purl to 1 st before shoulder m, pbf, sm, p2, sm, pbf, purl to end.

Repeat last 2 rows 3 more times. Remove back shaping markers on last row. 9 sts each front; 60 (60, 63, 65, 70, 75, 80) sts in back; 2 sts each shoulder.

Continue shoulder shaping and begin neck shaping:

Row 1: K1, [kfb, knit to 1 st before m, kfb, sm, k2, sm] twice, kfb, knit to last 2 sts, kfb, k1

Row 2: [Purl to 1 st before m, pbf, sm, p2, sm, pbf] twice, purl to end. Repeat last 2 rows 2 (1, 2, 2, 2, 2, 2) more time(s). 18 (15, 18, 18, 18, 18, 18) sts each front; 72 (68, 75, 77, 82, 87, 92) sts in back; 2 sts each shoulder.

Row 3: K1, [kfb, knit to 1 st before m, kfb, sm, k2, sm] twice, kfb, knit to last 2 sts, kfb, k1

Row 4: P1, [pbf, purl to 1 st before m, pbf, sm, p2, sm] twice, pbf, purl to last 2 sts, pbf, p1. Repeat last 2 rows 1 (1, 1, 1, 1, 2, 2) more time. 26 (23, 26, 26, 26, 30, 30) sts each front; 80 (76, 83, 85, 90, 99, 104) sts in back; 2 sts each shoulder.

Size XS only:
Skip to sleeve shaping and neck shaping.

Sizes S, M L, XL, 2X, & 3X:
Row 5: KCO3 (see Abbreviations & Techniques), [knit to 1 st before m, kfb, sm, k2, kfb] twice, knit to end.

Row 6: KCO3, [purl to 1 st before m, pbf, sm, p2, sm, pbf] twice, purl to end.

Repeat last 2 rows twice more.

Row 7: KCO 6, [knit to 1 st before m, kfb, sm, k2, sm, kfb] twice, knit to end.

Row 8: KCO 6, [purl to 1 st before m, pbf, sm, p2, sm, pbf] twice, purl to end. – (46, 49, 49, 49, 53, 53) sts each front; – (92, 99, 101, 106, 115, 120) sts in back; 2 sts each shoulder.

Begin sleeve shaping and neck shaping:

Size XS only:
Row 1: KCO3, [knit to 3 sts before m, kfb, pm, k1, kfb, rm, k2, rm, kfb, k1, pm, kfb] twice, knit to end.

Rows 2 & 4: KCO3, [purl to 1 st before m, pbf, sm, p1, pbf, purl to 2 sts before m, pbf, p1, sm, pbf] twice, purl to end.

Rows 3 & 5: KCO3, [knit to 1 st before m, kfb, sm, k1, kfb, knit to 2 sts before m, kfb, k1, sm, kfb] twice, knit to end.

Row 6: KCO3, purl to m, sm, p1, pbf, purl to 2 sts before m, pbf, p1, sm, pbf, purl to 1 st before m, pbf, sm, p1, pbf, purl to 2 sts before m, pbf, p1, sm purl to end.

Row 7: KCO6, [knit to 1 st before m, kfb, sm, k1, kfb, knit to 2 sts before m, kfb, k1, sm, kfb] twice, knit to end.

Row 8: KCO6, [purl to m, sm, p1, pbf, purl to 2 sts before m, pbf, p1, sm] twice, purl to end. [XS only: 45 sts each front; 90 sts in back; 22 sts each sleeve]

Sizes S, M L, XL, 2X, & 3X:
Row 1: [Knit to 3 sts before m, kfb, pm, k1, kfb, rm, k2, rm, kfb, k1, pm, kfb] twice, knit to end.

Rows 2 and 4: [Purl to 1 st before m, pbf, sm, p1, pbf, purl to 2 sts before m, pbf, p1, sm, pbf] twice, purl to end.

Row 3: [Knit to 1 st before m, kfb, k1, kfb, knit to 2 sts before m, kfb, k1, kfb] twice, knit to end. – (48, 51, 51, 51, 55, 55) sts each front; – (96, 103, 105, 110, 119, 124) sts in back; 14 sts each sleeve.

Continue sleeve and body shaping:

All sizes:
Row 1: [Knit to 1 st before m, kfb, sm, k1, kfb, knit to 2 sts before m, kfb, k1, sm, kfb] twice, knit to end.

Row 2: [Purl to m, sm, p1, pbf, purl to 2 sts before m, pbf, p1, sm] twice, purl to end.

Repeat last 2 rows 0 (4, 3, 7, 12, 11, 15) more times. 46 (53, 55, 59, 64, 67, 71) sts each front; 92 (106, 111, 121, 136, 143, 156) sts in back; 26 (34, 30, 46, 66, 62, 78) sts each sleeve.

Sizes M, L, XL, 2X, & 3X only:
Row 3: [Knit to 1 st before m, kfb, sm, k1, kfb, knit to 2 sts before m, kfb, k1, sm, kfb] twice, knit to end.

Row 4: Purl.

Repeat last 2 rows – (–, 2, 6, 7, 9, 8) more times.

Sizes XS, S, M L, XL, 2X only:
Row 5: Knit to m, sm, k1, kfb, knit to 2 sts before m, kfb, k1, sm, kfb, knit to 1 st before m, kfb, sm, k1, kfb, knit to 2 sts before m, kfb, k1, sm, knit to end.

Row 6: Purl.

Repeat last 2 rows 2 (4, 3, 1, 0, 0, –) more times. 46 (53, 58, 66, 72, 77, 80) sts each front; 98 (116, 125, 139, 154, 165, 174) sts in back; 32 (44, 44, 64, 82, 84, 96) sts each sleeve.

Continue sleeve increases:

All sizes:
Row 1: [Knit to m, sm, kfb, knit to 1 st before m, kfb, sm] twice, knit to end.

Row 2: Purl.

Repeat last 2 rows 16 (13, 17, 8, 8, 9, 4) more times. 46 (53, 58, 66, 72, 77, 80) sts each front; 98 (116, 125, 139, 154, 165, 174) sts in back; 66 (72, 80, 82, 100, 104, 106) sts each sleeve.

Work 0 (2, 2, 2, 12, 0, 10) rows in St st.

Work body and underarm shaping:

Sizes XS, S, M, XL, & 2X only:
Row 1: [Knit to 1 st before m, kfb, sm, knit to m, sm, kfb] twice, knit to end.

Row 2: Purl.

Repeat last 2 rows 4 (4, 4, –, 4, 4, –) more times.

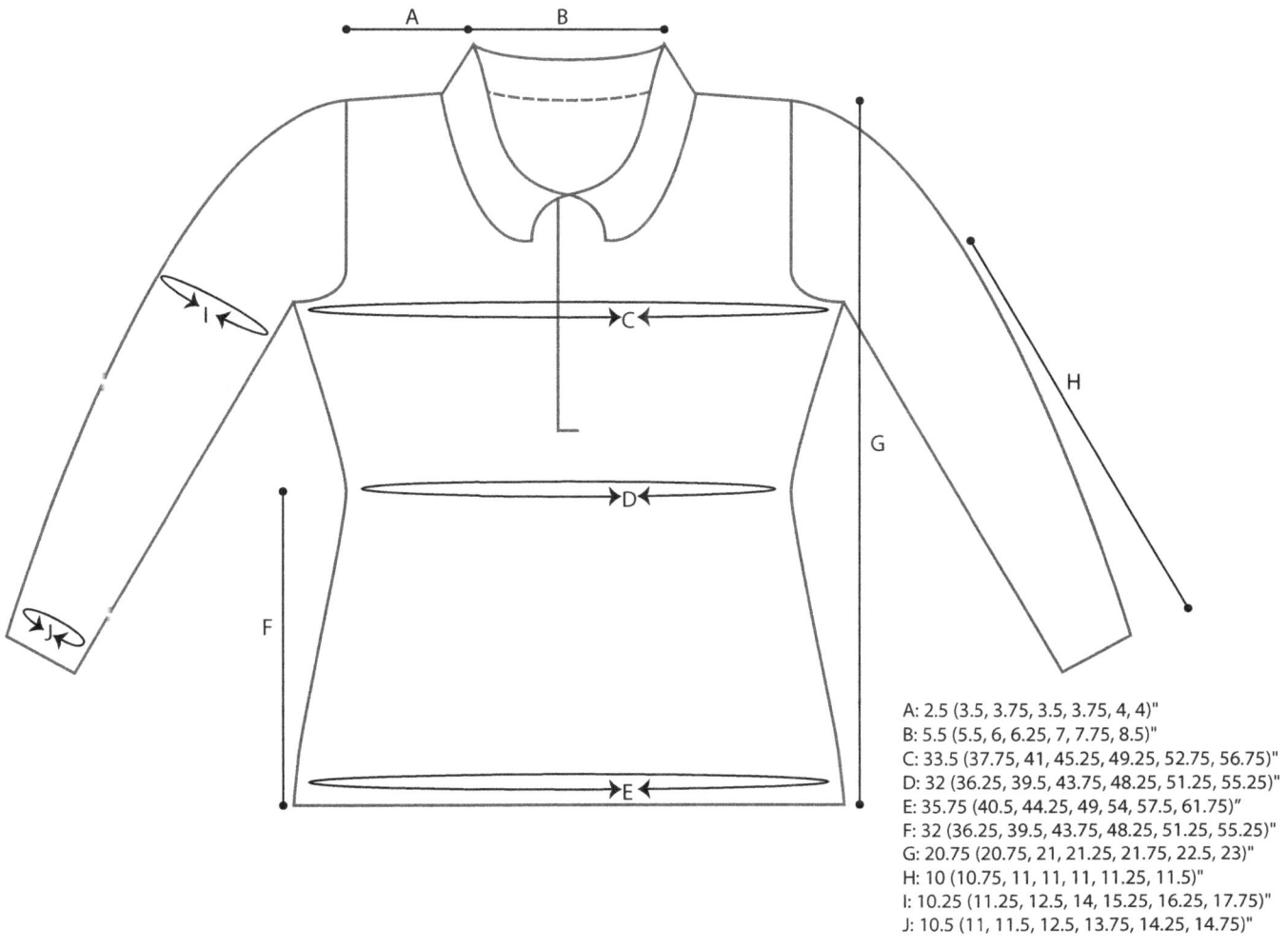

A: 2.5 (3.5, 3.75, 3.5, 3.75, 4, 4)"
B: 5.5 (5.5, 6, 6.25, 7, 7.75, 8.5)"
C: 33.5 (37.75, 41, 45.25, 49.25, 52.75, 56.75)"
D: 32 (36.25, 39.5, 43.75, 48.25, 51.25, 55.25)"
E: 35.75 (40.5, 44.25, 49, 54, 57.5, 61.75)"
F: 32 (36.25, 39.5, 43.75, 48.25, 51.25, 55.25)"
G: 20.75 (20.75, 21, 21.25, 21.75, 22.5, 23)"
H: 10 (10.75, 11, 11, 11, 11.25, 11.5)"
I: 10.25 (11.25, 12.5, 14, 15.25, 16.25, 17.75)"
J: 10.5 (11, 11.5, 12.5, 13.75, 14.25, 14.75)"

Sizes L & 3X only:
Row 1: [Knit to 1 st before m, kfb, sm, k1, kfb, knit to 2 sts before m, kfb, k1, sm, kfb] twice, knit to end.

Row 2: Purl.

Repeat last 2 rows – (–, –, 4, –, –, 4) more times. 51 (58, 63, 71, 77, 82, 85) sts each front; 108 (126, 135, 149, 164, 175 184) sts in back; 66 (72, 80, 92, 102, 104, 116) sts each sleeve.

Lower Body

Divide for sleeves:

All sizes:
Row 1: [Knit to m, rm, place sleeve sts on waste yarn, KCO 10 sts (placing a marker after 5 sts)] twice, knit to end. 56 (63, 68, 76, 82, 87, 90) sts each front; 118 (136, 145, 159, 174, 185, 194) sts in back.

Row 2: Purl.

Work 3 (5, 5, 4, 3, 3, 4) rows in St st.

Begin waist shaping:

Decrease Row: [Knit to 3 sts before m, ssk, k2, k2tog] twice, knit to end.

Repeat Decrease Row every 12 (10, 9, 8, 8, 8, 8)th St st row, 3 more times. 52 (59, 64, 72, 78, 83, 86) sts each front; 110 (128, 137, 151, 166, 177, 186) sts in back.

Work 11 (9, 8, 7, 7, 7, 7) rows in St st.

Begin working in the round:

KCO6, join, and pm for beginning of round. 110 (124, 134, 150, 162, 172, 178) sts in front; 110 (128, 137, 151, 166, 177, 186) sts in back.

Work 7 (7, 8, 8, 8, 9, 9) rounds in St st.

Begin hip shaping:

Increase Round: [Knit to 2 sts before side m, kfb, k1, sm, k1, kfb] twice, knit to end.

Repeat Increase Round every 9 (7, 9, 7, 6, 6, 5)th St st round, 3 (4, 3, 4, 5, 5, 7) more times. 118 (134, 142, 160, 174, 184, 194) sts in front; 118 (138, 145, 161, 178, 189, 202) sts in back.

Work 8 (6, 8, 6, 5, 5, 4) rounds in St st.

Work in St st until garment measures 5.5 (5.5, 5.75, 5.75, 5.75, 5, 5.25)" / 14 (14, 14.5, 14.5, 14.5, 12.5, 13.5)cm from beginning of rounds.

Remove center front m. Change to smaller needle.

Work in St st to next side marker; side marker is now the beginning of round marker.

Work 10 rounds in [k1, p1] ribbing.

BO in [k1, p1] ribbing pattern.

Right Front Button Band

Change to smaller needles. Beginning with RS facing, at lower edge, pick up and knit 77 (77, 77, 79, 81, 83, 85) sts.

Next row (WS): Knit.
Work 8 rows [k1, p1] ribbing.
BO in [k1, p1] ribbing pattern.

Left Front Button Band

Beginning with RS facing, at upper edge, pick up and knit 77 (77, 77, 79, 81, 83, 85) sts.

Next row (WS): Knit.
Work 3 rows in [k1, p1] ribbing.

Next row (RS): Rib 6, [(k2tog, yo2, ssk; rib 5) 7 (7, 7, 8, 8, 8, 8) times], (k2tog, yo2, ssk) 1 (1, 1, 0, 0, 0, 1) times, rib 4 (4, 4, 1, 3, 5, 3).

Next row (WS): [Rib 4 (4, 4, 1, 3, 5, 3), (k1, p1) in yo loops] 1 (1, 1, 0, 0, 0, 1) times, [rib 5, (k1, p1) in yo loops 7 (7, 7, 8, 8, 8, 8) times], rib 6.

Work 3 rows in [k1, p1] ribbing.
BO in [k1, p1] ribbing pattern.

Collar

With smaller needles and WS facing, beginning at Left Front Neck edge (do not include buttonband), pick up and knit 25 (27, 31, 31, 31, 33, 33) sts along Left Front neck edge to shoulder, pick up and knit 35 (35, 39, 41, 45, 51, 55) sts across Back Neck edge, pick up and knit 25 (27, 31, 31, 31, 33, 33) sts along Right Front Neck edge. 85 (89, 101, 103, 107, 117, 121) total collar sts.

Next row (WS): Knit.
Work 6 rows in [k1, p1] ribbing.
BO in [k1, p1] ribbing pattern.

Sleeves

Slip 66 (72, 80, 92, 102, 104, 116) sleeve sts from waste yarn onto larger dpns, pick up and knit 12 sts at underarm CO edge, placing a marker after 6 sts. 78 (84, 92, 104, 114, 116, 128) sts.

Knit to m.
Work 8 rounds in St st.

Next round (Decrease round): K1, k2tog, knit to 3 sts before m, ssk, k1.

Repeat Decrease Round every 14 (12, 8, 6, 5, 5, 3)th St st round, 4 (5, 8, 10, 11, 11, 15) more times. 68 (72, 74, 82, 90, 92, 96) sts.

Work in St st until piece measures 8.75 (9.5, 9.75, 9.75, 9.75, 10, 10.25)" / 21.9 (23.8, 24.4, 24.4, 24.4, 25, 25.6)cm from beginning of underarm.

Switch to smaller dpns. Work 10 rounds [k1, p1] ribbing.

BO in [k1, p1] ribbing pattern.

Finishing

Lightly steam block before working fabric band.

Cut a strip of fabric 13.75 (13.75, 13.75, 14, 14.5, 14.75, 15.25)" × 2" / 35 (35, 35, 35.5, 37, 37.5, 38.5) cm × 5cm. Press in 0.5" / 1.5cm seam allowance on all sides, cutting out corner squares where pressed edges meet. Pin in place to RS center of Right Front Button band. Hand sew down with matching thread and sewing needle. Sew buttons to fabric button band under buttonholes.

Weave in ends.

Note: If buttonholes are too big, use sewing thread on WS to close sides of holes a bit.

Thornhill Cowl

Stephannie Tallent

SIZE

One size

FINISHED MEASUREMENTS

Circumference: 27.5" / 70cm
Height: 7.5" / 19cm

MATERIALS

Little Red Bicycle Penny Farthing Sock (80%
superwash merino, 10% nylon, 10% cashmere;
385 yds / 352m per 115g skein)

- [Color A] Basque, 1 skein
- [Color B] Vixen, 1 skein

Recommended yarn substitutions:

Sincere Sheep Cushy Fingering (80% superwash
merino, 10% nylon, 10% cashmere; 375 yds / 343m
per 113g skein)

- [Color A] Bare, 1 skein
- [Color B] Kung Hey Fat Chow, 1 skein

OR

Knitted Wit Cashy Wool (70% superwash merino,
10% nylon, 20% cashmere; 400 yds / 366m per 113g
skein)

- [Color A] Naked, 1 skein
- [Color B] Black Magic, 1 skein

20-inch US #3 / 3.25mm circular needle, or size
needed to obtain gauge
20-inch US #2.5 / 3mm circular needle

Stitch markers (at least 1 for beginning of round,
more if desired)
Waste yarn for provisional cast on
Yarn needle

GAUGE

28 sts and 36 rounds = 4" / 10cm in stranded St st,
on larger needle

REQUIRED SKILLS

Knitting in the round; stranded colorwork
techniques; kitchener stitch (grafting); provisional
cast on

PATTERN NOTES

If you'd like a cowl with a larger circumference,
increase in repeats of 16 sts (which works out to
be about 2.25" / 5.5cm) and increase your yarn
requirements proportionately.

PATTERN

With smaller needles, provisionally CO 192 sts in
color B. Join to work in the round, being careful not
to twist. Pm for beginning of round.

Work 6 rounds of garter stitch in color B, beginning
with a knit round.

Change to larger needles. Work boxed repeat on
Arrows Chart twelve times around (knit all sts).

Change to smaller needles. Work 6 rows of garter
stitch in color B, beginning with a knit round.

Change to larger needles. Work boxed repeat on
Diagonal Arrows Chart twelve times around (knit
all sts). Do not break yarn.

Finishing

Place sts from provisional cast on onto smaller
needles. Using color A, graft live sts tog with sts
from provisional cast on. Cowl will naturally fold at
the garter stitch borders.

Weave in all loose ends. Note you can hide them on
the inside of the cowl. Block.

*This gorgeously soft indulgent cowl was inspired by the vagaries of fortune. Which way to go? Who can be
trusted? Wear this cowl with either side showing; it's completely reversible.*

Arrows Chart

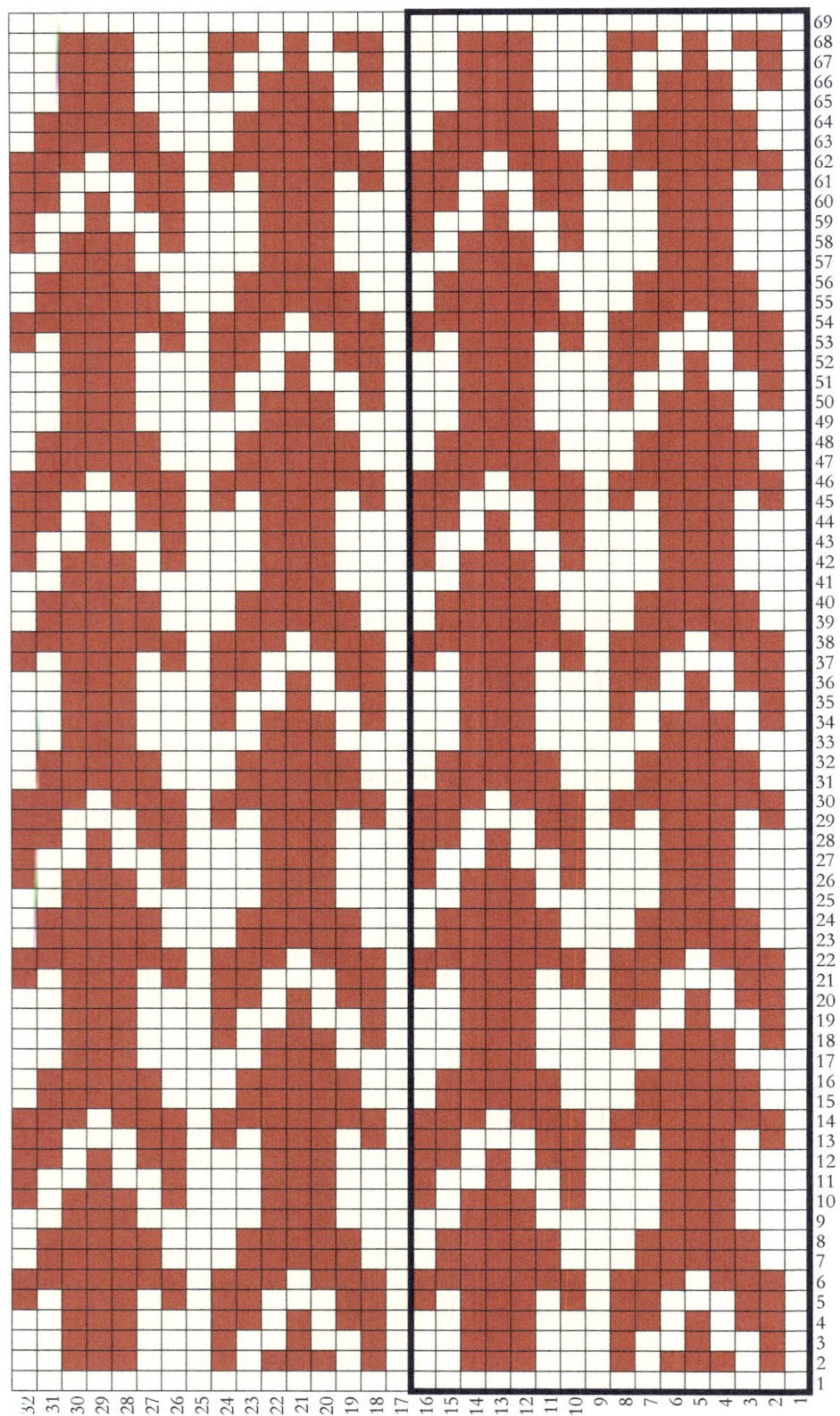

□ Color A Basque

■ Color B Vixen

▬ Repeat

Diagonal Arrows Chart

☐ Color A Basque
▨ Color B Vixen
━ Repeat

Melanie Shawl

Nina Machlin Dayton

SIZE

One size

FINISHED MEASUREMENTS

Wingspan: 60" / 152.5cm
Depth: 30" / 76cm

MATERIALS

String Theory Caper Sock (80% superwash merino wool, 10% cashmere, 10% nylon; 400 yds / 366m per 113g skein), color: Pewter; 2 skeins

32-inch US #4 / 3.5mm circular needle, or size needed to obtain gauge
Crochet hook small enough to fit into your beads (I used a size 12 / 1mm steel hook)

282 size 5/0 or "E" seed beads. Color used on sample: Noir Lined Crystal
4 stitch markers
Yarn needle

GAUGE

21 sts and 30 rows to 4" / 10cm in Feather Rib Body pattern blocked.

Gauge is not critical in this pattern, but a different gauge will affect yardage and size of finished object.

REQUIRED SKILLS

Increases/decreases (see Special Stitches below for specifics); garter stitch tab start (explained in pattern); working lace from charts and / or written instructions; twisted knit and purl stitches; working intricate lace from charts and written instructions; beading a knit stitch with a crochet hook

PATTERN NOTES

This triangular shawl is worked from the neck down, starting with a garter stitch tab, which is fully described in the pattern. Beads are placed with a crochet hook on the lace feathers near the border.

Size 5/0 or "E" seed beads can be difficult to find. They are available online at Twisted Sistah Beads. If size 5/0 "E" beads cannot be obtained then you

My childhood best friend and I were big fans of old movies, and we spent many nights and weekends watching black-and-white reruns on TV. One director whose movies we loved was Alfred Hitchcock. We found his films incredibly exciting and often scary, but we also found them irresistible for their depictions of a glamorous life—beautiful women, exquisite clothes, dark secrets, handsome men, exciting locations, and those moments where something normal suddenly tilted, and everything became terrifying.

Though The Birds was never my favorite Hitchcock film—to me birds are beautiful, not evil—I chose this film as my inspiration so I could celebrate the birds themselves, who probably had something important to say that went ignored. Why didn't anyone try harder to figure out what the birds were trying to say?

The cashmere in String Theory's Caper Sock yarn has the perfect drape and softness for depicting the lines of bird wings flowing gently into feathery tips. The beads sparkle like the sun glints off feathers, iridescent and magical.

may substitute the more common, and easier to find, size 6/0, but they will be slightly smaller than the beads shown on the sample.

PATTERN

CO 2 sts. Work in garter stitch (knit every row) for 6 rows (3 ridges).

Next row: Knit 2 sts. Turn work 90 degrees and pick up 3 sts along long edge of rectangle. Turn work 90 degrees; pick up 2 sts along short edge of rectangle. 7 sts.

Next row: K2, pm, p1, pm, p1, pm, p1, pm, k2. These markers delineate the 2-st garter stitch border on

each edge of the needles, and the center st. After this row, slip markers as you come to them.

Work Chart 1. 31 sts.
Work Chart 2.

Work the 12 rows of Chart 2 a total of 10 times. Each repeat adds 24 sts, or 4 new repeats of the ribbed body. 271 sts.

Work Chart 3. 289 sts.
Work Chart 4. 349 sts.
Work Chart 5. 523 sts.

Finishing

Cut yarn and pull through last st. Wet block shawl to finished measurements. Weave in all ends.

Chart 1

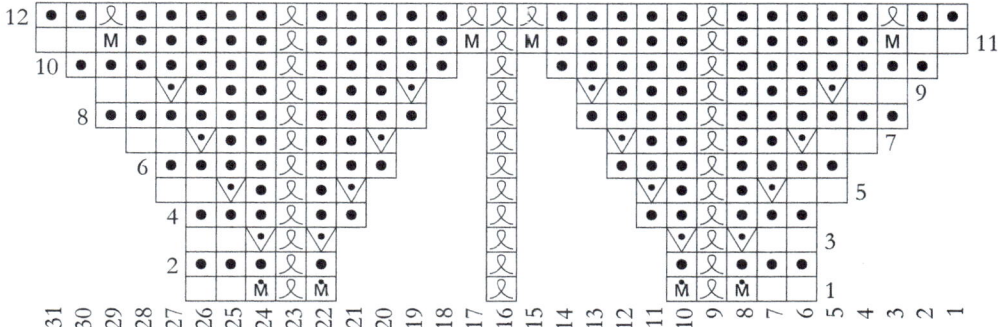

Chart 2

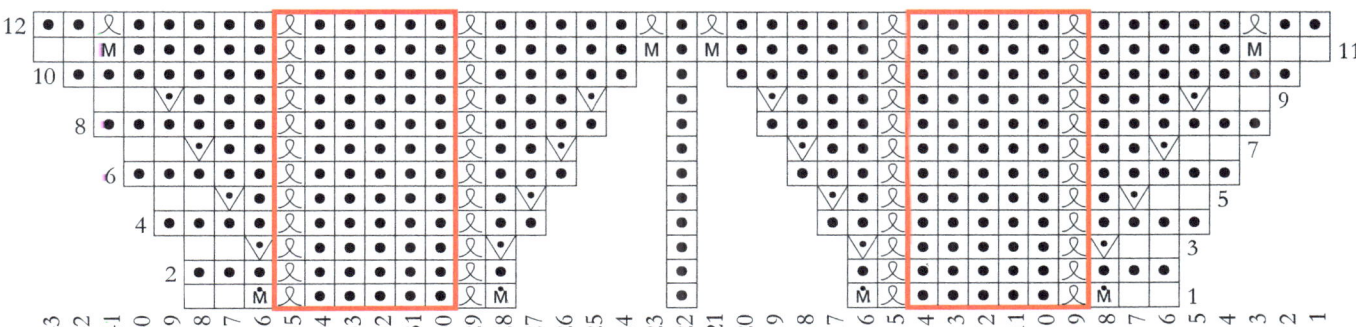

Chart 3

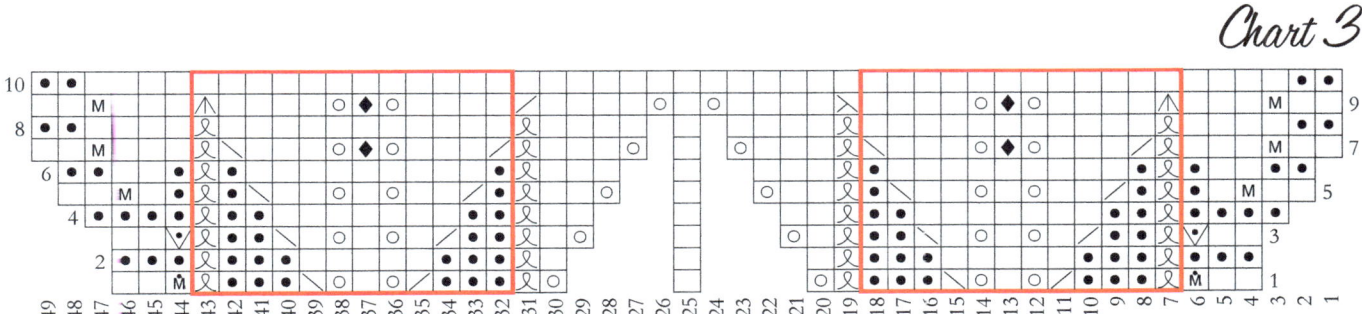

□ RS: k; WS: p		⊠ skp
• RS: p; WS: k		⟁ s2kp
ℓ RS: k tbl; WS: p tbl		◆ PB
○ yo		Ṁ M1P
╱ k2tog		M M1
╲ ssk		⊡ pfb

Chart 4

Chart 5

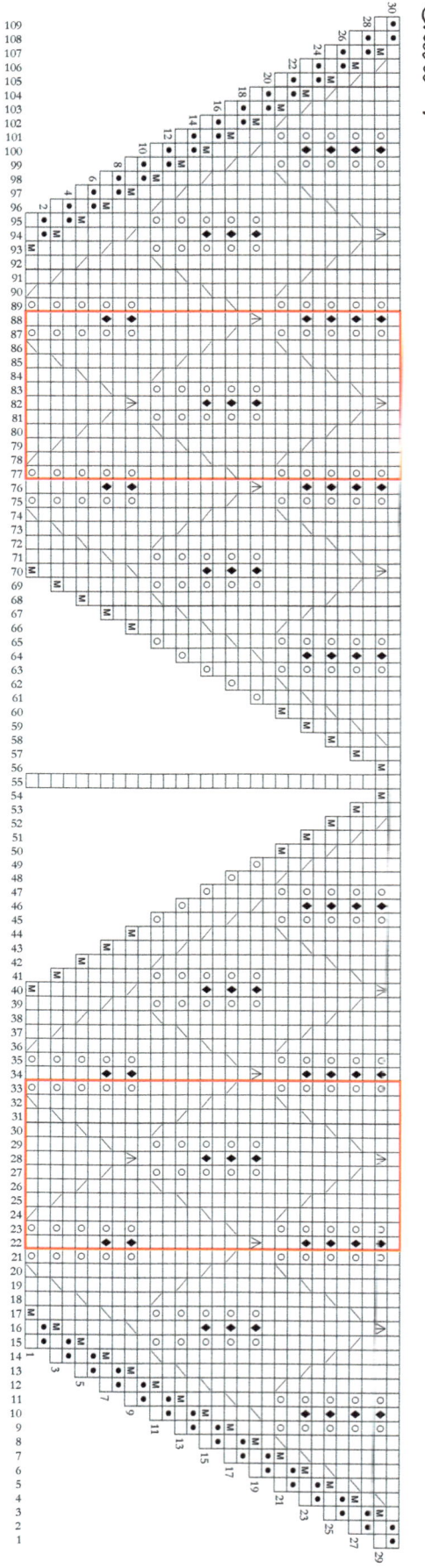

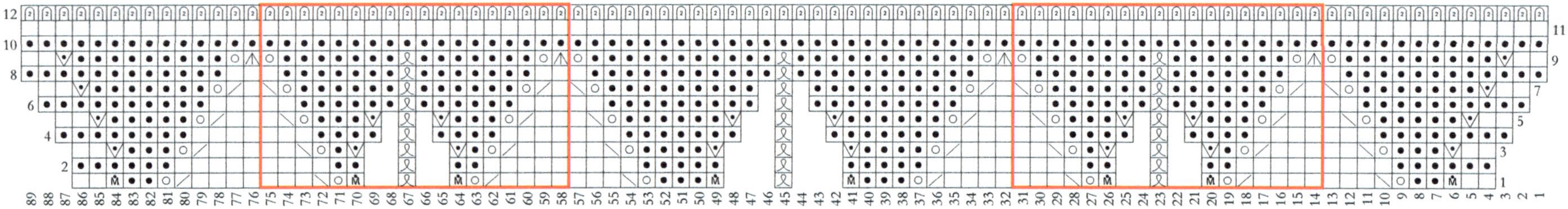

Key:

☐	RS: k; WS: p
●	RS: p; WS: k
⊠	RS: k tbl; WS: p tbl
○	yo
╱	k2tog
╲	ssk
▲	s2kp

◆	PB
Ⓜ	M
Ⓜ	M1
Ⓜ	M1P
⌵	pfb
⋒	WS: k2togtbl bo

Bodega Bay Stole

Anne Podlesak

SIZE

One size

FINISHED MEASUREMENTS (BLOCKED)

Length: 78" / 198cm
Width: 20.5" / 52cm

MATERIALS

Wooly Wonka Fibers Arianrhod Sock (70% merino, 25% silk, 5% glitter; 435 yds / 398m per 100g skein); color: Raven's Wing; 3 skeins

36-inch US #4 / 3.5mm circular needle, or size needed to obtain gauge

Minimum 2 stitch marker(s)
Waste yarn or a spare 36-inch circular needle
Yarn needle

GAUGE

20 sts and 30 rows = 4" / 10cm in St st, blocked

Gauge is not critical in this pattern, but a different gauge will affect yardage and size of finished item.

REQUIRED SKILLS

Working simple lace from chart or written instructions; kitchener stitch (grafting)

PATTERN NOTES

The stole is constructed by casting on at one end, knitting the three charts as indicated, and then placing the first half on scrap yarn or a spare circular needle. Repeat for the second half. The two sections are then grafted together along the center back of the stole.

Knit 2 sts at the beginning and end of every row, to work the garter stitch border.

Pattern repeats on the chart are delineated by the outlined boxes.

When blocking the finished piece, be sure to pull the scalloped edges into evenly undulating curves. You may find several pins in each of the scallops will help to ensure a prettier, less pointed edging.

PATTERN

Using the long-tail cast on, CO 104 sts.
Set up row (WS): K2, pm, k100, pm, k2.

Begin working the Raven's Tail chart, knitting the first and last 2 sts of every row.

Work Rows 1–8 once.
Work Rows 9–16 ten times.
Work Rows 17–20 once.

Begin the Crow Wings chart, knitting the first and last 2 sts of every row. Work Chart ten times.

Begin the Starling's Flight chart, knitting the first and last 2 sts of every row. Work Chart four times.

This elegant rectangular stole was inspired by the original movie advertisement posters for Alfred Hitchcock's The Birds and the sophisticated costume designs of Edith Head. The stole features three different-sized, wing-shaped motifs, including a tail-wing-shaped scalloped edging. It is knit in two halves from each end, and then grafted in the middle. The lace patterning is elegant and simple, and because there is no shaping, it would be a great first lace project.

Break yarn and slip live sts to a long piece of scrap yarn or a spare needle.

Repeat for the second half of the stole. Keep sts on the needle. Leave a 50" / 127cm tail for grafting.

Graft the live sts of the two halves tog using Kitchener stitch.

Weave in all ends on wrong side of stole, but do not trim ends. Allow stole to soak in a lukewarm bath until completely saturated. Press or spin excess water out gently. Block flat to finished dimensions, pulling the Raven's Tail motifs along the cast-on edge into gently undulating scallops. Allow to dry thoroughly, and then unpin. Trim darned-in ends from wrong side of fabric.

Raven's Tail Chart

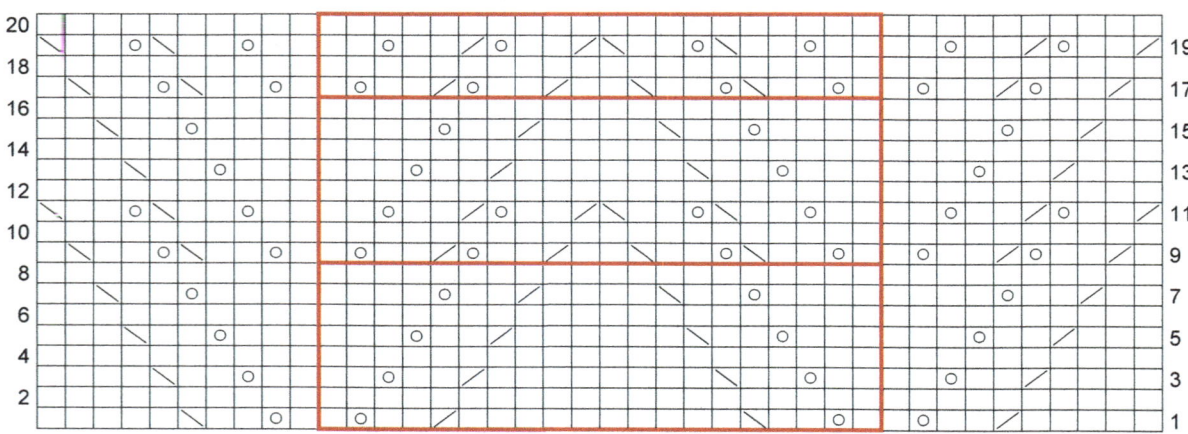

Crow Wings Chart

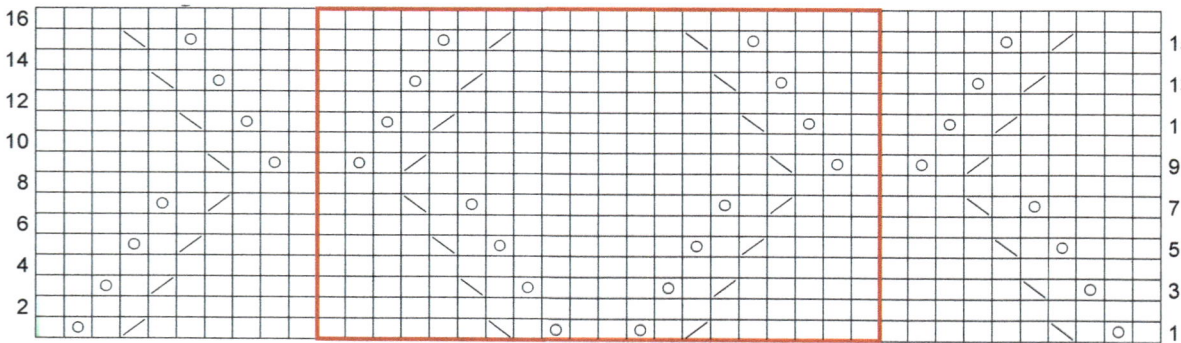

Starling's Flight Chart

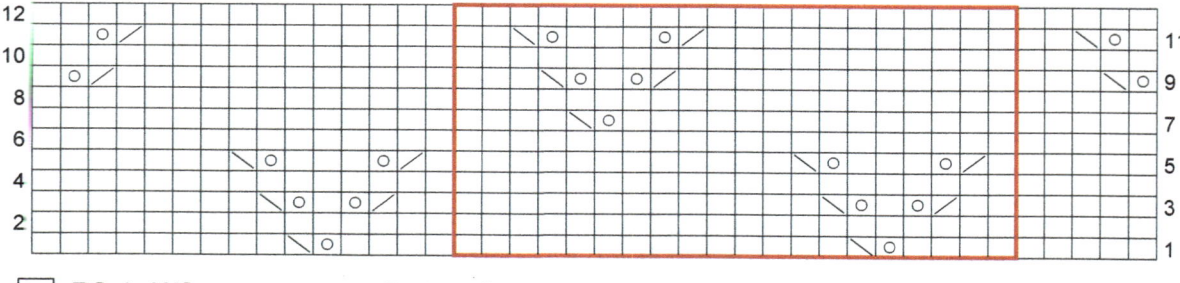

☐	RS: k; WS: p	— Pattern Repeat
⊡	yo	
⟋	k2tog	
⟍	ssk	

Tippi Toes

Jill Bigelow Suttell

Tippi Toes are inspired by the films The Birds *and* Marnie, *both starring Tippi Hedren. Each element of these toe-up socks captures an element of Hedren's characters in these films. The stitch patterns represent both bird wings and the "V" formation of birds in flight. The red cuffs signify Marnie's fear of red. Also, Marnie has a habit of pulling at her skirts to be sure her knees were covered so I thought it might be fun to make the sock ribbing cover the knee or be folded over below the knee.*

SIZES

Women's M (L); shown in size M
Sized to fit foot circumferences: 8 (10)" / 20.5 (25.5)cm

FINISHED MEASUREMENTS

Foot circumference: 7.5 (9.75)" / 19 (25)cm
Foot length: 9.25" / 23.5cm (adjustable)
Leg length: 13.5" / 34.5cm

MATERIALS

SweetGeorgia Tough Love Sock (80% superwash wool, 20% nylon; 425 yds / 463m per 4oz skein)

- [MC] Slate; 2 skeins
- [CC] China Doll; 1 skein

Two 20-inch US #1 / 2.25mm circular needles, or size required to obtain gauge

2 removable stitch markers
Yarn needle

GAUGE

37 sts and 50 rounds = 4" / 10cm in Birds Chart patt
33 sts and 47 rounds = 4" / 10cm in St st

REQUIRED SKILLS

Knowledge of basic sock construction; knitting in the round on two circulars; increases/decreases; figure 8 cast on; short rows; working simple cables and lace from chart or written instructions; twisted stitches

PATTERN NOTES

First half of stitches are sole stitches, second half of stitches are instep stitches.

STITCHES AND TECHNIQUES

Figure 8 cast on

Hold 2 needles in parallel with points facing right. Leaving a 4" / 10cm tail, place tail between the needles with tail coming toward you. [Wrap tail around bottom needle and back up between needles. Wrap tail around top needle and back down between needles.] Repeat until 5 sts are on each needle.

Slip bottom sts to cable. K3 from top needle. Let remaining loops unravel until there are 3 sts on each needle. K3 from bottom needle through the back loop.

Wrap and turn (w&t)

Knit side: Move yarn from back to front, slip st from left to right, move yarn from front to back, slip st back to left. Turn.

Purl side: Move yarn from front to back, slip st from left to right, move yarn from back to front, slip st back to left. Turn.

Work wraps

Knit side: Lift wrap up and over st it wraps so that is on the left side of the st. Knit st and wrap tog through the back loop.

Purl side: Pick up wrap from the knit side and pass it over st it wraps so that is on the left side of the st. Purl wrap and st tog.

PATTERN

Toe

Using figure 8 cast on method, CO 6 sts (3 on each needle). Adjust needles so working yarn is available.

Knit 3 sts on needle 1. Unwrap the rest so there are 3 sts on each needle. Turn and knit sts on needle 2 through the back.

Round 1: [M1R, k1] 6 times. 12 sts.
Round 2 and all even rounds: Knit.
Round 3: [M1R, k2] 6 times. 18 sts.
Round 5: [M1R, k3] 6 times. 24 sts.
Continue in this way through Round 19, when you will [m1R, k10] 6 times. 66 sts.
Round 20: Knit.

Size M only:
Round 21: Knit.

Size L only:
Round 21: [M1R, k11] 6 times. 72 sts.
Round 22: Knit.
Round 23: [M1R, k12] 6 times. 78 sts.
Round 24: Knit.
Round 25: [K1, m1R, k42] twice. 80 sts.

Note for both sizes: If additional length is needed, add it here.

Foot

Size M only: Start Birds Chart with st 6 and end with st 17. Do not work sts 1–5 or sts 17–22. Work Birds Chart, repeating sts 6–16 four times across instep.

Size L only: Work complete Birds Chart, repeating sts 6–16 four times across instep.

Both sizes:

Work 10 rnds of Bird Chart 4 times total, knitting sole sts as established.

Foot Gusset

Knit sole sts, work first 17 (22) sts of instep in patt, pm, start Gusset Chart, pm, work remaining instep sts in patt.

Continue pattern as established while working Gusset Chart in between markers. Note: the numbers in red on the left side of chart show corresponding line of Birds Chart. 96 (110) sts.

Heel Turn

Heel is worked on sole needle only. 32 (40) sts on sole needle.
Row 1: Knit to 2 sts left, w&t.
Row 2: Purl to 2 sts left, w&t.
Row 3: Knit to 3 sts left, w&t.
Row 4: Purl to 3 sts left, w&t.
Row 5: Knit to 4 sts left, w&t.
Row 6: Purl to 4 sts left, w&t.
Continue in this way through Row 16, when you will purl to 9 sts left, w&t.

Row 17: Knit to last 2 sts, working wraps (see Pattern Notes), ssk, turn.
Row 18: Purl to last 2 sts, working wraps, p2tog, turn. 30 (38) sts on sole needle.

Heel Flap

Transfer 15 sts from each end of instep sts to sole sts. Slip sts until working yarn is available. 60 (68) sts on sole needle.

Work appropriate Heel Chart back and forth on sole sts. At end of chart row, turn.
Note that Rows 1 & 10 are only worked once. Repeat Rows 2–9 only.
Repeat Heel Chart rows until 34 (42) sts remain on sole needle. 68 (82) sts total.

Next row: Sl 1, work Row 1 of Heel Chart to last 3 sts on sole needle, ssk, p1. Work Round 1 of Birds Chart on instep sts. 67 (81) sts.

Size M only:
Slip last st on instep needle to sole needle. Sl 1, p1, k2tog, start Birds Chart with Round 2, st 9. 66 sts.

Size L only:
K1, k2tog, start Birds Chart with Round 2, st 4. 80 sts.

Both sizes:
Work 10 rounds of Birds Chart 6 times.

Calf Gusset

On next Round 1 of Birds Chart, work 17 (22) sts on sole needle, pm, work Round 1 of Calf Chart, pm, continue round in patt. Continue pattern as established while working Calf Chart in between markers. 110 (124) sts.

At the end of Calf Chart, resume Birds Chart across all sts to complete the last pattern repeat. For additional length, work Birds Chart once more.

Cuff

Change to CC.

Size M only:
On first round, dec 2 sts, maintaining rib pattern. 108 sts.

Both sizes:
[K2, p2] around for 5" / 12.5cm.
BO all sts.

Finishing

Weave in ends. Block.

Gusset Chart

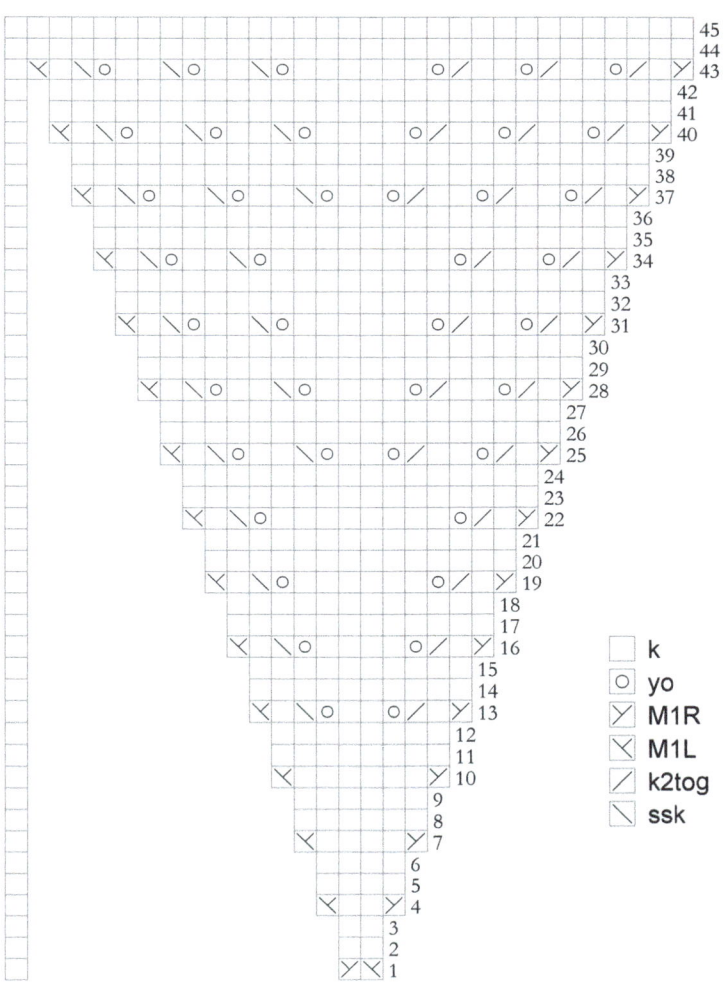

Legend:
- □ k
- ○ yo
- ⋋ M1R
- ⋌ M1L
- ╱ k2tog
- ╲ ssk

Birds Chart

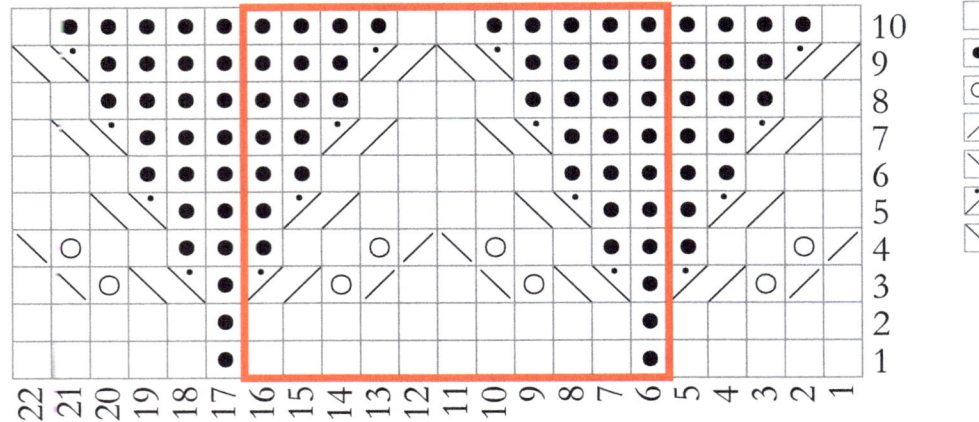

☐	k
●	p
○	yo
◺	k2tog
◹	ssk
◿	1/1 RCp
◸	1/1 LCp

Medium Heel Chart

Note: worked flat

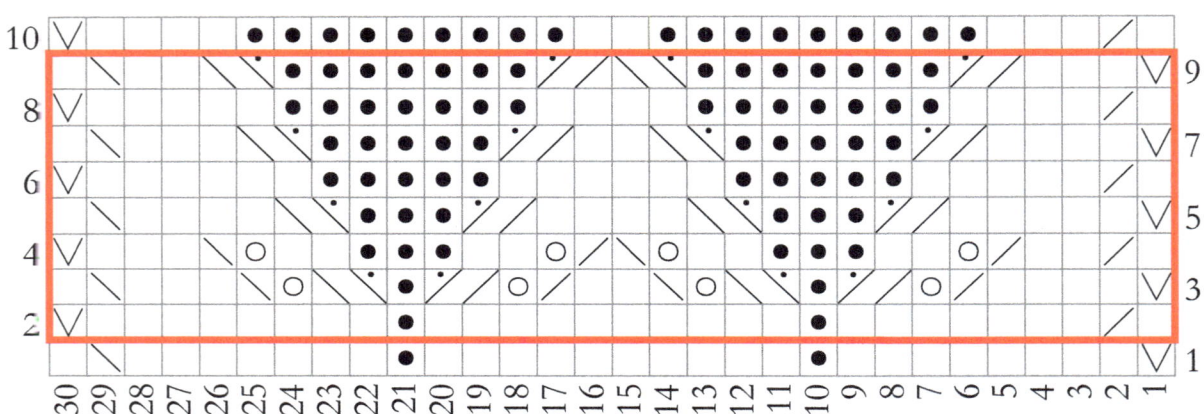

Large Heel Chart

Note: worked flat

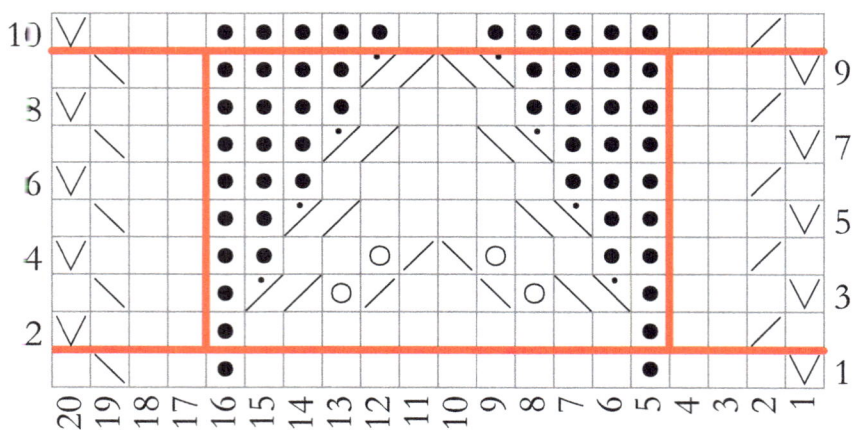

☐	RS: k; WS: p
●	RS: p; WS: k
∨	RS: sl1; WS: sl1 wyif
○	yo
◺	RS: k2tog; WS: p2tog
◹	RS: ssk; WS: ssp
◿	1/1 RCp
◸	1/1 LCp

Calf Chart

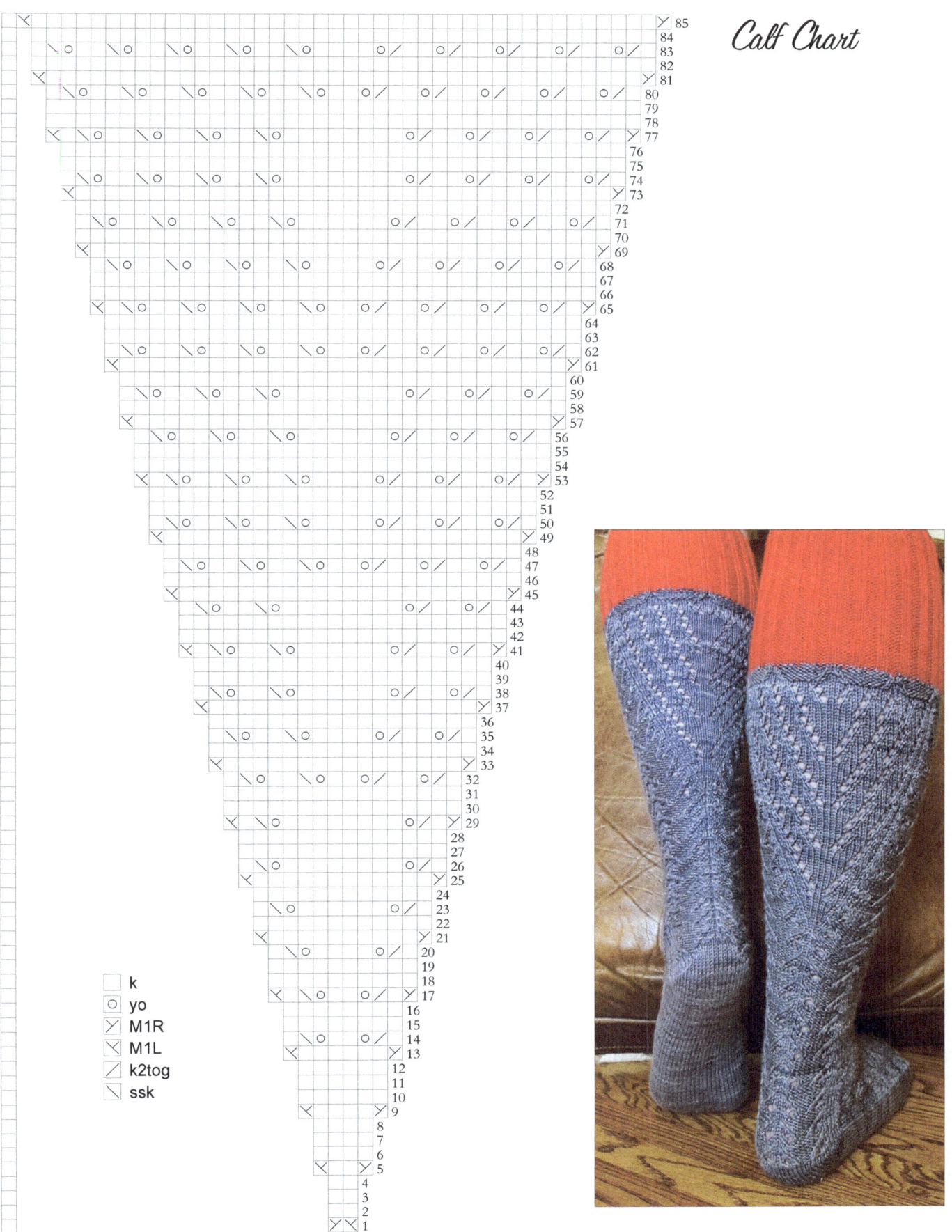

Legend:
- ☐ k
- ○ yo
- ⋎ M1R
- ⋏ M1L
- ╱ k2tog
- ╲ ssk

Annie Pullover

Christina Werge

SIZES

Women's XS (S, M, L, XL, 2X, 3X); shown in size M
Intended to be worn with 1" / 2.5cm of positive ease

FINISHED MEASUREMENTS

Bust: 30 (34, 38, 42, 44, 48, 52)" / 76 (86.5, 96.5, 106.5, 111.5, 122, 132)cm

MATERIALS

Posh Yarn Sylvia DK (50% merino, 50% silk; 230 yds / 212m per 100g skein); color: Tragic Ending; 4 (4, 5, 5, 6, 7, 7) skeins

32-inch US #6 / 4mm circular needle, or size needed to obtain gauge
32-inch US #5 / 3.75mm circular needle

2 removable stitch markers
2 stitch holders or waste yarn
Yarn needle

GAUGE

21 sts and 30 rows = 4" / 10cm in St st, on larger needle

REQUIRED SKILLS

Knowledge of basic sweater construction; increases/decreases; knitted cast on; seaming

PATTERN NOTES

This sweater is worked flat from the bottom up. The sleeve stitches are joined to the body stitches along the way. Front and back pieces are identical, so you have to go through the instructions twice to create both pieces. It is recommended to start knitting the sleeve parts for your piece first to have them ready when they need to be joined to the body stitches. The sleeves of this sweater are angled to improve the fit. Because of this construction (and to emphasize the typical rounded shoulder line of the mid-century) the sleeves have generous ease on the upper arms that tapers down to just 1" / 2.5cm ease on the cuffs.

PATTERN

The underarm increases in both following sleeve sections are always made using the knitted cast on (see Abbreviations & Techniques). Work across the cast-on sts to complete the row.

Right Sleeve Part

CO 4 sts using larger needle.
Row 1 (RS): Knit to end.
Row 2 (WS): CO 4, p3, k1, k tbl, k3. 8 sts.

Row 3: Kfb, knit to end. 9 sts.
Row 4: CO 4, p4, p tbl, purl to last 5 sts, k5. 13 sts.

Row 5: Knit.
Row 6: CO 4, p4, p tbl, purl to last 4 sts, k3, kfb. 18 sts.

In The Birds, *Annie Hayworth is the tragic teacher, who has already lost the guy and who will also lose her life in the course of this movie. I can picture the sad, but down-to-earth Annie wearing this flattering boatneck sweater with her gray slacks or dressed up with a skirt.*

The sweater itself is all mid-century classic with its three-quarter-length sleeves and defined waistline. The simple lines of the Annie Sweater are perfect for this hand-painted silk / merino blend. While the silk lends the required drape, the grays glow like a gloomy day in Bodega Bay.

Row 7: Knit.
Row 8: CO 4, p4, p tbl, purl to last 5 sts, k5. 22 sts.

Row 9: Kfb, knit to end. 23 sts.
Row 10: CO 4, p4, p tbl, purl to last 5 sts, k5. 27 sts.

Row 11: Knit.
Row 12: CO 4, p4, p tbl, purl to last 4 sts, k3, kfb. 32 sts.

Row 13: Knit.
Row 14: CO 4, p4, p tbl, purl to last 5 sts, k5. 36 sts.

Row 15: Kfb, knit to end. 37 sts.
Row 16: CO 4, p4, p tbl, purl to last 5 sts, k5. 41 sts.

Row 17: Knit.
Row 18: CO 4, p4, p tbl, purl to last 4 sts, k3, kfb. 46 sts.

Row 19: Knit.
Row 20: CO 4, p4, p tbl, purl to last 5 sts, k5. 50 sts.

Row 21: Kfb, knit to end. 51 sts.
Row 22: CO 4, p4, p tbl, purl to last 5 sts, k5. 55 sts.

Row 23: Knit.
Row 24: CO 4, p4, p tbl, purl to last 4 sts, k3, kfb. 60 sts.

Size XS only:
Put all sts on a holder.

Sizes S, M, L, XL, 2X, & 3X only:
Row 25: Knit.
Row 26: CO 4, p4, p tbl, purl to last 5 sts, k5. 64 sts.
Row 27: Kfb, knit to end. 65 sts.

Size S only:
Put all sts on a holder.

Sizes M, L, XL, 2X, & 3X only:
Row 28: CO 4, p4, p tbl, purl to last 5 sts, k5. 69 sts.
Row 29: Knit.

Size M only:
Row 30: Purl to last 4 sts, k3, kfb. 70 sts.
Put all sts on a holder.

Size L only:
Row 30: CO 2, p2, p tbl, purl to last 4 sts, k3, kfb. 72 sts.
Row 31: Knit.
Row 32: CO 2, p2, p tbl, purl to last 5 sts, k5. 74 sts.
Row 33: Kfb, knit to end. 75 sts.
Put all sts on a holder.

Sizes XL, 2X, & 3X only:
Row 30: CO 4, p4, p tbl, purl to last 4 sts, k3, kfb. 74 sts.
Row 31: Knit.

Size XL only:
Row 32: CO 2, p2, p tbl, purl to last 5 sts, k5. 76 sts.

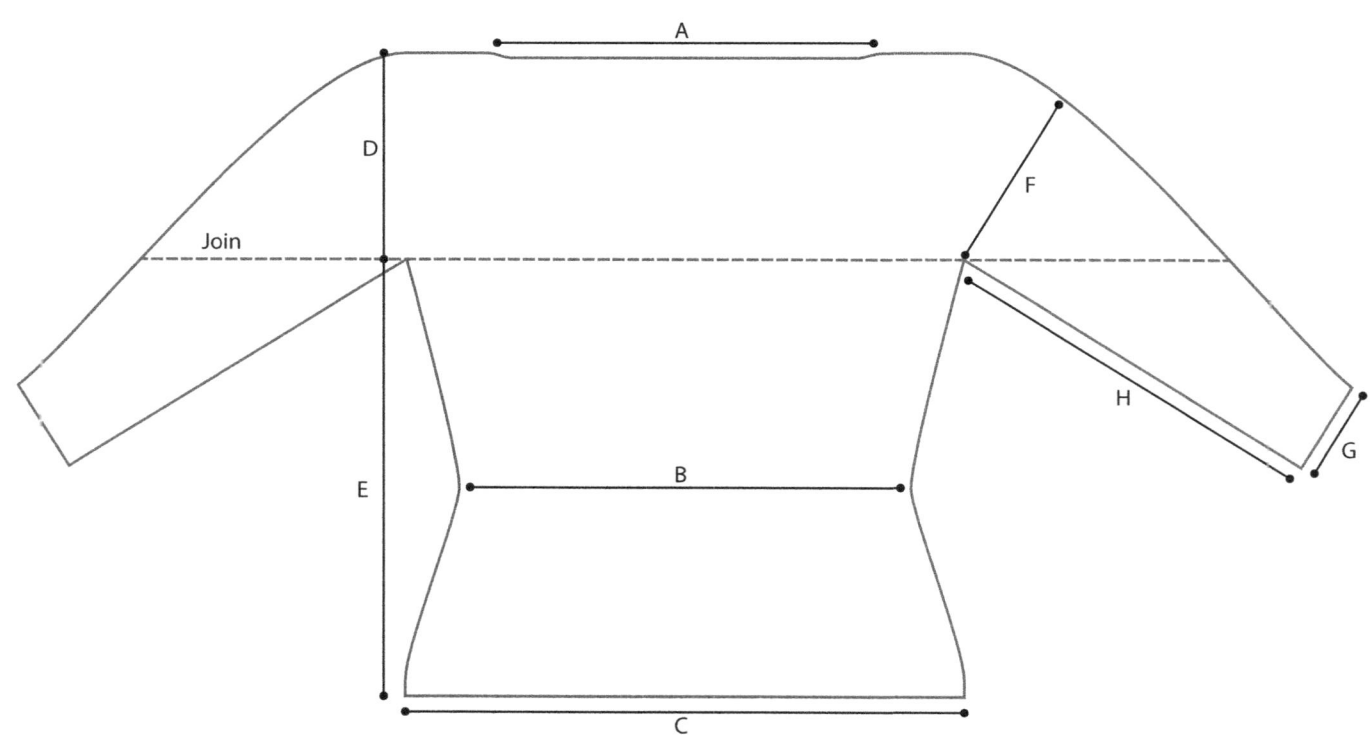

A: 9 (9.5, 10, 10.25, 10.75, 11, 11.5)"
B: 11 (13, 15, 17, 19, 21, 23)"
C: 15 (17, 19, 21, 23, 25, 27)"
D: 6 (7.5, 8, 8.5, 9, 10, 10.5)"
E: 12 (12.25, 12.5, 12, 12, 12)"
F: 5.5 (6, 6.5, 7, 7.5, 8.5, 9)"
G: 4 (4.5, 4.75, 5.25, 5.75, 6.25, 6.5)"
H: 10.5 (11.25, 12, 13, 13.75, 15, 15.75)"

Row 33: Kfb, knit to end. 77 sts.
Row 34: CO 2, p2, p tbl, purl to last 5 sts, k5. 79 sts.
Row 35: Knit.
Row 36: Purl to last 4 sts, k3, kfb. 80 sts.
Put all sts on a holder.

Sizes 2X & 3X only:
Row 32: CO 4, p4, p tbl, purl to last 5 sts, k5. 78 sts.
Row 33: Kfb, knit to end. 79 sts.
Row 34: CO 4, p4, p tbl, purl to last 5 sts, k5. 83 sts.
Row 35: Knit.
Row 36: CO 2, p2, p tbl, purl to last 4 sts, k3, kfb. 86 sts.
Row 37: Knit.
Row 38: CO 2, p2, p tbl, purl to last 5 sts, k5. 88 sts.
Row 39: Kfb, knit to end. 89 sts.

Size 2X only:
Put all sts on a holder.

Size 3X only:
Row 40: CO 2, p2, p tbl, purl to last 5 sts, k5. 91 sts.
Row 41: Knit.
Row 42: CO 2, p2, p tbl, purl to last 4 sts, k3, kfb. 94 sts.
Put all sts on a holder.

Left Sleeve Part

CO 4 sts using larger needle.

Row 1 (WS): Knit to end.
Row 2 (RS): CO 4, k4, k tbl, k3. 8 sts.

Row 3: Kfb, k3, purl to end. 9 sts.
Row 4: CO 4, k4, k tbl, knit to end. 13 sts.

Row 5: K5, purl to end.
Row 6: CO 4, k4, k tbl, knit to last st, kfb. 18 sts.

Row 7: K5, purl to end.
Row 8: CO 4, k4, k tbl, knit to end. 22 sts.

Row 9: Kfb, k3, purl to end. 23 sts.
Row 10: CO 4, k4, k tbl, knit to end. 27 sts.

Row 11: K5, purl to end.
Row 12: CO 4, k4, k tbl, knit to last st, kfb. 32 sts.

Row 13: K5, purl to end.
Row 14: CO 4, k4, k tbl, knit to end. 36 sts.

Row 15: Kfb, k3, purl to end. 37 sts.
Row 16: CO 4, k4, k tbl, knit to end. 41 sts.

Row 17: K5, purl to end.
Row 18: CO 4, k4, k tbl, knit to last st, kfb. 46 sts.

Row 19: K5, purl to end.
Row 20: CO 4, k4, k tbl, knit to end. 50 sts.

Row 21: Kfb, k3, purl to end. 51 sts.
Row 22: CO 4, k4, k tbl, knit to end. 55 sts.

Row 23: K5, purl to end.
Row 24: CO 4, k4, k tbl, knit to last st, kfb. 60 sts.

Size XS only:
Put all sts on a holder.

Sizes S, M, L, XL, 2X, & 3X only:
Row 25: K5, purl to end.
Row 26: CO 4, k4, k tbl, knit to end. 64 sts.
Row 27: Kfb, k3, purl to end. 65 sts.

Size S only:
Put all sts on a holder.

Sizes M, L, XL, 2X, & 3X only:
Row 28: CO 4, k4, k tbl, knit to end. 69 sts.
Row 29: K5, purl to end.

Size M only:
Row 30: Knit to last st, kfb. 70 sts.
Put all sts on a holder.

Size L only:
Row 30: CO 2, k2, k tbl, knit to last st, kfb. 72 sts.
Row 31: K5, purl to end.
Row 32: CO 2, k2, k tbl, knit to end. 74 sts.
Row 33: Kfb, k3, purl to end. 75 sts.
Put all sts on a holder.

Sizes XL, 2X, & 3X only:
Row 30: CO 4, k4, k tbl, knit to last st, kfb. 74 sts.
Row 31: K5, purl to end.

Size XL only:
Row 32: CO 2, k2, k tbl, knit to end. 76 sts.
Row 33: Kfb, k3, purl to end. 77 sts.
Row 34: CO 2, k2, k tbl, knit to end. 79 sts.
Row 35: K5, purl to end.
Row 36: Knit to last st, kfb. 80 sts.
Put all sts on a holder.

Sizes 2X & 3X only:
Row 32: CO 4, k4, k tbl, knit to end. 78 sts.
Row 33: Kfb, k3, purl to end. 79 sts.
Row 34: CO 4, k4, k tbl, knit to end. 83 sts.
Row 35: K5, purl to end.
Row 36: CO 2, k2, k tbl, knit to last st, kfb. 86 sts.
Row 37: K5, purl to end.
Row 38: CO 2, k2, k tbl, knit to end. 88 sts.
Row 39: Kfb, k3 purl to end. 89 sts.

Size 2X only:
Put all sts on a holder.

Size 3X only:
Row 40: CO 2, k2, k tbl, knit to end. 91 sts.
Row 41: K5, purl to end.
Row 42: CO 2, k2, k tbl, knit to last st, kfb. 94 sts.
Put all sts on a holder.

Body

CO 81 (91, 101, 111, 121, 131, 141) sts using smaller needle.

Row 1 (RS): K1, [p1, k1] to end.
Row 2 (WS): P1, [k1, p1] to end.

Row 3: K1, [p1, k1] to end.
Row 4: P1, k1, p2tog, [p1, k1] to last 5 sts, p1, ssp, k1, p1. 79 (89, 99, 109, 119, 129, 139) sts.
Row 5: K1, p1, k2, [p1, k1] to last 3 sts, k1, p1, k1.
Row 6: P1, k1, p2, [k1, p1] to last 3 sts, p1, k1, p1.
Row 7: K1, p1, k2, [p1, k1] to last 3 sts, k1, p1, k1.
Row 8: P1, k1, p2tog, [k1, p1] to last 5 sts, k1, ssp, k1, p1. 77 (87, 97, 107, 117, 127, 137) sts.

Repeat Rows 1–8 another 3 times. 65 (75, 85, 95, 105, 115, 125) sts.
Repeat Rows 1–7 once more. 63 (73, 83, 93, 103, 113, 123) sts.

Change to larger needle. Starting with a WS row, work 5 (5, 5, 5, 5, 3, 3) rows in St st.

Next row (RS): K2, m1L, knit to last 2 sts, m1R, k2. 65 (75, 85, 95, 105, 115, 125) sts.

Repeat the last 6 (6, 6, 6, 6, 4, 4) rows 8 more times. 81 (91, 101, 111, 121, 131, 141) sts.

Work 3 (3, 1, 1, 1, 9, 7) rows in St st. Break yarn.

With RS facing, rearrange the sleeves and body sts onto the same long needle. Make sure the small garter stitch bands (the sleeve cuffs) are both facing to the outside (see schematic). 201 (221, 241, 261, 281, 309, 329) sts.

For easy seaming always BO sts on RS rows knitwise and on WS rows purlwise.

Row 1 (RS): BO 2, knit to last 4 sts, p4. 199 (219, 239, 259, 279, 307, 327) sts.

Row 2 (WS): BO 2, purl to last 3 sts, k3. 197 (217, 237, 257, 277, 305, 325) sts.

Row 3: BO 2, knit to end. 195 (215, 235, 255, 275, 303, 323) sts.

Row 4: BO 2, purl to end. 193 (213, 233, 253, 273, 301, 321) sts.

Repeat the last 2 rows 16 (17, 18, 22, 20, 20, 21) more times. 129 (145, 161, 165, 193, 221, 237) sts.

Next row (RS): BO 3, knit to end. 126 (142, 158, 162, 190, 218, 234) sts.

Next row (WS): BO 3, purl to end. 123 (139, 155, 159, 187, 215, 231) sts.

Repeat the last 2 rows 4 (5, 6, 5, 8, 11, 12) more times. 99 (109, 119, 129, 139, 149, 159) sts.

Next row (RS): BO 3, knit to end. 96 (106, 116, 126, 136, 146, 156) sts.

Next row (WS): BO 3, p19 (23, 27, 31, 35, 39, 43), pm, k55 (57, 59, 61, 63, 65, 67), pm, purl to end. 93 (103, 113, 123, 133, 143, 153) sts.

Next row: BO 3, knit to end. 90 (100, 110, 120, 130, 140, 150) sts.

Next row: BO 3, purl to next marker, sm, knit to next marker, sm, purl to end. 87 (97, 107, 117, 127, 137, 147) sts.

Next row: BO 3, knit to end. 84 (94, 104, 114, 124, 134, 144) sts.

Next row: BO 3, purl to next marker, remove marker, knit to next marker, remove marker, purl to end. 81 (91, 101, 111, 121, 131, 141) sts.

BO all remaining sts.
Make a second piece, identical to the first.

Finishing

Weave in all ends. Wet block both pieces gently to size. Sew both upper arm seams from cuff to neck, ending after sewing the first 4 sts of the garter stitch neckline border on each shoulder. Sew the side and underarm seams.

Abbreviations & Techniques

See page 168 for cable abbreviations.

* ...	rep from *; repeat the instructions between the asterisks the number of times specified
[...]	repeat the instructions between the brackets the number of times specified
[purse]	[yo, p2tog]; worked over 2 sts
CC (CC1, CC2, etc)	contrasting color
cdi	knit back and front; pick up the vertical line running down in between the 2 sts you just made, and knit into the back of it
ch	chain (crochet)
cn	cable needle
dec	decrease or decreasing
dpn(s)	double point needle(s)
inc	increase or increasing
k	knit
k tbl	knit through the back loop
k2tog	knit 2 sts tog as one
k2tog tbl	knit 2 sts tog through the back loop
k2togtblBO	Knit 2 sts.* Insert left-hand needle into 2 sts on right-hand needle in front of right needle, so as to be positioned to k2tog through the back loop. Knit these 2 sts tog through the back loop, then k1*. Repeat from * to * until all sts are bound off. This creates a very loose and stretchy bind off.
k3tog tbl	knit 3 sts tog through back of loop
k3tog	knit 3 sts tog
KCO	knitted cast on
kfb	knit into front and back of a single stitch
kwise	knitwise, as if to knit

LH	left-hand
LLI	left-lifted increase: pick up leg of stitch 2 rows beneath stitch on the RH needle and knit into it
m1	make one (increase)
m1L	use tip of LH needle to lift strand between sts from front to back; knit this loop through the back loop
m1P	make 1 purlwise: lift the strand between the sts with your LH needle from front to back; purl this new stitch through the back loop, twisting it closed
m1R	bring tip of LH needle under strand between sts from back to front; knit this loop
m1RP	from the back, use LH needle to lift the horizontal strand between sts; purl through the front loop
MC	main color
MR	make ringlet: p2, slip these 2 sts back to LH needle wyif, move yarn to back around front of sts, slip sts back to RH needle
p	purl
p tbl	purl through the back loop
p2tog	purl 2 sts tog as one
p2tog tbl	purl 2 sts tog through the back loop
p3tog	purl 3 sts tog as one
patt	pattern
PB	place bead by crochet hook method
pbf	purl into back and front of a single stitch
pfb	purl into front and back of a single stitch
pfbf	purl into front, back, and front again of a single stitch
pm	place marker

pos	pass second stitch on LH needle over first stitch; slip to RH needle
posk	pass second stitch on LH needle over first stitch and knit
pospo	slip knitwise, pass second stitch on LH needle over first stitch; slip to RH needle; pass slipped stitch over
pospok	slip knitwise, pass second stitch on LH needle over first on LH needle; slip to RH needle; pass slipped stitch over; pass back to LH needle and knit
psso	pass slipped stitch(es) over
p tbl	purl through the back loop
pwise	purlwise, as if to purl
RH	right-hand
RLI	right lifted increase: pick up leg of stitch beneath stitch on the LH needle and knit into this loop
rm	remove marker
RS	right side (public side)
s2kp	slip 2 sts tog knitwise, k1, psso
sc	single crochet
sk2p	slip 1 stitch knitwise, k2tog, psso
skp	slip 1 stitch knitwise, k1, psso
sl	slip
sm	slip marker
ssk	slip 2 sts knitwise one at a time, then knit them tog through the back loop
ssp	[wyif, sl 1 knitwise] twice; return these 2 sts to LH needle, then p2tog tbl, inserting RH needle through bottom stitch first
sspo	slip, slip, pass slipped stitch over
sspok	slip, slip, pass slipped stitch over, pass back to the LH needle and knit
sssk	slip 3 sts knitwise one at a time, then knit them tog through the back loop
St st	stockinette stitch
st(s)	stitch(es)
tbl	through the back of the loop

tog	together
w&t	wrap & turn
WS	wrong side (private side)
wyib	with yarn in back
wyif	with yarn in front
yo	yarn over
yo2	yarn over twice: wrap yarn counter-clockwise two times

Cable Cast On

[With RH needle pull the loop between first and second sts of the LH needle and place it on LH needle making it first st] until you have CO the required number of sts minus 1. Before placing last loop on LH needle, bring yarn to front, place loop on LH needle, turn work. Sl the first st from RH needle to LH needle, k2tog.

Knitted Cast On (KCO)

Turn work so that all sts are on LH needle. Make a knit st with your RH needle, but do not take the old st off. Instead, slip the new st onto LH needle.

Jeny's Surprisingly Stretchy Bind Off

This method is worked similarly to the standard bind off, except you add a yarnover to each stitch before binding off:

To bind off a knit stitch: work 1 st as it appears, work a yo by bringing yarn up and over the needle so that yarn is in front, then work the next knit st. Pass both the original st and yo over the second st.

To bind off a purl stitch: work 1 st as it appears, work a yo by bringing yarn up and over the needle so that yarn is in back, then work the next purl st. Pass both the original st and yo over the second st.

You can find more information on the Knitty site: <knitty.com/ISSUEfall09/FEATjssbo.php>

Or watch Cat Bordhi demonstrate the technique on YouTube here: <bit.ly/12M2Rux>

Sewn Bind Off

Find a photo tutorial on the Knitty site: <knitty.com/ISSUEsummer06/FEATsum06TT.html>

Cable Abbreviations

1/1 LC	Sl 1 to cn, hold in front. K1. K1 from cn.
1/1 LCp	Sl 1 to cn, hold in front. P1. K1 from cn.
1/1 LCt	Sl 1 to cn, hold in front. K tbl. K tbl from cn.
1/1 LCtp	Sl 1 to cn, hold in front. P1. K tbl from cn.
1/1 RC	Sl 1 to cn, hold in back. K1. K1 from cn.
1/1 RCp	Sl 1 to cn, hold in back. K1. P1 from cn.
1/1 RCt	Sl 1 to cn, hold in back. K tbl. K tbl from cn.
1/1 RCtp	Sl 1 to cn, hold in back. K tbl. P1 from cn.
1/2 LC	Sl 1 to cn, hold in front. K2. K1 from cn.
1/2 LCp	Sl 1 to cn, hold in front. P2. K1 from cn.
1/2 RC	Sl 2 to cn, hold in back. K1. K2 from cn.
1/2 RCp	Sl 2 to cn, hold in back. K1. P2 from cn.
2/1 LC	Sl 2 to cn, hold in front. K1. K2 from cn.
2/1 LCp	Sl 2 to cn, hold in front. P1. K2 from cn.
2/1 LCp2tog	Sl 1 st to cn, hold in back. K2. Sl st back to LH needle. P2tog.
2/1 LCt	Sl 2 to cn, hold in front. K tbl. K2 from cn.
2/1 LCtp	Sl 2 to cn, hold in front. P1. K2 tbl from cn.
2/1 RC	Sl 1 to cn, hold in back. K2. K1 from cn.
2/1 RCp	Sl 1 to cn, hold in back. K2. P1 from cn.

2/1 RCp	Sl 1 to cn, hold in back. K2. P1 from cn.
2/1 RCp2tog	Work to 1 st before symbol. Sl st to RH needle. Sl next 2 sts to cn, hold in front. Sl first sl st back to LH needle. P2tog. K2 from cn.
2/1 RCt	Sl 1 st to cn, hold in back. K2. K tbl from cn.
2/1 RCtp	Sl 1 to cn, hold in back. K2 tbl. P1 from cn.
2/2 LC	Sl 2 to cn, hold in front. K2. K2 from cn.
2/2 LCkp	Sl 2 to cn, hold in front. K1, p1. K2 from cn.
2/2 LCp	Sl 2 to cn, hold in front. P2. K2 from cn.
2/2 LCp2tog	Sl 2 to cn, hold in front. P2tog. K2 from cn.
2/2 LCpp2tog	Sl 2 to cn, hold in back. K2. Sl sts from cn back to LH needle. P1, p2tog.
2/2 LCpt	Sl 2 to cn, hold in front. P1, k tbl. K2 from cn.
2/2 LCt	Sl 2 to cn, hold in front. K2 tbl. K2 tbl from cn.
2/2 LCtp	Sl 2 to cn, hold in front. K tbl, p1. K2 from cn.
2/2 RC	Sl 2 to cn, hold in back. K2. K2 from cn.
2/2 RCp	Sl 2 to cn, hold in back. K2. P2 from cn.
2/2 RCp2tog	Sl 2 to cn, hold in back. K2. P2tog from cn.
2/2 RCp2togp	Work to 1 st before symbol. Sl st to RH needle. Sl next 2 sts to cn, hold in front. Sl first sl st back to LH needle. P2tog, p1. K2 from cn.
2/2 RCpk	Sl 2 to cn, hold in back. K2. P1, k1 from cn.

2/2 RCpt	Sl 2 to cn, hold in back. K2. P1, k tbl from cn.
2/2 RCt	Sl 2to cn, hold in back. K2 tbl. K2 tbl from cn.
2/2 RCtp	Sl 2 to cn, hold in back. K2. K tbl, p1 from cn.
2/3 LC	Sl 2 to cn, hold in front. K3. K2 from cn.
2/3 LCp	Sl 2 to cn, hold in front. P3. K2 from cn.
2/3 LCp2tog	Sl 2 to cn, hold in front. P1, p2tog, K2 from cn.
2/3 RC	Sl 3 to cn, hold in back. K2. K3 from cn.

2/3 RCp	Sl 3 to cn, hold in back. K2. P3 from cn.
2/3 RCp2togp	Sl 3 to cn, hold in back. K2. P2tog, p1 from cn.
3/3 RCyo	Sl 3 to cn, hold in back. K2tog, yo, k1. K1, yo, skp from cn.
4/4 LRC	Sl 4 to cn, hold in front. [P1, k1] twice; [p1, k1] twice from cn.
4/4 RRC	Sl 4 to cn, hold in back. [K1, p1] twice; [k1, p1] twice from cn.
6/6 LRC	Sl 6 to cn, hold in front. [P1, k1] 3 times; [p1, k1] 3 times from cn.
6/6 RRC	Sl 6 to cn, hold in back. [K1, p1] 3 times; [k1, p1] 3 times from cn.

Filmography

All of the following films referenced in this book can be found on DVD and Blu-ray formats and are available from Netflix.

- *Spellbound* (1945), starring Ingrid Bergman and Gregory Peck.

- *Notorious* (1946), starring Claude Rains, Cary Grant, and Ingrid Bergman.

- *Rope* (1948), starring James Stewart, John Dall, and Farley Granger.

- *Dial M For Murder* (1954), starring Ray Milland, Grace Kelly, and Robert Cummings.

- *Rear Window* (1954), starring James Stewart, Grace Kelly, Thelma Ritter, and Raymond Burr.

- *To Catch a Thief* (1954), starring Cary Grant and Grace Kelly. As of April 2013, Amazon Prime members can watch this film free on streaming.

- *Vertigo* (1958), starring James Stewart, Kim Novak, and Barbara Bel Geddes.

- *North by Northwest* (1959), starring Cary Grant, Eva Marie Saint, James Mason, and Martin Landau.

- *The Birds* (1963), starring Rod Taylor, Tippi Hedren, Jessica Tandy, and Suzanne Pleshette.

- *The Man Who Knew Too Much* (1934/1956). The 1934 version stars Peter Lorre. The 1956 version stars James Stewart and Doris Day.

About the Designers

Stephannie Tallent is a movie buff as well as an indie designer. Her first book, *California Revival Knits*, was published by Cooperative Press in 2012. She lives in Hermosa Beach, California, with her husband Dave, dog Rigel, and cats Obi, Meggie, and Cali. Find her on Ravelry as StephCat and online at sunsetcat.com.

Dani Berg has been a passionate knitter since she first took up the needles in 2001. She designs to stay sane while raising two children and a husband in their suburban Chicagoland home. Surrounded by homework, housework, and the daily drama that life can bring, there's nothing more satisfying than sitting down with a glass of red wine, a fresh skein of yarn, and dogs at her feet to make her appreciate how full and fabulous life has become. And the truth is, she wouldn't change it for anything. (Well, maybe for a basket full of money and a maid, but that's another story…) She blogs at turnknit.blogspot.com; find her on Ravelry as daniknits.

Rebecca Blair is a lace and glove aficionado in Canada. Her favorite Hitchcock movie is *Vertigo*, with *Rear Window* a close runner-up. Her username on Ravelry is bewilderbeast and she blogs her knitting exploits at doiliesarestylish.blogspot.com.

Glenna C., aka Glenna Harris, took up knitting as stress relief while studying for her PhD in Toronto, then kept right on going. Her knitting and design philosophy is guided by a desire to constantly seek new challenges with interesting techniques and beautiful results, through cables, colorwork, and more. She loves reading, photography, yoga, film, and television, and believes in knitting fearlessly and often. She blogs twice weekly at crazyknittinglady.wordpress.com, and is on Ravelry as GlennaC.

Kristen Hanley Cardozo lives in the San Francisco Bay Area with her family, designing knitwear and writing. When she's not knitting or writing, she's probably thinking about knitting or writing. You can follow her online at knittingkninja.com or find her on Ravelry as Jejune.

Brenda Castiel has been knitting on and off since she was in her teens, but became somewhat obsessed with it in 2007. She loves squishy wools for the short, mild Los Angeles winters, and likes cottons and blends for the rest of the year. Brenda firmly believes that even beginner knitters can create something beautiful and useful, so she strives to keep patterns simple yet original. Her designs have been in *Interweave Knits*, *Vogue*, and more. She goes by Goodstuff on Ravelry, and blogs from time to time about knitting and life at knitandtravelandsuch.blogspot.com.

Rachel Coopey loves designing and knitting socks and recently self-published her first collection of sock patterns. You can read about her constant quest for warm feet, ever-growing sock yarn collection, and her knitting and spinning adventures on her blog: coopknits.co.uk and find her on Ravelry as Coopknit.

Jennette Cross started watching Hitchcock movies with her dad as a kid. Now she watches them with her lazy cocker spaniels while she knits too much and dreams of buying a loom one day. She blogs at doviejayknits.com and is doviejay on Ravelry.

Anna Dalvi is originally from the west coast of Sweden, but has traded the rugged cliffs of Bohuslän for the Canadian wilderness. In her knitting, Anna enjoys variety more than anything else: from intricate lace to sprawling cables, and differences in color and texture. Find her online at knitandknag.com and as knitandknag on Ravelry. She has authored two books with Cooperative Press: *Shaping Shawls* and *Ancient Egypt in Lace and Color*.

Nina Machlin Dayton has been knitting, designing, and teaching for 35 years. A native New Yorker, Nina currently lives in western Massachusetts with her husband, daughter, two cats, and a dog, in an old Victorian house filled to the rafters with yarn and books. You can find out more about her designs at ravelry.com/designers/nina-machlin-dayton. She is ninaknits on Ravelry.

Elizabeth Green Musselman recently became a full-time knitting editor, designer, and teacher, after spending 13 years as a history professor. She works primarily as the book designer for Cooperative Press. Find her online at darkmatterknits.com and as elizabethgm on Ravelry.

Becky Herrick isn't a big fan of suspenseful movies because they keep her up at night. She lives on the western slopes of the green mountains in Vermont where she can be found in the garden, hiking, canoeing, and snowshoeing. Check out what she's up to right now on her blog: beckyinvt.wordpress.com. She can also be found on Ravelry as BeckyinVT.

This is *Elanor King*'s first design. If you like it, watch out for more patterns coming soon at catchloops.com. Elanor is Irish, worked as an engineer pre-kids, and loves maths and sci-fi. Elanor is probably logged on to Ravelry right now as catchloops if you'd like a natter, even about knitting!

Triona Murphy is thrilled to be back where knitting with wool makes sense, after recently returning to the U.S. Midwest from Los Angeles. When she's not designing, she writes young adult novels and hopes to get them published someday. Her website and blog are at trionadesigns.com, and she's otismurph on Ravelry.

Carolyn Noyes, after years of working 24/7 as a magazine editor in Manhattan, is now getting all those stored-up designs out of her head and onto the needles in her home state of Maine. Check out her other designs at CarolynNoyes on Ravelry and her knitting blog at carolynnoyes.com.

Cables and twisted stitches are *Luise O'Neill*'s first love when it comes to designing; the interplay of the fluid lines these techniques create fascinate her. She can be found on Ravelry as impeccableknits and at impeccableknits.ca.

Heather Ordover is host of the *CraftLit* podcast, editor of the *What Would Madame Defarge Knit?* series, mother of boys, knitter of socks, teacher of things. All of Heather's doings can be found via Crafting-a-Life.com. She is MamaOKnits on Ravelry.

Anne Podlesak is the owner/dyer of Wooly Wonka (woolywonkafiber.com) and signs in as bunnyspinner on Ravelry. She has published patterns in the summer 2012 issue of *Jane Austen Knits* magazine, *Spin-Off* magazine, the online Ennea Collective, and also offers self-released patterns for knitters and hand-spinners.

Stefanie Pollmeier—whenever she's not working on her master's thesis in archaeology—lives, knits and designs in Münster, Germany. You can read about her knitting and designing adventures and constant battles against cat hairs, stash growth, and WIP-overload on rewolluzza.wordpress.com, or find her as chaoscat on Ravelry.

Jaala Spiro runs Knitcircus Publications and co-hosts the Knitcircus Podcast with Amy Detjen. She's happiest in a room full of knitters or watching episodes of Buffy with a new project. Find her on Ravelry as jaaladay, tweeting as @knitcircus and on Knitcircus.com.

Nadya Stallings was born and grew up in the beautiful Ural Mountains of Russia. She was curious about needlework from a very tender school age. Knitting has always been her favorite craft among all others. She moved to the United States in 2002 to become the loving wife of a great American guy, with whom she lives in northeast Ohio. Nadya started writing her knitwear designs in 2009 when she became a laid-off worker, and has not spent a day without designing since. She is Nastknit on Ravelry and blogs at nadyasdesigns.blogspot.com.

Jill Bigelow Suttell (pandora on Ravelry) is an independent knitwear designer and teacher living in lower Michigan with her incredibly supportive husband and dog. For more information, visit b-ewe-tiful.com.

Katherine Vaughan has been knitting for more than 25 years and designing for more than five. She primarily designs children's wear and accessories for adults and the home. Her knitting world has been greatly enhanced by a subscription to Netflix, which enables her to watch classic movies while knitting for hours on end. Katherine daylights as an academic librarian in Virginia, where it is sometimes cold enough to wear her handknits. Find her online at ktlvdesigns.com and on Ravelry as KTLV.

For *Christina Wall*, a part-time teaching job in a local yarn boutique turned her into a knitting designer. Professionally, Christina Wall worked as a court reporter (stenographer) and never imagined she would be designing patterns for a living. "But I'd never go back," she says. "I love what I do." Find her on Ravelry as ClassicCableKnits or Christina Wall, and online at aknitterslife.blogspot.com.

Christina Werge is a longtime movie geek (and Hitchcock fan). Creating and crafting since childhood, she has finally settled on knitwear design. Perhaps her background in engineering explains her thing for simple lines, good fit, and complicated math. Find her online at herrlichkeiten. net and on Ravelry as schneefloeckchen.

A Dutch knitter living in the United Kingdom, *Linda Wilgus* loves designing all things seamless. Many of her designs are vintage-inspired. Linda shares a house in Cambridgeshire with her husband, two daughters, sock-stealing retriever, and heaps of yarn. See more of her designs at woollymammothknits.com, or find her on Ravelry as linw.

Karin Wilmoth teaches knitting at Anacapa Fine Yarns in Ventura, California, and is a homeschooling mom. She began her knitting journey 12 years ago in an insane attempt to knit socks for the whole family in three months. Her natural ability to teach—combined with her nerdy love of math humor and science, and love of fine details—inspire her to explore unusual knitting constructions. Whether she's working top-down, sideways, circles or other geometrics, she enjoys creating knits that offer a different perspective. You can find her musings and other knitterly ponderings at knittingkirigami.wordpress.com. She is knitspinner69 on Ravelry.

Yarn Information

Thank you so much to the following yarn and notions companies for providing support!

Anzula | anzula.com

Anzula hand dyes luxury yarns and spinning fibers. With 16 lines of yarn available in over 80 colorways each, you're sure to find the perfect thing for your next project.

Bijou Basin Ranch | bijoubasinranch.com

Bijou Basin Ranch is a small, family-owned and -run yak ranch and boutique yarn company located in the Colorado outback about 65 miles southeast of Denver. Our primary goal has been to bring the luxurious yak fiber to hand-knitting and crochet consumers throughout the US and abroad. To do this, we market the yak fiber under the Bijou Spun brand and work with wonderfully talented independent designers to develop designs that show the beauty of our unique fiber. Softer than cashmere, warmer than wool and incredibly wearable, the yak fiber of Bijou Spun is a truly unique but affordable luxury yarn.

Blue Moon Fiber Arts | bluemoonfiberarts.com/newmoon

Blue Sky Alpacas | blueskyalpacas.com

Brooklyn Tweed | brooklyntweed.net

Brooklyn Tweed is a yarn company dedicated to high-quality domestic yarns, contemporary knitwear design, and fostering creativity and innovation in knitters and designers worldwide. Our yarns are spun in historic Harrisville, New Hampshire, from the fleece of Wyoming-grown Targhee-Columbia sheep. We fleece-dye our wool to achieve 32 rich heathers that give even the simplest fabrics depth and sophistication.

Cephalopod Yarns | cephalopodyarns.com

Cephalopod Yarns creates quirky, unique colorways inspired by nature, literature, and geek culture.

Drachenwolle | drachenwolle.com

Located in the south of Germany, Drachenwolle specializes in what dragons have been specializing in since the beginning of time: Treasure. In this particular lair, you will find hand-dyed yarns of vibrant color and lush texture that measure up to highest quality standards – created in old-fashioned workshop ambience complete with flickering flames, bubbling cauldrons and the faint scent of woodsmoke in the air.

Fyberspates LTD | fyberspates.co.uk

Fyberspates is based in the UK and specializes in making luxury yarns; hand dyed and commercially dyed. We lean towards a strong palette of colors, and are currently obsessed with metallics. Basically we just love yarn, fibers, textures, and colors more than anything else in the world.

Harrisville Designs | harrisville.com

Hazel Knits | hazelknits.com

Hazel Knits is the brainchild and consuming passion of Seattleite Wendee Shulsen and her partner in crime, Dave Decoteau. Working part-time at a local yarn shop, Wendee realized there was an unsatisfied demand for more color and yarn options. After experimenting on her own and loving the results, she went into business in 2007 and currently offers a full line of original colorways on custom-milled stock. When the duo is not in the studio perfecting their next creation, they spend their free time hanging precariously from rock walls, sleeping under the stars, and nibbling on figs and goat cheese.

Hedgehog Fibres | hedgehogfibres.com

Hedgehog Fibres is an independent artisan fiber and yarn dyeing studio located in County Cork, Ireland. We have a passion for fiber arts, and special care is paid to every skein, to create one of a kind luxurious colorways.

Indigodragonfly | indigodragonfly.ca

Rich, intoxicating, multi-tonal colors created with love and a sense of humor.

Knit Picks | knitpicks.com

Knit Picks yarn is both luxe and affordable—a seeming contradiction trounced!

Little Red Bicycle

Unfortunately, Little Red Bicycle yarns are no longer available.

Madelinetosh | madelinetosh.com

Old Maiden Aunt Yarns | oldmaidenaunt.com

Unique and beautiful yarns, hand-painted in Scotland.

Posh Yarn | poshyarn.co.uk

Posh Yarn Limited is a small artisan yarn company, based in Wales. We believe in individuality, creativity, and working with the best materials that you possibly can. To that end, all our colourways are unique and unrepeated, and we use the most luxurious yarn bases. Our yarn reflects the love, joy, and inspiration that we put into every skein.

Quince & Co | quinceandco.com

Shibui | shibuiknits.com

Shibui Knits fuses modern taste with classic silhouettes, creating a line of elegant and functional designs. We pride ourselves on producing affordable luxury yarns and inventive, elegant patterns.

Sincere Sheep | sinceresheep.com

Springtree Road | springtreeroad.com

String Theory Hand Dyed Yarn | stringtheoryyarn.com

String Theory Hand Dyed yarns are all dyed by Tanis and Karen in our homes on the rugged and beautiful coast of Maine, which provides endless inspiration. We have a yarn shop in a lovely historical house near the village of Blue Hill. Artisan yarns for adventurous knitters.

Sunday Knits | sundayknits.com

Sunday Knits, created by designer Carol Sunday, combines classic luxury yarns (masterfully spun in Italy from humanely sourced fibers), with her own harmonious color palette. Our yarns are especially soft, light, and lofty with a nice hand, a lovely drape, and colors that look really good on people.

SweetGeorgia Yarns Inc | sweetgeorgiayarns.com

SweetGeorgia Yarns is an artisan yarn company that makes exquisite hand-dyed knitting yarns and spinning fibers in stunningly saturated colors. Based in Vancouver, Canada, we are dedicated to inspiring knitters worldwide to express themselves unapologetically through color.

Tactile Fiber Arts | tactilefiberarts.com

Textilegarden | textilegarden.com

Verdant Gryphon | verdantgryphon.com

The Verdant Gryphon is a quirky, small dyeworks nestled in Maryland's wild and wonderful Eastern Shore. We're your one-stop source for luxury hand-dyed yarns in mythically beautiful colors sprinkled with ancient history, entomology, exotic locales, and all sorts of other fun and esoteric chicanery.

Wollfarm | en.dawanda.com/shop/wollfarm

Woolen Rabbit | thewoolenrabbit.com

Wooly Wonka | woolywonkafiber.com

Wooly Wonka Fibers is an indie dye company based in northern New Mexico. We specialize in kettle-dyed yarns, from laceweight to worsted, as well as hand-painted roving, and knitting patterns for the discriminating hand-knitter.

Zen Yarn Garden Inc. | zenyarngarden.com

Zen Yarn Garden, Inc. is based in Ontario, Canada. We opened our doors in 2005 and since then have evolved into a full-time husband-wife team. We take pride in providing the most luxurious fibres available for yarns as well as creating colourways that have a richness and depth to them that is one-of-a-kind.

About Cooperative Press

More period-inspired pattern books from Cooperative Press

California Revival Knits
by Stephannie Tallent

Ancient Egypt in Lace and Color
by Anna Dalvi

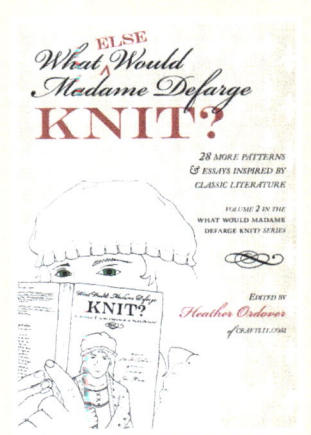

What (else) Would Madame Defarge Knit?
edited by Heather Ordover

Needles and Artifice
by the Ladies of Mischief

Cooperative Press (formerly anezka media) was founded in 2007 by Shannon Okey, a voracious reader as well as writer and editor, who had been doing freelance acquisitions work, introducing authors with projects she believed in to editors at various publishers.

Although working with traditional publishers can be very rewarding, there are some books that fly under their radar. They're too avant-garde, or the marketing department doesn't know how to sell them, or they don't think they'll sell 50,000 copies in a year.

5,000 or 50,000. Does the book matter to that 5,000? Then it should be published.

In 2009, Cooperative Press changed its named to reflect the relationships we have developed with authors working on books. We work together to put out the best quality books we can and share in the proceeds accordingly.

Thank you for supporting independent publishers and authors.

Join our mailing list for information on upcoming books!

www.cooperativepress.com

CPSIA information can be obtained at www.ICGtesting.com
Printed in the USA
BVOW10s0248141113

33€294BV00004B/13/P